Lacy Dona

BLEEP!

BLEEP!
Larry Bowa Manages

Larry Bowa with Barry Bloom

Bonus Books, Chicago

92   91   90   89   88   5   4   3   2   1

Library of Congress Catalog Card Number: 88-70285

International Standard Book Number: 0-933893-59-0

Bonus Books, Inc.
160 East Illinois Street
Chicago, Illinois 60611

Typography: Point West, Inc.

Printed in the United States of America

CONTENTS

MANAGER LARRY BOWA

HT: 5-10 WT: 160
BORN: Dec. 6, 1945 in Sacramento, CA
RESIDENCE: Bryn Mawr, PA

PERSONAL: Lawrence Robert (Larry) Bowa . . . he and wife Sheena have a daughter, Tori (7-29-83) . . . Larry graduated from McClatchy High School in Sacramento where he starred in basketball . . . he then played baseball for two years at Sacramento City College . . . Larry's father, Paul Bowa, was a AAA player and A-league manager in the St. Louis Cardinals' chain in the 1940's and his uncle, Frank, played for 5 seasons, also in the Cardinals' organization . . . Larry's off-field interests include billiards, racquetball and golf.

MANAGERIAL EXPERIENCE: Larry was named as the 11th manager of the San Diego Padres on October 28, 1986 after leading the Las Vegas Stars to the Pacific Coast League championship in his only season at the helm . . . he earned the job by convincing Jack McKeon that he was capable of managing at the AAA level during a meeting late in 1985, even though Bowa still had the option of returning as a player with the New York Mets . . . his transition from player to manager was a smooth one, as the Stars posted a 36-34 mark in the first half race . . . as Bowa became more familiar with managing, the better the team played as evidenced by the 44-28 ledger in the second half of the campaign, with Las Vegas running away in the Southern Division . . . in the first round of the playoffs against Phoenix, Bowa's crew fell behind in the best-of-5 format, 2 games to 1, however, won the remaining games to advance to the PCL finals with Vancouver . . . the Stars duplicated the feat by winning the last 2 games against the Canadians to win the league title.

PLAYING CAREER: Larry's professional career spanned 20 years, the last 16 coming with 3 major league clubs . . . he spent the majority of his big league career with the Philadelphia Phillies, signing with their organization as a free agent on October 12, 1965 . . . after 4 minor league seasons, 5 games of which came as a member of the PCL San Diego club in 1966, Larry joined the Phils . . . he spent 12 years in Philly, playing in 5 All-Star games, 4 NLCS' and a World Series . . . he was traded to the Chicago Cubs on January 27, 1982 with Ryne Sandberg for shortstop Ivan DeJesus . . . while with Chicago, he participated in his 5th NLCS, a dramatic 5-game series against the Padres in 1984 . . . Larry finished his major league career with the New York Mets, signing as a free agent on August 20, 1985 . . . during his playing career, Bowa established himself as one of the best defensive shortstops to play the game . . . he holds the major league record for the highest lifetime fielding percentage for a shortstop with a .980 mark, winning a pair of Gold Gloves (1972 and 1978) . . . he holds the N.L. record by leading the loop in fielding on 6 different occasions . . . his .987 fielding mark in both 1971 and 1972 is the best single-season percentage in league history, and he committed a National League record-low 9 errors in 150 games in 1972 . . . he also holds the major league standard for highest fielding pct. by a shortstop in over 100 games, fielding at a .991 clip in 146 games in 1979 . . . he owns the longevity record in the N.L. by playing in 2,222 games at short, ranking 2nd in major league history to Luis Aparicio's 2,581 total games . . . offensively, he had a .260 lifetime batting average, including 4 big league seasons over the .280 mark, peaking at .305 in 1975 . . . the switch-hitting Bowa finished his career with 2,191 hits . . . he had an outstanding 1980 World Series, batting .375 against Kansas City in leading the Phils to the title in 6 games . . . he also set a Fall Classic record by starting 7 double plays.

(adapted from 1987 San Diego Padres Media Guide)

RECORD AS PLAYER

YEAR	CLUB	AVG.	G	AB	R	H	2B	3B	HR	RBI	SB
1966	Spartanburg	.312	97	429	70	134	14	4	2	36	24
	San Diego	.316	5	19	0	6	0	1	0	1	0
1967	Bakersfield	.188	7	32	4	6	2	0	0	3	2
	Reading	.281	22	89	11	25	4	0	0	9	0
1968	Reading	.242	133	480	47	116	14	2	3	36	14
1969	Eugene	.287	135	568	80	163	11	6	1	26	48
1970	PHILADELPHIA	.250	145	547	50	137	17	6	0	34	24
1971	PHILADELPHIA	.249	159	*650	74	162	18	5	0	25	28
1972	PHILADELPHIA	.250	152	579	67	145	11	*13	1	31	17
1973	PHILADELPHIA	.211	122	446	42	94	11	3	0	23	10
1974	PHILADELPHIA	.275	162	669	97	184	19	10	1	36	39
1975	PHILADELPHIA	.305	136	583	79	178	18	9	2	38	24
1976	PHILADELPHIA	.248	156	624	71	155	15	9	0	49	30
1977	PHILADELPHIA	.280	154	624	93	175	19	3	4	41	32
1978	PHILADELPHIA	.294	156	654	78	192	31	5	3	43	27
1979	PHILADELPHIA	.241	147	539	74	130	17	11	0	31	20
1980	PHILADELPHIA	.267	147	540	57	144	16	4	2	39	21
1981	PHILADELPHIA	.283	103	360	34	102	14	3	0	31	16
1982	CHICAGO (NL)	.246	142	499	50	123	15	7	0	29	8
1983	CHICAGO (NL)	.267	147	499	73	133	20	5	2	43	7
1984	CHICAGO (NL)	.223	133	391	33	87	14	2	0	17	10
1985	CHICAGO (NL)	.246	72	195	13	48	6	4	0	13	5
	NEW YORK (NL)	.105	14	19	2	2	1	0	0	2	0
M.L. Totals		.260	2247	8418	987	2191	260	99	15	525	318

*Led League

DIVISION SERIES RECORD

YEAR	CLUB, OPP.	AVG.	G	AB	R	H	2B	3B	HR	RBI	SB
1981	Phl. vs. Cin.	.176	5	17	0	3	1	0	0	1	0

LEAGUE CHAMPIONSHIP SERIES RECORD

YEAR	CLUB, OPP.	AVG.	G	AB	R	H	2B	3B	HR	RBI	SB
1976	Phl. vs. Cin.	.125	3	8	1	1	1	0	0	1	0
1977	Phl. vs. L.A.	.118	4	17	2	2	0	0	0	1	0
1978	Phl. vs. L.A.	.333	4	18	2	6	0	0	0	0	0
1980	Phl. vs. Hou.	.316	5	19	2	6	0	0	0	0	1
1984	Chi. vs. S.D.	.200	5	15	1	3	1	0	0	1	0
L.C.S. Totals		.234	21	77	8	18	2	0	0	3	1

WORLD SERIES RECORD

YEAR	CLUB, OPP.	AVG.	G	AB	R	H	2B	3B	HR	RBI	SB
1980	Phl. vs. K.C.	.375	6	24	3	9	1	0	0	2	3

ALL-STAR GAME RECORD

YEAR	CLUB, SITE	AVG.	G	AB	R	H	2B	3B	HR	RBI	SB
1974	N.L. at Pit.	.000	1	2	0	0	0	0	0	0	0
1975	N.L. at Mil.	.000	1	0	0	0	0	0	0	0	0
1976	N.L. at Phl.	.000	1	1	0	0	0	0	0	0	0
1978	N.L. at S.D.	.667	1	3	1	2	0	0	0	0	1
1979	N.L. at Sea.	.000	1	2	0	0	0	0	0	0	0
A.S.G. Totals		.250	5	8	1	2	0	0	0	0	1

RECORD AS MANAGER

YEAR	CLUB	LEAGUE	FINISH	W	L	PCT.
1986	Las Vegas	Pacific Coast (1st Half)	3rd	36	34	.514
		(2nd Half)	*1st	44	28	.611
1987	San Diego	NL	6th	65	97	.401

*Defeated first half Southern Division winner Phoenix, 3 games to 2, then defeated Northern Division champion Vancouver, 3 games to 2.

ACKNOWLEDGEMENTS ♦

This is a book that describes all the trials and tribulations of my first year as big-league manager—the ups and downs of winning and losing. Mostly losing. There were times during the season when I could have strangled my young players, but as the season progressed, I learned how to deal a little better with losing. My frustrations during the season were taken out by screaming and hollering at my players. But in the end, I learned that my players cared about winning just as much as I did.

The Jeffersons, Jones and Coras were my big experiments. As I look back, they are much stronger individuals now than when we first started. They made adjustments just as I made adjustments.

Throughout the book you will see that inexperience was the reason for a lot of my outbursts. I can honestly say I respect every one of the players that went through my first year with me. I hope we grow together and become a much better team.

Jack McKeon was the man who took a chance and made me a manager after only one year of minor-league experience. Because of his patience and confidence in me, he enabled me to get through what would have been a trying season for even an experienced manager.

Thanks to Joan Kroc, Ballard Smith and Chub Feeney: First of all, for giving me the opportunity, and secondly, for offering their continued support during a season in which so many front office people might have turned their backs.

Thanks also to the San Diego fans for their support and their understanding that we were and still are going through a complete rebuilding program.

And most importantly, I would like to thank my family for their patience during my playing career and my managing career. To be married to the same wife for 17 years is something special. My wife Sheena falls into that special category. I'd also like to thank my little girl Tori who made life bearable after our horrendous start. Then there are my parents, Paul and Mary, who sacrificed everything while I was growing up just to enable me to play baseball—they were there through good and bad, but always remained my number one fans. There's my sister Paula, who has taken a backseat to all the publicity that big brother has gotten throughout his career. She, too, has been a great fan, but an even greater sister.

I love them all. And I owe all my success to them.

Last, but not least, I would like to thank Barry Bloom for putting up with me for a 162-game season and 30 spring training games. I was not the easiest person to get along with during the season.

Larry Bowa, February, 1988, Bryn Mawr, Pennsylvania

To Larry Bowa, for selecting me from a host of talented writers across America to chronicle with him his first season as a big-league manager.

To my dad, Lenny, and my mom, Gloria, whose 60th birthdays and 40th wedding anniversary all just happened to pass during the time it took to write and research this manuscript.

To my younger bro, Steve, for being an accomplice at arms at so many games during our crazy New York City childhood.

To my wife, Alicia, for a season of unyielding love and support during what just happened to be the first year of our marriage.

To our children, Rafi and Joanna, for all the giggles.

Barry M. Bloom, February, 1988, San Diego, California

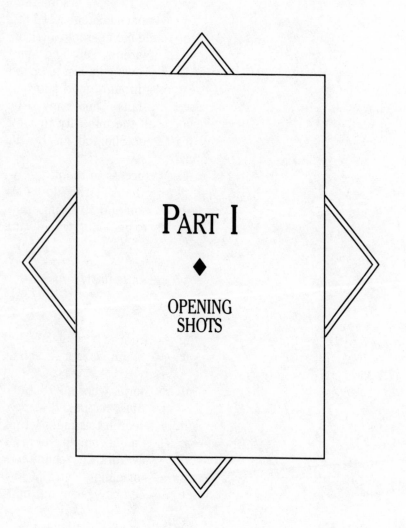

PART I

◆

OPENING
SHOTS

AUG. 15, 1985 ◆
CHICAGO, IL

I learned when I left Philadelphia in 1982 not to burn bridges. I ripped the hell out of Bill Giles back then. I called him a liar and all that about my contract. Now here it was more than three years later and I'm playing out the string with the Chicago Cubs. There were only six weeks left and I had decided back in the spring that this was going to be my last season whatever the bleep happened, anyway. So Dallas Green calls me into his office at Wrigley Field. And we've got, what, two weeks before you extend rosters from 25 to 40 players? And the season's shot. We're going nowhere.

So he calls me in and says, "I've got to do the toughest thing I've ever had to do in my baseball career. I've got to release you."

I mean, I was bleepin' stunned. I said, "You've got to do what?"

He said, "I've got to release you. We want to bring up Sha-won Dunston."

I even suggested: "Put me on the disabled list. It's only two weeks. Let him play. Then I'll be on the 40-man roster and I'm out of here anyway."

"Nope," he says. "Jim Frey doesn't want you around while Dunston is playing."

I said, "You've got to be kidding me. He thinks I make the kid nervous?"

Of course, all the writers wanted to know what was going on. But I didn't want to get into it. I said, "Oh well, they think it's best for the organization so I'll just be on my way."

So I accepted it. I just left. I didn't rip anybody, really. Until now. It's probably the most emotional I've ever been as a player, getting released. The next day I came in for a news conference. To face the Chicago press for the last time and I just bleepin' broke down. I couldn't believe it. I cried openly. I mean, it was a blow. Not to my ego. I had a lot of pride and I thought I was doing a good job. I had just played the game of the week. I made about four plays in the hole. I got three hits off that young Mets' right-hander Dwight Gooden, who was just coming into his own throwing all that heat.

Dallas just kept saying, "I'll explain it all to you one day when we're both away from this game."

I told him, "You don't have to explain anything. I know exactly what's coming down."

It was all between me and the manager. Me and Frey.

Frey was always an offensive oriented manager. He really didn't like singles. He came from Baltimore with the three-run homer. You know, the Earl Weaver thing. I never really fit into his plans. Not even from the very start. The guy was very critical of offensive performance. It stood out in my mind because he never played in the big leagues. I mean, if this guy was a great player, you could say he wants me to be like him. But he never played a game in the big leagues. You know, he was a minor-league bum, basically. But talking to him, you'd think he had played 30 years in the big leagues.

So basically right from the start, he disliked the way I played. I was a singles type hitter who did little things. He was for that big swing, baby. Let it go. It's not that I don't have respect for him. I just think he has a chip on his shoulder because he never played in the big leagues. You know, all his clubhouse speeches when he would hold a clubhouse meeting, they would start out exactly the same:

"Well, you're gonna bleep the little man, huh? You're gonna bleep with the little man. Well, this little man is not gonna be bleeped with."

He has that little man syndrome. He was paranoid about that.

I think there is merit to having done something in the big leagues. I'm not saying that just because a guy played big-league ball he knows more. I'm just talking about how the team views it. I can sit there all day and say to the Padres, "I think you ought to do it this way." And if they say to me, "What the bleep do you know about it?" I can say, "I've got a World Series ring. I've been in six playoffs. I've been in five All-Star games. That's what the bleep I know about it."

But you go up to a guy who has never played, what's he gonna say? I've managed twenty years in the minor leagues? The players say, "So bleepin' what!" That's just the way the big-league players operate. I'm not sayin' it's right because I know some guys in the minor leagues who have never played a day of big-league ball that are more knowledgeable than guys who have played in the majors for twenty years. That's just the way the system is.

See, I'm not saying I think I have the respect of everybody, but I think they know that I'm not gonna put up with crap. That I'm gonna stick by what I said the rules are and that's the way it's gonna be. And those same rules are going to apply to everybody. I don't think they're gonna test that anymore. I don't think I have the respect of everybody, but I think I have the respect of a lot of guys. And I think I have this part down: You better not screw with him because he's gonna stay on you. That's been established.

I think it's better to come on strong and then back off, than to try and do it the other way. I did the same thing in Vegas. Once you establish yourself, you can always say, "Hey, let's cut it back a little." But you can't start off real loose and then in June say, "Let's kick it in the butt. I'm gonna get tough." You can't go that way. It's better to start off a little bit rougher than you want to. And then say, "Hey, Larry, you're a little too rough. Back off a little bit. They're getting the message. You're just making them a little too uptight."

If a player wants to complain to me, I like to say, "Come on in and we'll talk about it. We'll go over your viewpoint and my viewpoint and you might have some merit to what you say." With Frey, you would go in and he would say, "OK, let me hear you out." And then he would tell you his viewpoint and that would be it. With Frey, he wouldn't say jack to you. You'd come in and you wouldn't know whether you're playing or sitting. I can understand it being like that with guys who are just coming up. But a guy who has played 15, 16, 17 years, I think you owe it to him to say, "Hey, Larry, tomorrow you're not playing" or "tomorrow you are playing." I think you owe the guy at least that much respect.

About the Dunston situation, Frey wanted the kid to take the job, but he was a rookie and just wasn't bleepin' ready. So he would sit me down three or four days at a time and then all of a sudden he would say, "OK, now you're playing." I'd come into the locker room that day mentally not ready to bleepin' play. As a player, every morning I used to get up and I knew what I was going to do. I knew what pitcher I was facing. I had everything down. I'm not blaming that all on him. That was probably a tough adjustment for me. I had been a regular for 15 years. I should have adjusted better mentally.

Hell. Frey said I made Dunston nervous. That Dunston could not play to his capabilities with me watching his every move. It was a joke. We were 25 games out at the time. There was no reasoning for this except that Frey wanted me out. It shows how intimidated Frey was. That's what it says to me. Dallas caved in to him because Dallas is a man, who in the end can say: "You did it your way and it was lousy. So get the bleep out!" You know what I'm saying? And that's exactly what happened to Frey early in 1986, anyway. He followed me out the door as manager by only a few months.

You see, if you're the manager for Dallas, you can do it your way, but if you screw up, big boy, you take all the heat. Which is good. I respect Dallas for that. He told me, "Some day you're gonna be a manager and you better hope that your general manager gives you the power I give my managers." And looking back, Dallas has been that way all the time. If he gives you a job and things are going rough, don't go to him for help. Get yourself out of the jam you got yourself into. Because when it's over, he's gonna say, "Hey, here it is. You bleeped up." It makes it easier for him to make a decision.

You know, Frey could have come back to him and said, "I wanted Bowa out of here. He caused a lot of problems. That's why Dunston didn't play." But Dallas wasn't going to give him that.

One thing about Dallas to me, and I know this as a fact, Dallas does not like yes-men. When you sit down and talk to Dallas, he sort of likes you to disagree with him. He likes to argue. Which is one reason I think we got along. We respect each other. We've had our arguments. Like the year in Philly when we finally won the World Series—1980. It was like a last hurrah in '80. Phillies management said, "OK, you guys don't do it this year and bleep you. We're tearing up this team." Dallas was our manager and he just went bleepin' nuts. Yeah, we won it all that year. Beat Frey's Kansas City team in six games to win the Phillies only world championship in this century.

But there was a time in Philly when Dallas just came in and ripped the hell out of us. "They don't know how to win. They don't know how to play." In the papers. I'm talkin' bleepin' headlines. So a writer came over to me and I was angry anyway. We were going bad and he caught me at a bad time and he said, "Man, did you hear what Dallas said?"

I said, "No, what?"

"He said you guys don't know how to win. You're selfish. All you do is think of yourselves, not of the team."

And I said, "Go ask Dallas what the bleep he ever did in the big leagues?" It was the headline story the next day: "Bowa to Green: What Have You Done in the Big Leagues!"

So we happened to be going on a road trip the day the story came out. And we were in the airport. At the gate. Waiting for the plane. Dallas was on one side reading the paper and I was standing on the other side with Greg Luzinski and somebody else. Now Dallas looks over at me and I'm waiting to be taken apart. But he smiles and says, "Hey Bow—touché."

That's the kind of relationship we had. That's why when he called me into his Wrigley Field office that day, I was bleepin' stunned. I looked at him like, " I can't believe this is happening."

But he said, "You know what's going on down there."

So I walked away. Because aside from Frey, the people in Chicago, the fans and the writers, treated me great. I had a good time there. It was a real change. I wouldn't have wanted to play there my entire career, because I think it would take three or four years off your career. Playin' during the day. No doubt in my mind. I mean, at the end of your career, I think it's a great change. You're used to playing all night games. Now you go there. You play all day games. You live a normal life. You get up at eight, eat breakfast. You come home at night, barbecue. I mean, it was like a regular eight to five job. But playin' under the sun every day, if you're a regular player, it would kill you. Dallas even asked me if I wanted to stay in the organization. He said, "I want you to stay in the organization as a manager."

And I said, "Well, I appreciate it. I liked playing for you. I liked working for you. But I'm not going to make a decision."

Then I went home and I figured I wasn't going to play anymore. My wife Sheena and I sat down and I said, "The only way I'd play is if the Mets call. They're three games out. They've got a shot." I knew their backup shortstop was just put on the disabled list and they needed another one. So after about three days, Davey Johnson of the Mets called.

He said, "We want you to come to New York."

So I went there. Played there. And they came up short. That was it.

Aug. 21, 1987 ♦
New York, NY

L arry Bowa was snorting fire from his nostrils. He was seeing red as he had so many times in this lugubrious season, his first as a big-league manager. A season in which his San Diego Padres club had found a way to lose precisely 60 percent of its games.

On the field, at least, Bowa had exhibited a certain amount of cool. He hadn't been thrown out of a baseball game in three months. It had last occurred on May 20, to be exact, right here in New York at Shea Stadium in a loss to the Mets that was just another nugget in the club's brutal 12-42 start.

But in the fifth inning of this night's game, Bowa completely lost it. Bowa tossed his brown cap to the dirt. Eyes wide with passion, blue veins protruding dangerously from his forehead and neck, Bowa charged homeplate umpire Steve Rippley, apparently grazing Rippley with his chest and hips in the onslaught.

"That's a bump," screamed Rippley at the manager he had already thumbed from the game.

"A bump, a bump?" Bowa said after the Padres had handed the defending world champions a 6-2 loss. "The last bump he got was when he bumped his wife last night."

Jack McKeon, the Padres burly general manager with the salt and pepper mustache and the endless cigar dangling from his thick lips, sat nearby, shaking his head in corroboration of Bowa's story.

In Bowa's mind, he had a damn good reason for being ejected for the fourth time in a rookie managerial season. By season's end, he would be banished by umpires on five occasions. To put it into perspective, this was only two times less than most of his tenure as a shortstop with the Philadelphia Phillies, which began in 1970 and ended in 1982 when Bowa was traded to the Chicago Cubs.

Bowa was angry at the umpire for not warning Mets right-hander Ron Darling about the pitch that had dumped John Kruk to the seat of his pants. In his previous at bat against Darling, the left-handed swinging Kruk had skied a two-run homer into the Padres bullpen in left-field to give San Diego a 3-0 lead. Pitchers can be awfully touchy about such things.

Unwritten baseball law allows a pitcher to fire a warning shot at the very same hitter during his next at bat. Sometimes these tactics have sickening results. On July 7 in Chicago, for instance, Padres right-hander Eric Show apparently decided that it was time to back hot-hitting slugger Andre Dawson away from the plate. Dawson, a right-handed hitter, hung his arms ominously across the strike zone. Show came in too high and too inside. Dawson didn't have enough time to react.

The result was an ensuing melee and 24 stitches in Dawson's left cheek and upper lip. The injury made the National League's leading home run hitter sullen and angry. Dawson, who had homered twice off Padres pitchers the day before, had also homered off Show in his previous at bat.

A sudden spate of pitchers utilizing the unwritten law had moved first-year league president A. Bartlett Giamatti to order that umpires issue a firm warning to pitchers after such incidents whether the umpire deemed the incident flagrant or not. Giamatti, a former president of Yale University, probably had never had to issue such edicts about unwritten college pranks.

Thus, with two out in the fifth inning and nary a Padres soul on base, Darling took the opportunity to fire the first pitch over Kruk's head. Kruk was the native West Virginian, who on his first trip to Chicago a year earlier, had turned to a teammate during a bus ride along Lake Shore Drive, pointed to Lake Michigan and asked in his most innocent southern drawl, "What ocean is that? The Mediterranean?"

That same Mr. Kruk was now busy sifting himself out of New York clay dirt.

What stunned Bowa was that umpire Rippley, a vacation fill-in from the Pacific Coast League (PCL), did not follow Giamatti's orders. Bowa was run from five ballgames and suspended twice during his one season of managing the Padres Class AAA Las Vegas affiliate in the PCL.

In managing the Stars to the 1986 PCL title in only his first season removed from the playing field, Bowa had set the groundwork for making a quick jump back to the big leagues. Bowa bounced out of the visitor's dugout, which is on the third base side of the field at Shea Stadium. He issued a severe protest to the umpire, who was not in a receiving mood.

"I don't mind playing that way," Bowa said. "OK. Knock him down. Bleep it. I'm just saying follow the rules. Do it the right way. In Chicago, it's a bleepin' warning. In New York, it's nothing. All I'm asking for is one rule that applies to every city we go to. That pitch was no closer than the one that hit Dawson. I guarantee it. He got out of the way and Dawson didn't.

"We had a big melee there. Here nothing happened. I'm not saying we wanted to fight. I'm just saying they overblew it in Chicago. That didn't happen here. Let's just get consistent. The guy hits the ball 400 feet and then he goes on his butt? I like to play like that. But let's just put the rule in."

When Bowa had finished saying his piece and began to turn back toward the dugout, he became incensed by Rippley's parting shot. "I'm running the show here," he said. "I'm calling the shots. I'll tell you when a guy is throwing at him."

That was too much for the already well-carbonated Bowa to handle. "Bleep you," Bowa railed. "Who the bleep are you, bleepin' God?"

That is when Bowa was run from the game. And that is when the Larry Bowa Show usually begins. He "snaps," as he calls it.

"Sometimes I don't even remember what I say. All I know is that after it is over, I always feel better. I know I'm not going to have a heart attack or an ulcer," Bowa says.

Usually, these snaps follow a pattern. They are the zenith of a series of losses or angry disappointments—several days in which Bowa is trying to forgive the mental mistakes and forget the lack of emotion he sees in his players. Sometimes these snaps take the form of tyrannical clubhouse meetings. Sometimes they simply are contained in remarks about players to the press.

And sometimes . . .

For instance, this particular snap came after two tough losses to the Phillies at Veterans Stadium. It came at the end of a week in which Bowa had been at odds with pitchers Show and Storm Davis.

On the previous Tuesday in Philadelphia, Davis had publicly asked to be traded, culminating a subpar season in which his relationship with Bowa had completely deteriorated. Just the previous night in Philly, Bowa had once again lambasted Show for his performance in a 10-2 loss.

Show's effort had so disturbed Bowa that he called him into his office at 5:30 on this particular evening. Uncharacteristically, Bowa missed most of batting practice meeting with Show. When Bowa emerged 45 minutes later he found that Chris Brown had decided once again he couldn't play. Brown, who had been glanced in the upper left arm by a Fred Toliver pitch in the first inning just the night before, took batting practice and decided that he could not swing.

Bowa was beginning to wonder if Brown, who had had his jaw shattered by St. Louis Cardinals right-hander Danny Cox several months earlier when Brown was still a member of the San Francisco Giants, might be reticent about facing hard-throwing right-handers. Darling is a hard-throwing right-hander.

About Show, Bowa said: "We talked about life. I learned a few things from him about life outside baseball, and I think he learned a few things from me about life in baseball."

But clearly, Bowa was in no laughing mood going into a game in which his club effected another one of those neat reversals which had so characterized this strange season. It was Bowa's bad fortune that not only Giamatti, but the entire Padres brass—owner Joan Kroc, president Chub Feeney, former president Ballard Smith, who is now a member of the board of directors, and McKeon—was in the stands to witness the explosion.

Feeney, the just retired National League president, who joined the club in June, was not pleased about his manager's antics. When the Padres returned to San Diego several days later, he called Bowa in to tell him so.

"He told me, 'you don't help your team,'" Bowa said later, recalling the meeting. 'It's not very professional.' He made sense. He thought what I did was right, sticking up for John and all that, but after the umpire said no way, I should have dropped it. And I said I would have. But then the umpire said, 'I'm runnin' the show here.' And when he said that as I was walkin' away, that just upset me. He doesn't like managers to get thrown out of the game. I think I've done pretty well in that category."

Feeney should be well aware of the Bowa psyche. As league president, he read the reports about Bowa's well-documented snaps during his playing days. "He suspended me once for pushing Jim Quick. And I deserved it. I didn't push him. I bumped him. The fines . . . Oh hell, he's done that so many times I can't count. He was president of the league for practically my entire career. I know he's got more than $5,000, easy. When I first started getting kicked out it was a hundred. Then it started going up—three hundred, five hundred, seven hundred. In 16 years I'd have to say I was kicked out 40 or 50 times. I'm serious."

Actually, Bowa wasn't nailed nearly that many times as a player, even if he was in his own memory. From 1974–81, Bowa was only ejected from seven games. Neither the Phillies nor the league office have records charting the first four years of Bowa's career. But by his own admission, "I was a lot more toned down during my first five years."

During his four years in Chicago (1982-85) Bowa was ejected five times. In his brief one-month stay with the Mets before his retirement at the end of the '85 season, Bowa was thumbed just once—in his third game in New York after his untimely release by the Cubs.

As a player, Bowa found that he could relieve some of his tension by wreaking havoc on material items. Light bulbs, toilet bowls, fixtures, bats and helmets. Once, Bowa was billed by former Cubs president Dallas Green for the commode he smashed apart in the home dugout at Wrigley Field after a particularly galling strikeout.

But, said Bowa, "I always made sure none of my teammates were around me when I went crazy. That way, nobody got hurt."

As a manager, Bowa has become even more demonstrative, though he can no longer succumb to his usual display of raw emotions on inanimate objects. Instead, he is reduced to biting his fingernails to the bone and building up anger over the course of several days like a pressure cooker.

In his first few months managing Vegas, Bowa learned the hard way that he had to begin to control his temper.

"He was so intense on every pitch," said Stars general manager Larry Koentopp, who had more than his share of soul-searching talks with the novice manager. "Every time the umps made a call, he was out on the field. He was driving himself and everyone else crazy."

During the spring prior to the 1986 season when Bowa was invited to Yuma, Arizona, to help coach the Padres major leaguers, the players opened a cash pool to pick the game of Bowa's first ejection as Las Vegas manager. He was nailed in the Stars 21st game by Pam Postema, the first woman to umpire at the triple-A level. Postema, whose ambition is to ump in the major leagues, was involved in a running feud with Bowa and was responsible for three of his first four ejections, all coming in one week.

Postema's report about the debacle to the PCL office has become a minor-league legend. In the report, she claimed that she did not so much mind being referred to as a particular part of the female anatomy, but she was aghast when Bowa questioned her femininity. The feud led to Bowa's first suspension.

"Jack McKeon called me and told me to lighten up a little," Bowa recalled. "And for the rest of the season I was good. I didn't get tossed until the league playoffs."

But he was back to his irascible self when the Padres opened his first season as manager with five straight losses. On opening night in San Diego, Bowa treated hometown fans to one of his famous snaps when he argued long and hard with second base umpire Bob Engel after Engel allowed a San Francisco Giants double play. He ruled that Tim Flannery had slid out of the baseline to drill shortstop Matt Williams, who bounced his pivot throw by first base.

Certainly, that the call negated a Padres run and turned what would have been a one-run game into a Giants blowout, was a determining factor. But when Engel ignored Bowa, who was pointing at skid marks which seemed to indicate that Flannery had not slid out of the baseline, the real fun began.

With veins a-popping, his neck jerking violently and his cap on the ground, Bowa stunned everyone by ranting and raving for more than two minutes after he had been ejected. Bowa had ardently noted that it certainly would be a feather in Engel's cap because he ran him from his first game since Bowa became a big-league manager.

Similarly, on this night months later, after the season had long turned sour, Bowa had to be restrained from Rippley by a combination of the other three umpires before he begrudgingly went to the clubhouse amidst the growing jeers and catcalls of 41,000 Mets faithful.

"I deserved to be kicked out," Bowa said. "I'm not saying I didn't deserve it. I needed it. I had some built up frustrations in me. I just didn't want to pay that much. I'm sure this fine will be a big one. I'll just have to appeal it like everyone else. Just prolong it."

Bowa was fined $500 by Giamatti, who really didn't have to read the umpire's report. Bowa didn't appeal it.

Did he overreact?

"I think he did," said Mets manager Davey Johnson. "But that's Larry."

OCT. 28, 1986 ♦
SAN DIEGO, CA

T he klieg lights were set up in this horseshoe shaped room called the Stadium Club—a utilitarian space in San Diego Jack Murphy Stadium where the Padres hold important media conferences. The television cameras and tape recorders were ready to roll.

For weeks it had been rumored that Lawrence Robert Bowa, that 41-year-old spark plug from Sacramento, would become the 11th manager in the short, chaotic history of a Padres franchise that had joined the National League during its last expansion in 1969. Today, it would become reality.

Only days before, Padres president Ballard Smith, disillusioned by the club's 74-88, fourth-place finish in the National League's Western Division only two years removed from its first pennant, had disposed of Steve Boros. Bowa would become the Padres' third manager in eight months. Or since that spring day—February 24—when Dick Williams stunned everyone by resigning his post on the opening day of spring training after four winning seasons.

Williams' resignation was only part of a sordid tale which involved a power struggle, cross accusations and recriminations. In the end, that struggle nearly toppled the organization that the late Ray Kroc saved for the city back in 1974. Smith, who would resign as club president midway through the 1987 season, would divorce his wife Linda.

Joan Kroc, who inherited the club when her husband, the founder of the McDonald's hamburger empire, passed away in January 1984, would suffer through periods of stress with Linda, her only daughter.

It was safe to say that the Padres were no happy family when Bowa, capitalizing on one successful season as a minor-league manager, faced the local media with all his usual bravado.

"I'll tell you this," Bowa said. "I played for a long time in the big leagues and I hate to lose. And I want that attitude to spread among our players. I'll also say this: There's no doubt in my mind that I can run a baseball team. No doubt. I'll make some mistakes. This team is going to let it all hang out. I can't guarantee that we'll win X amount of games. But I guarantee that this team will give 100 percent every day. If a guy doesn't give 100 percent, he won't play. It's as simple as that. Really, is it too much to ask for a guy to give his best for 27 outs?"

Bowa, who was allowed to add only one coach, Greg Riddoch, to a veteran staff, would find out that managing in the big leagues was nothing like managing in Vegas.

"In the Coast League, it's basically self-motivated because players haven't reached their goal," Bowa would say later. "They know they have to go out and bust their butt. They know that I turn in a report every day to Jack McKeon and the front office. If a guy doesn't hustle, doesn't run out a ground ball, it goes right in the report. They know up here that they've reached the big leagues. There's not a league above the big leagues."

Early in the 1986 season, when Boros was in the process of losing his grip on the Padres at the major-league level, Bowa was having no easy time making the transition from his playing days to his managing days. Bowa had been so anxious to obtain his first managerial job, he turned down a $250,000 contract to be a utility player for the 1986 New York Mets, who only the day before had beaten the Boston Red Sox in seven tough games to win the World Championship. Not only had Bowa rejected a six-figure salary, but he had lost out on big post-season money and a chance to earn his second championship ring. Instead, Bowa opted for $28,000 and the 100-degree summer days of Vegas, where the lights may shine on the strip, but rarely waver to the north side of town where the Stars play their baseball at cozy, modern Cashen Field.

"I set myself in a situation in which I could manage in the minor leagues for about three years," Bowa recalled. "At that money. I said, OK, I want to do this. I want to give it a shot. But if it doesn't happen in three years, forget it."

There were many reasons why it happened much faster than he expected. But, of course, it had to begin with Bowa. The Pacific Coast League uses a playoff system which breaks the season down into halves. At mid-season, records revert to zero and the first-half winners meet the second-half winners in the playoffs. Bowa was fortunate. His team finished 36-35 during a first half in which he was suspended several times because of a running feud with umpire Pam Postema.

During one of the suspensions, Bowa was involved in a clubhouse confrontation with outfielder Gary Woods, a former Chicago Cubs teammate, who was thrown out at the plate to end a game.

When a reporter from the *Las Vegas Star* wrote up the incident, Bowa wound up having a shouting match with the writer, too.

But with the Padres signing former major-league slugger Steve Kemp to a minor-league contract, and Bowa softening his hard-edged attitude, the team soared into first place during the second half.

"It wasn't easy playing for him at first," said pitcher Ed Wojna, who pitched for Bowa at Vegas in '86 and for a short time in San Diego in '87. "He was tough. He pushed us. Some guys resented him. But he got the most out of us. He got us to do our best. We respected him. And he changed as a manager over the course of the year. He still drove us, but he became more tolerant. More relaxed."

Said Bowa: "Last year in Vegas in May, a coach of mine, Rob "Peach" Picciolo, came up to me and said, 'Larry, these guys are scared of you. They're scared, they're scared, they're scared.' He had a clubhouse meeting to tell them that they, 'Don't understand what Larry is trying to get across to you. That he cares about you. That he wants you to get out of triple-A, because that's not where you're supposed to play.' And I'll tell you what:

That meeting must have broken the ice or something. Because it seemed like from that day on they started responding.

"Peach was the guy who came up with the idea: Don't listen to the level of his voice. Listen to what he is saying. Don't listen to his harshness or look into his eyes when he squints. Listen to the words he's saying. That's all."

Someone must have begun listening because the Stars started playing. But it still irked Bowa that he couldn't get the locals or the tourists out of the casinos and away from the Shecky Green Show long enough to watch his little team play Bowa ball—a combination of aggressive running tactics, bunts and squeezes, mixed with a power game that capitalized on the light desert air. The Stars even offered fans a "Guarantee a Win Night." Anyone attending the July 28 game against Vancouver would be admitted free the next night if the Stars lost.

The idea wasn't a hit. When Vegas lost 9-5 before 2,900 people, General Manager Larry Koentopp estimated that the ruse had cost him a possible $11,000 in ticket revenue.

But that was hardly Bowa's problem. He had exhibited sizeable growth as a manager. During the tumultuous first half, when Bowa was alienating his players and being ejected from games at a record pace, Padres general manager Jack McKeon noted that Bowa was probably, "A few years away from managing in the big leagues."

But with the playoffs on the horizon as the minor-league season concluded on August 31, McKeon had already changed his mind.

"In August I realized Larry was probably ready. He had learned how to deal with players. He had made adjustments in his managing style. His players were responding. He'd come an awfully long way."

Now, with Bowa facing the klieg lights, McKeon was in full bloom.

"I was asked for my recommendation and I suggested Larry," McKeon said after Bowa had stepped away from the podium for more personal interviews. "Larry was a highly competitive individual as a player and I think he has shown it will carry over as a manager. I think he's got a chance to be an outstanding major-league manager . . . He was the only man I recommended for the job."

Noted columnist Nick Canepa in the *San Diego Tribune* about a similar McKeon decision made eight months earlier: "You may recall Boros was the only man McKeon recommended for the job."

What happened to Boros in such a short span of time is another contributing element to the Bowa odyssey. It was pure timing and good luck that Bowa's amazing acceleration coincided precisely with the deterioration of the major-league club. On July 13, 1986, when the Stars had yet to round into shape, the Padres were but three games out of first place, having ridden the crest of a 45-43 first half.

At an All-Star game function that summer in Houston, Smith, taken with the team's seemingly positive position, had proclaimed these Padres as superior to the 1984 team that came back from a two-zip deficit to beat Bowa's Cubs in the last of the five-game playoffs.

It was to be the zenith. By early August, Boros had lost control of a club that took a severe nose dive into the cellar, 10 games out of first place.

And Smith? Bowa found Smith at Cashen Field viewing the young prospects—catcher Benito Santiago, pitcher Jimmy Jones, shortstop Gary Green. It is highly implausible to find a major-league club president in a minor-league clubhouse talking baseball philosophy with a novice manager.

"I'd never heard of anything like that before," Bowa said.

But it was at that point Smith made a decision not to break up the Stars unless it was absolutely necessary. They might win the title. The Padres were dead in the water and as punishment would be left to flounder for the remainder of what had been nothing short of an ugly season.

The Padres troubles had really begun in November 1985 after the defending National League champions had concluded a disappointing run at a second consecutive pennant. In September of that season, with only one year remaining on his contract, Williams began telling cronies that he would not return to the club in 1986 as a lame duck manager. Williams was convinced, and remains so to this day, that McKeon was plotting to come down to the field to replace him at the opportune moment. And so he sought a contract extension.

He may have been correct in his assumption, but the truth is that Williams, as he had done in four managerial jobs prior to his tenure with the Padres, had alienated almost everyone in the organization. Smith eventually called Williams simply, "A bad guy." Williams called both Smith and McKeon "liars."

It was too bad. Williams was the best baseball man the Padres had ever had as a manager. The numbers speak for themselves. The Padres won 337 games, a division title and a pennant under Williams. They were a .500 team or better for his four years as manager, something they had only accomplished once in 13 seasons prior to Williams' arrival in 1982 and have not accomplished in the two years since his departure.

Williams, as suits his style, noted last summer as he managed the Seattle Mariners to their best record in franchise history: "I don't want to comment on what's happening down there except to say that we follow it, and needless to say, we enjoy what's happening."

What began as a Shakespearean tragedy had long since evolved into a "Comedy of Errors."

The details are murky, but the Williams debacle is what really began the Padres fall from grace. The story has been pieced together through conversations with all parties over the course of several years.

After the 1985 season, Smith called Williams into his office for a meeting with McKeon and asked him point blank if he wanted to return to manage the club. According to Smith, Williams said no. But Williams did mutter something about a buyout on the last year of his contract. Smith allegedly said he would look into it and told Williams, who was about to depart with his wife Norma on a cruise, to think about his decision. They would talk again in several weeks.

What the Padres announced is that Williams would honor his contract and return as manager. Williams believes he left that meeting with a buyout promise in hand.

With Williams out of town, McKeon thought it prudent to begin notifying certain members of the coaching staff that they might try to seek employment elsewhere. Ozzie Virgil, who has worked with Williams for many years, interpreted it as a sign that the Padres were trying to force Williams out by undermining his authority. Virgil, who had no clue what had occurred at the November meeting, blasted the Padres and then signed a deal to coach for the San Francisco Giants.

At this point, Kroc, who was not fully briefed about the situation, became irate when she read the Virgil accounts in the paper. Kroc called the Associated Press to say that Williams would remain the manager on her authority because she adheres to her late husband's philosophy that the Krocs honor all contracts.

The four parties—Kroc, Williams, Smith and McKeon—met in a private setting at Kroc's La Jolla home. Williams was again confronted with the same question that had been posed to him a month earlier by Smith: Did he want to return as manager under the terms of his contract? This time, Williams said yes. Smith couldn't believe it.

Williams would remain along with Virgil, who was also rehired. As bounty, Williams asked for the head of coach Harry Dunlop, a long-time McKeon ally. He was granted the request. Williams explained that action years later.

"Harry was a pipeline," Williams said. "Harry was a pain in the ass. I didn't ask for Harry, basically didn't want Harry."

The affair left the organization with a complete breakdown in credibility. Kroc had effectively neutered her son-in-law in public. Smith, who was undergoing his own more personal problems at the time, was becoming more and more belligerent in his dealings with the media. McKeon was left hanging. And Williams was kept in a job he did not want with his only supporter, the owner, who was not a factor on a day-to-day basis.

One close friend of Kroc's noted that the hamburger heiress had been forced to head off a "palace coup" in her own baseball organization.

Sadly, it was only the beginning. By February it became increasingly plain to Williams that he had isolated himself within the organization and that he was not prepared to return to the club for spring training. Days before the opening of camp, Kroc allegedly called Williams to ask him if he was ready for the season ahead. Williams said no.

Recognizing a crisis on her hands, Kroc had to make an around-the-world telephone call to Smith, who just happened to be in Australia for the opening of a new McDonald's restaurant. Her message to Smith, who is still a member of the McDonald's Board of Directors, was succinct: "Williams does not want to return as manager. Come home."

On February 24, with the team gathered in its Yuma clubhouse, Joan and Dick faced the media in the same Stadium Club where Bowa was taking the reins today. They each made brief statements. Answered no questions. Kissed. And left the room. The Padres announced that Williams had resigned, but in truth, he had been fired and would be paid the full term of his contract. As a prerequisite of the deal, neither party would talk about the situation for a year.

That left the Padres scattering for a manager. McKeon was asked to draw up a list of names, but he had already hired Boros as the minor-league coordinator in anticipation that just such a situation might arise. Boros, who was at camp in uniform, was whisked to San Diego, where after one session with the hierarchy, he was promoted to manage the club for the season on the stipulation that he could return to his former position if the club was not satisfied with his ability to manage.

Boros, who had been fired as manager of the Oakland A's early in 1984 when disagreements arose between him and management, brought Dunlop back as one of his coaches.

It wouldn't be an easy season for Boros, a scholarly man whose soft approach was a neat comparison to the grumpy Williams in the early going. But he could never earn the respect of many of the same players who blasted Williams.

His most significant handicaps seemed to come off the field. The day after Boros was hired, pitcher LaMarr Hoyt was whisked away for drug rehabilitation. It was learned that he had been arrested for trying to smuggle over-the-counter drugs across the Mexican-American border and had also been cited in San Diego during a routine traffic stop for carrying a small amount of marijuana and a switchblade. Hoyt, a Cy Young Award winner with the Chicago White Sox in 1983 and a 16-game winner and All-Star with the Padres in 1985, would never be a factor.

Then there was that fateful day in May when the Padres decided to ban beer and liquor from the home clubhouse in San Diego. This incited a mini-revolution led by relief pitcher Goose Gossage, who would eventually be suspended for his nation-wide diatribes against Kroc and Smith.

Gossage began the salvo by calling Kroc a hypocrite for banning beer when she, "Poisons the world with her cheeseburgers."

After one particular clubhouse meeting about player gripes, Smith was so surprised when he was confronted by a group of anxious reporters, that he called them a bunch of "bleepin' flies."

Bowa's problems with Pam Postema seemed infinitesimal in comparison. Despite a series of injuries to Padres pitchers and all the off-field distractions, both McKeon and Smith had seen enough of Boros. McKeon, a long-time friend, who had hired both Boros and Dunlop as coaches when McKeon managed the Kansas City Royals, was despondent. He and Boros had never built the communication he had anticipated.

Smith lamented the fact that Boros could not handle disciplinary matters. Smith said he had implored Boros to handle player problems and had assured him that his decisions would be backed by management. But Boros was either incapable or unwilling to make those decisions. Smith blamed the Gossage suspension on Boros because he felt it should have been handled at the club level by the manager. Instead, it turned into another public fight with the Major League Baseball Players Association, who, in 1985, had contested the way the Padres handled second baseman Alan Wiggins when he was treated for the second time for cocaine abuse. Now they were threatening to take the Padres to arbitration because of their suspension of Gossage. Gossage and the Padres settled their dispute, but later on, the association would claim that the Padres were a franchise acting above baseball rules in the handling of both Hoyt and Wiggins in regard to their serious drug problems.

Undoubtedly, all these elements had to coincide for Bowa suddenly to earn his first shot as a big-league manager. And here he was today, taking over an aging team in serious decline with this kind of boldness:

"Don't expect me not to get thrown out of games. Don't expect me to be a choirboy. I've never done that. I'm very competitive. I'm not saying I'm going to get kicked out of 50 ballgames, but I want us to take the field with a little cockiness—let the other clubs know, hey, we've got a good ballclub."

By nightfall, though, Bowa began to find out what it is like to be associated with the Padres. That evening, Hoyt was arrested again—this time trying to smuggle 400 Quaalude and Valium pills across the border. Hoyt was then severed from the ballclub which stuck hard by its edict that second-time drug offenders would not be tolerated.

Several days later, McKeon traded veteran catcher Terry Kennedy to Baltimore for pitcher Storm Davis. The restructuring had begun. The trading of Kennedy opened the position to Santiago, who was valued highly by the organization, but had played only a handful of major-league games. Davis, who might have been a cog in another trade, became a valuable commodity because of the problems facing Hoyt. But Davis had missed the final five weeks of the '86 season when he tore ligaments in his foot, trying to cover first base.

Veterans Graig Nettles, Jerry Royster and Dave LaPoint were not extended new contracts, further lowering the experience level of Bowa's team.

And then in December, the Padres traded their one pure power hitter, Kevin McReynolds, to the Mets for a group of youngsters including Kevin Mitchell, Stanley Jefferson and Shawn Abner. Mitchell, a rookie in 1986, was expected to replace the aging Nettles at third base. It was hoped that Jefferson would replace McReynolds in center field while offering the Padres their first real catalyst at the top of the order since Wiggins succumbed to cocaine use for the second time and was banished from the club.

With that, the transition was all but complete. Only three starters remained from the 1984 pennant-winning club—right-fielder Tony Gwynn, who was the Padres only reliable talent, shortstop Garry Templeton, who was hampered by severely sore knees, and left fielder Carmelo Martinez, who was coming off a disappointing season.

The pitching staff was in shambles. Like Davis, Eric Show and Dave Dravecky had also missed the final five weeks of the '86 season because of elbow tendinitis. Gossage, who appeared only twice in game action during the final five weeks because of the suspension, was a real question mark. Would age be a factor? He would be 36 before the season was out.

The Padres were also about to audition Joey Cora—another in a series of green second basemen. And there was plenty of suggestion within the organization that incumbent first baseman Steve Garvey, at 38, had outlived his usefulness. Add to all this the mere fact that Kroc, tired of dealing with the incessant public criticism and the ever-expanding drug issue, had decided to place the Padres up for sale, fueling a city council suspicion that the sale would be consummated prior to the signing of a new stadium lease which was close to expiration.

This was the club that the brash Lawrence Robert Bowa had agreed to guide with so much panache for a mere $100,000 salary in his first season as a big-league manager.

"Larry would have accepted a half-year contract. That's how much confidence he has in himself," said McKeon.

Bowa would find out soon enough just what kind of mess he had really drawn himself into.

PART II

◆

SPRING
1987

MONDAY, FEB. 23, 1987 ♦
YUMA, AZ

Y uma is a small town nestled on the Arizona side of the Colorado River just an hour north of the Mexican border. For 11 months a year, Yuma is a haven for snowbirds who wheel their way south in camper-trailers of all shapes and sizes to free themselves of the frigid Canadian winters; for soldiers from the nearby military base, and for the locals, who dine at such roadside greaseries as Brownie's Cafe or Chester's Chuckwagon, where you can still hit the Tuesday night "All You Can Eat" Chicken Fry for $3.99.

Yuma has been alternately termed an armpit and the only thing between here and hell that interrupts Interstate-8 in its 400-mile blacktop run from San Diego to Tucson. During the summer, when temperatures rarely dip below 100 degrees in the shade, the only outdoor activities seem to be conducted by Gila monsters and buzzards. A columnist, who has long since made his way back East, once noted that the only bit of excitement piercing those deadly summer months is the Colorado River rafting championships. Another writer who once covered the Padres, called Yuma, "A place where old white people go to die." You can well imagine how the chamber of commerce received that.

But for one glorious month each year Yuma comes alive with the dreams that young men fancy in spring. The crack of the bat. The sound of symmetrical pieces of woven horsehide filled with thread and cork, thudding into the middle of leather gloves. The grunts and groans of a baseball team running itself through the paces in preparation for what Steve Garvey calls the major-league championship season—162 games, the All-Star game, seven playoff games and seven World Series games. For the San Diego Padres, it all begins right here in the Ray Kroc Complex. (It was once called the Desert Sun Complex, but has now been renamed in honor of the late Ray Kroc.) For five weeks, the boys of summer shed themselves of the pounds and kinks of winter in this far-off desert outpost some three hours east of San Diego and four hours southwest of the Phoenix area where five other teams train in what has commonly become known as the Cactus League.

The Padres have been training in Yuma since the inception of the franchise in 1969. Noting that for 12 months each year, Yuma was simply a depot for those weary travelers who needed nothing more than a room for the night and a full gas tank, city fathers, in all their wisdom, put together a package which C. Arnholt Smith, the Padres' first owner, could not turn down. The city would build the complex which now may be unrivaled in the Cactus League circuit—a cloverleaf of fields circling a yellow, corrugated, aluminum field house which umbrellas clubhouse facilities, offices, weight rooms, training rooms, a press room and a dining room.

On one side of the cloverleaf would rest Desert Sun Stadium, a cozy, 7,000 seat, well-lit park where the Padres play all their home exhibition games. The Padres would simply pay the city rent and help maintain the grounds.

For all the jokes one can make about Yuma, one thing is certain, the city treats all members of the Padres party like royalty each spring. The Cabelleros de Yuma, the group in charge of spring-training preparation and execution, are constantly at hand to give proper direction. As in any city or town that lines the byways of America, Yumans are fiercely proud of their home, even if visitors are somewhat sarcastic about the environs.

Aside from the common griping of players who would rather not be sequestered in such a remote area, the marriage between Yuma and the Padres has always been a good one. The Padres view it as beneficial that their own fans are simply hours away and can drive to Yuma to see the spring games. Indeed, for the one month when Yuma comes alive and the Gila monsters hide under various rocks and cacti, nary a hotel room can be found, either out on the interstate or on Fourth Avenue—the business route which slices east to west cross town.

But at this time of spring when the players straggle in for several days and before the major influx of beer-drinking San Diegans, Yuma is at its most peaceful. A wind whips across the desert bringing in the smell of flowers and the hint of warmth to come. It was chilly, though, today when manager Larry Bowa assembled his pitchers and catchers for the first time in what would be a spring of hard knocks and lessons learned.

"I told them I didn't want any bleepin' around," Bowa said of his first meeting with the players. "I expect them to be professionals. I told them that their 74-88 record last year was nothing to be proud of. And coming in fourth place was nothing much either."

Bowa's immediate concerns would be with the arms of Dave Dravecky and Eric Show, and with the psyche of reliever Goose Gossage, who was suspended by the club in late August for behavior deemed detrimental to the team.

During the workout, in which pitchers threw to catchers off several workout mounds located between two practice fields, Bowa watched intently as Gossage reared back and popped a few fastballs into a catcher's mitt, sixty feet, six inches away.

"Yeah, I'll take my chances with that," Bowa said.

Show and Dravecky, two parts of an eventual five-man pitching rotation, threw quite a bit more gingerly. Both pitchers had taken long periods of rest between the end of the season and the beginning of different courses of therapy. Dravecky was intent on building up the muscles around the left elbow. Show was content to simply build up his right arm.

After mixing up fastballs and breaking pitches for 10 minutes, Show walked off the mound and claimed that he still felt a strange twinge in the elbow. "It could be scar tissue," he said. "Something in there is causing the irritation. I don't really feel it right now when I throw. I feel it when I do awkward things. Like lift things in a strange way. I suppose that if it was bad today, I'd really be disappointed right now. But it wasn't. So far so good. I have to keep positive. Be optimistic about it."

Bowa, who was still trying to make a decision whether or not Dravecky would open the season in the bullpen, was fully aware of how important the health of these two pitchers was to the success of the season.

"If they're hurt, we're in trouble, no question about it," Bowa said. "They're two quality pitchers. It would be like telling the Mets they had to go without Ron Darling or Dwight Gooden. How do you think they'd do? No, there's no sense in sugar coating that. I'll tell you what I told both of them: 'Take it slow.' I don't care whether they go out and let up 20 runs every time they pitch, just as long as they're ready by April. They're veterans. They know what they have to do. I'd press some young kids, but I'm not going to press them."

The highlight of the day might have been the weigh-in of Carmelo Martinez, the left-fielder. He had concluded 1986 with nine homers and 25 RBIs and had then returned to his native Puerto Rico where scouts reported he had gained so much weight he was floating around like a dirigible. Several months earlier, Bowa had sent Martinez a letter while he was playing in the winter league, notifying him that for every pound he came into camp above 200, Bowa was going to fine him 10 dollars. The message was clear: "You can tell him that he can get in shape in Las Vegas," Bowa said at the time.

By the first of the year, when Bowa was in a Padres party that scouted San Diego players in the Puerto Rican winter league, Martinez, playing in Caguas, a town 30 miles south of San Juan, had claimed to have shed 12 pounds off his meaty frame. "I'm about 216," Martinez said back then. "I've got about 16 pounds more to go. Yeah, I got the letter. That's too much money."

Martinez eventually weighed in at 205. "That's fifty bucks," Bowa said. "I told him he could take me out to a steak and lobster dinner in New York. That should about cover it."

It was the brightest moment of a grim and determined five-hour workout. Perhaps the most determined workout at the complex since the team had won the pennant in 1984.

"Did you see anybody out there laughing?" said Tony Gwynn, one of several position players on hand who still didn't need to report to camp for several days. "I sure didn't."

Adding to the no-nonsense atmosphere of this camp was a memo directed at the media and typed on San Diego Padres stationery.

The title: "Club Communication."

The topic: "Spring training policies."

One sensed that Bowa meant business when this bold-faced, capitalized, underlined statement jumped off the middle of the page:

DO NOT APPROACH THE MANAGER OR THE COACHES AT ANY TIME DURING THE WORKOUT!!!

"Oh lighten up," Bowa said when asked about the rules. Then he added, "They're not my rules."

Say what?

"Let's look at them," he said. "That's my rule. That's my rule. And that's especially my rule."

The rules:

> Larry will be happy to cooperate with every interview request. Workouts are scheduled to begin at 9 a.m. daily through March 5. He will be available for interviews prior to workouts except when he is meeting with a player or a member of his staff... He will be available for interviews following each workout. Please don't camp out in the manager's office. He will invite you in at the conclusion of field work.

Said Bowa with a big grin: "That's not true. I ain't invitin' anybody in. If they're there, I'll talk to them."

> You may conduct player interviews anytime prior to the workout. When the workout is in progress, please use discretion as to when to approach a player. If they are not actively involved in a

workout at the time and are in foul territory around the batting cage, you may attempt to talk with players. We would appreciate no television interviews during the workout only because they are more time consuming and could interfere with a player completing his required assignments. Upon completion of the official workout, players are available both on the field and in the clubhouse.

Said Bowa: "You know those TV guys. They come down here and just expect you to quit your workouts. Stop 'em right in the middle so they can do a TV interview. That really shocks me because the main thing here is just trying to get the guys in shape. They come down like you're supposed to stop everything. It doesn't affect my job, but my main objective right here is getting the team ready to play. Not to worry about granting TV interviews from people, some of them, who you probably won't see all year. Once the season starts, if we happen to get off real bad, you probably won't even hear from them."

THE CLUBHOUSE IS CLOSED TO THE MEDIA FROM THE BEGINNING OF THE WORKOUT THROUGH ITS CONCLUSION.

Players will have only 10 minutes to change shirts during the session and do not have time to conduct interviews in the clubhouse area.

This was a first during spring training when the atmosphere is usually more relaxed and conducive for discourse between the media and the players. In fact, under Steve Boros last spring, camp was just that. Camp. Except nobody brought the marshmallows and the wieners. "When the games begin, we'll open up the clubhouse again," Bowa said. "That way, when Eric Show comes in after pitching three innings, you can get your interviews."

NOTE TO TELEVISION CAMERAMEN:

When taping the workout, do not go into fair territory without the manager's permission or beyond the first and third base bags in foul territory. This is a precautionary measure due to baseballs that stray during the workout.

In the following days, Bowa would discover that clubhouse access and regulating the media would be the least of his problems. Unbeknown to him, negotiations were now beginning to accelerate in regard to the possible sale of the franchise. A decision whether or not to sign free agent Tim Raines, the league's 1986 batting champion and a close friend of Gwynn, was being made at the top of the organization. That decision alone would have far-reaching effects on the makeup of his ballclub.

He would wonder why Kevin Mitchell, a San Diego native who was brought to the Padres in the McReynolds deal, was the only player who missed the start of the first full-scale workout by several hours. Mitchell's story was that he was stopped on the mountain pass just prior to the Imperial Valley between San Diego and Yuma because he had no chains on his tires and could not proceed because of a snowfall. He returned 50 miles to San Diego so a cousin could take him over the mountain in a four-wheel drive truck.

Would Mitchell, who grew up on the streets in tough Southeast San Diego, be an eventual problem? Bowa wondered.

All this was transpiring without Bowa's knowledge several days later when the manager arrived at the complex at seven-thirty in the morning to find Steve Garvey, already in full uniform, jogging.

WEDNESDAY, FEB. 25, 1987 ◆
YUMA, AZ

A t the winter meetings last December in Hollywood, Florida, it was one o'clock in the morning. Jack McKeon, me, our chief scout, Dick Hager, Ballard Smith, Dick Freeman, the club's vice president, and our advisor, Tal Smith, were all sitting in a hotel suite. We were going over our ballclub and Steve Garvey's name came up. When I left that room that night, I was unsure what Garvey's status was. Were we going to play Carmelo Martinez or John Kruk at first? The only guy who frowned on it was Dick Freeman. The reason, of course, being the public relations end of it. Someone at the meeting said, "You're putting Larry on the spot by not making a decision on the guy." The Padres thing was, "We'll keep him on the team, but you don't have to play him." The guy went on to say that, "Hey, you're just putting the manager on the spot, because if he's there, he's going to be playing. Why not just make a decision on him?" This was right before we made the Kevin McReynolds trade. We were going with youth anyway, so this would have been a great time to just say, hey, we're gonna go all the way. Ballard made the statement that when we signed Steve originally to a five-year deal back in 1983, everyone in the front office said that if we could get three or four years out of him, it would be great.

When I left the meeting, I went home to Clearwater. They said that they might make a decision on it after the holidays. After the first of the year because Ballard was going to go skiing or something. But as you know, it never came off.

It wasn't that Garvey's skills had deteriorated. It was just that they were getting lesser and lesser and we were going in another direction. We were going toward a youth movement and it would have been a perfect time. I think they were more than a little up-set that Garvey had made such a public showing about trying to buy the team when Joan put it up for sale last winter. Joan had a thing about it. Almost like she was embarrassed to be put in that sort of position by a ballplayer. I wasn't out there, but I heard Ballard took a pretty good shot at him in the papers because Garvey was critical of the direction the organization had taken. But Dick Freeman, who was looking at things from a purely business sense, kept saying, "What about the season-ticket holders?" And someone in the room countered that by saying, "For two weeks you're going to get a lot of flack, but after two weeks are over, they're going to forget about it."

When I got to spring training, Ballard and Jack said, "You're the manager. You can play whoever you want." In other words, the onus is on my back. I'm going to be made the bad guy when I say, "Steve, you're not playing." It's like the point that was made at the meeting, "You're just putting the manager in the middle instead of just cutting the ties and saying we're going with youth." In fact, they were even going to have it set up where Steve, if he wanted to, could say, "I'm going to retire." If he was worried about being embarrassed or not looking right, they were going to give him that option.

I thought it was a good idea. I don't have anything against Steve, but I thought because we were going with kids, maybe it was just better to go the whole way. Let's just not do it halfway. Everyone told me that he'd really lost a step in the field. And that when he goes through slumps now—where before he'd maybe go 1-for-20, or something—now he'd go 1-for-40 or 50. You know, I hadn't seen him play. I really hadn't. And it'll be hard to tell this spring when he plays only five or six innings a game.

When they asked my opinion that night, I couldn't really comment because I hadn't seen the guy play for two years. All I said was that if we're going for youth, let's do it the whole way. Let's not do it half-heartedly. Let's go the whole gambit and the oldest guy on the team would be shortstop Garry Templeton at 31, which is not ancient. Dick Freeman looked over to me and kept shaking his head, like—it can't be done, it can't be done. I knew, when I left the room that Dick would have some more in-put in the decision. He was worried about the season-ticket hold-ers and probably about paying off his $1.45 million. Freeman said season tickets were down and they would be going down further. "You don't know how important Garvey is to the commu-nity," he said. Someone said, "What's more important, the com-munity or just winning ballgames?" In Dick's situation, he also wants to win, but he's concerned with the community. Getting the season-ticket holders.

In our situation? Well, you have to do what you think is right if it means winning more games. But now it's all in my hands. There's nothing else that can be done about it.

As far as Steve goes now, he's the first baseman. But I'm not going to sit and just watch him wallow. If he's swinging the bat, he's going to play. I've got to get him out in the late innings if he's on the bases. He can't run. So it's like using two players. But what else am I going to do? I figure, when the season starts, I'll give him 150 at bats to see if he can cut it. After that, I'll have to make a decision. I mean, if he's struggling. It'll be up to me and it's go-ing to be a tough one if I have to make it. But I'll tell you one thing, he impressed the hell out of me today. Here's a guy who's been in the game for 17 years and he's out there jogging before I get here. That's why he's been a success. That's why when he takes the uniform off for good, he'll be a success at whatever he does. If you ask me, he was sending a message to all of us. If his skills are still at the same level as his work habits, maybe the best decision we ever made was the one we didn't follow through on.

Thursday, Feb. 26, 1987 ♦
Yuma, AZ

(D) ick Williams may be gone from the Padres but he certainly has not forgotten. It was almost a year ago to the day that Williams left the Padres high and dry when he elected not to show up for the first day of spring training. A few months later, Williams was named manager of the Seattle Mariners, the sixth club he has led in an illustrious managerial career that dates back to 1967. In 20 years, Williams has parted ways on sour terms in Boston, Oakland, California, Montreal and San Diego. This, despite pennants in Boston and San Diego and a pair of world championships in Oakland.

Williams, a marginal utility man during much of his 13-year playing career, has certainly been down the pike as a manager. Larry Bowa, who holds the major-league record for fielding percentage by a shortstop (.980) and has played more games at the position than any shortstop in National League history (2,222), has been down the pike as a player, but is just a novice as a manager. Thus, the genesis of today's newspaper ignited dispute.

Williams, whose Mariners train at Tempe's Diablo Stadium in the Phoenix area, must have bristled earlier this week when he picked up a copy of the *Arizona Republic* to read this particular Bowa comment about managing:

"I'm not hired to be fired. I'm hired to manage and when I'm tired of managing, I'll quit. I think if you approach it assuming you're hired to be fired as a manager, then you're thinking negatively before you start. I plan on managing as long as I want to because I believe in what I'm doing. I have confidence in myself."

The fact that Bowa had made this statement shortly after his hiring last November, evidently had no effect on Williams. Lloyd

Herberg, a reporter for the *Arizona Republic*, decided to seek Williams out and get his reaction to the remark.

Williams didn't disappoint:

"Well, very few managers can say that, but he's had a full year managing in the minor leagues," Williams said. "I think it's a standard thing. It's been going on all the while. It didn't apply to Connie Mack and he owned the ballclub. And it didn't apply to Walter Alston and it probably won't apply to Tommy Lasorda. I've put some good numbers on the board and I've moved around. Sparky Anderson's put some good numbers on the board and he's moved around. Same with Billy Martin. Same with Whitey Herzog. Here again, I've only been in it 20 years managing. Larry would know much better."

Bowa, who rarely shuns a good fight, responded with fervor when approached about Williams' retort by a group of San Diego reporters:

"I was only trying to say, 'Why go in on it on a negative? If it happens, it happens.' I didn't think he worried so much about me. I didn't think he followed my career so closely. It's a compliment. Tell him I had a 17-year career in the big leagues. That's why I didn't get my managerial experience as quick as he did."

Williams, of course, wouldn't let the matter die. He was intent on getting in the last word. When the Padres made their first spring appearance in Tempe several weeks later, Williams attempted to use the tried and true out utilized so often by baseball people. He blamed the entire incident on the writer from the *Arizona Republic*.

"It was only half the story," Williams said. "The guy from the Phoenix paper interviewed me and wanted to know about managers hired to be fired. I said, 'Hell, everyone I know—unless he's Connie Mack, Walter Alston or possibly Tommy Lasorda—is hired to be fired.' I also told him that I thought Bowa would do a hell of a job. But that part wasn't in the paper. For some reason, writers have a tendency to do that. I don't know why.

"I respect Larry Bowa. He's a bulldog. When he played, you could throw at him, and he would get on base and beat you."

Herberg, the writer in question, had one unequivocal statement when he was appraised about Williams' version of the story:

"He's a liar. He never said that."

Bowa, who had a big smirk on his face, decided to let the jury rest. Old managers never die, it seems. They never even fade away.

SUNDAY, MAR. 1, 1987 ♦
YUMA, AZ

"We have no plans to make any further offers to Tim Raines. We believe that our offer of $1.1 million per year over two years is the highest outstanding offer and to bid against ourselves would make no sense.

"Tim Raines has recently indicated he will not take a pay cut from the $1.5 million he made last year. We do not believe in today's baseball market that he is worth that sum of money. Tom Reich, Tim Raines' agent, has publicly and privately indicated that he will not allow Tim Raines to sign at a discount from the $5.5 million three-year contract offer made by Montreal. He has additionally indicated that he feels Tim Raines is a $2 million-a-year ballplayer.

"We reopened negotiations with Mr. Reich because we had received indications that Tom Reich would accept a contract in the range of $1.3 million a year. Both Tim Raines and Tom Reich have since denied those reports. Jack McKeon and Larry Bowa agree with this decision. They have indicated they would like to see a resolution of this matter now, as it is potentially disruptive to spring training. Since it is obvious we are not close to agreeing to terms with Tim Raines, we are ending contract negotiations."

—Padres President Ballard Smith.

L arry Bowa stood with his arms characteristically crossed along the piping at the back of the batting cage as the Padres partook in a typical batting practice fundamental drill. Each hitter would lay down a bunt, hit to the opposite side to move an imaginary runner from first base to second, and hit a fly to the outfield that might score a runner from third. After that, the batter would be free to swing away. From each side of the batting cage, coaches were hitting fly balls and ground balls to waiting fielders. On Bowa's mind was a player who was not on the field—

free agent Tim Raines—a man in the middle of baseball's war against the multi-million dollar, multi-year contract.

At last December's winter meetings, Commissioner Peter Ueberroth had noted in his annual state of the game address that baseball's 26 owners were paying nearly $50 million to players who were no longer on active rosters. Publicly he was telling the owners that they had to tighten purse strings. Privately, it was suspected that the commissioner had orchestrated a sudden cooling of the free agent market because for two consecutive winters, owners had chosen not to bid for attractive star ballplayers.

The Major League Baseball Players Association had loudly cried collusion, filing separate grievances in favor of the two groups of free agents—the class of 1986, in which the Padres had made no overtures, and the class of 1987, in which the Padres had casually wooed both outfielder Tim Raines, formerly of the Montreal Expos, and third baseman Bob Horner, formerly of the Atlanta Braves. Bowa could care less about collusion and such political manipulations. All he cared about was how he could improve a team that he was beginning to suspect might be considerably short in a number of areas. Since Horner had long ago bowed out of the Padres picture, Bowa's attention was on Raines and his own club's game of verbal rhetoric.

"Raines would take a lot of pressure off the young kids," Bowa was saying, the team's first intrasquad game only hours away. "I'm talking about a Stanley Jefferson or if a Joey Cora should make the team. With a Tim Raines, they wouldn't have to get on. Right now, they do. No ifs ands or buts about it. As it is, we're going to have trouble scoring runs. We can't make mistakes. We have to play almost error-free, mental-free baseball and it's hard to play that every game. It's tough for a pitcher to go out there every day and go nothing-nothing for six innings. You're afraid to make a mistake, and when you're afraid, that's when you usually make one.

"A guy like Raines could add a lot. I don't want to get into the money part, but what he's asking for seems to be fair market value. That is, with the numbers I heard. What is it, $1.3 million with the incentives to get to $1.5? But it's not my money. If it was my money, I'd do it in a second."

Little did Bowa suspect at the time that this would be just the end of round two in the Raines non-negotiations with critical round three coming up in several weeks. The first two rounds had ended similarly—with the Padres making inquiries to Raines' Los Angeles-based agent Tom Reich, who sternly rebuffed what he considered to be low-end proposals.

Smith, after much organizational soul-searching, had decided to delve into the big name free agent market for the first time since the Padres failed to sign Chicago Cubs pitcher Rick Sutcliffe after the 1984 pennant-winning season. To illustrate how much difference two years had made, Smith, who was integral in signing free agents Steve Garvey and Rich Gossage to lucrative, long-term contracts, thought he had nabbed Sutcliffe for the measly price of $2 million per year for four years. Sutcliffe opted instead to return to the Cubs where he figured he had unfinished business.

Sutcliffe, who won the Cy Young Award when he was traded from Cleveland to the Cubs in mid-1984, was the pitcher of record that crazy October day in San Diego when the Cubs blew a 3-0 lead, Game 5 and the National League pennant to the Padres. Larry Bowa, of course, was the Cubs shortstop that day.

Smith could never really explain why in 1983, Garvey was worth $1.45 million per year for five years; why in 1984, Gossage was worth $1.35 million per year for five years, plus a huge annuity; why in 1985, Sutcliffe was worth all those bucks, but why in 1987, Raines, who had just come off a season as the league's leading hitter, wasn't worth nearly that much.

"We were going to sign Garvey at whatever the cost," Smith said. "It was pretty much the same thing with Gossage, although we had reached our limit in his case. We were just lucky he accepted it. I was never comfortable with the Sutcliffe negotiations. They went on a little too long. Something just wasn't right. The money was too high. There was too much risk. I was going to go ahead with it, but I never had a good feeling about it. By the time we began pursuing Tim Raines, the marketplace had changed."

In terms of Sutcliffe, the Padres might have been fortunate. Sutcliffe had two successive injury-plagued seasons in Chicago under the terms of his new contract.

But by late last winter Smith did know he had to do something dramatic. After the disastrous '86 season, it became apparent that the Padres were the proud owners of the great shrinking season-ticket base. And so, a letter was addressed to all potential renewals stating that the Padres would indeed actively pursue free agents in the off season. Raines was mentioned as one of the likely candidates. This admission, in itself, had come at some personal embarrassment to the Padres chief executive. Late in the summer of '86, it was suggested by *San Diego Union* columnist Wayne Lockwood that Raines would be the perfect free-agent signee for a team that was sadly lacking a player with speed and hitting prowess at the top of the batting order. But Lockwood neglected one key factor. The Padres had taken a hard line on drug abuse and Raines had undergone rehabilitation for a cocaine habit during the early stages of his career. Though Raines was one of those rare athletes who never again succumbed to the problem and was described by Jack McKeon as a model citizen, the Padres decided to go on the offensive. Smith, who once claimed to have at least 100 files in his possession on different ballplayers with drug problems, reiterated the club position that players with a drug problem in their past would never don Padres brown and gold. In fact, he added, until the Padres had some protection against drug abuse in the form of mandatory urinalysis written into the basic agreement, he would sign no player to anything longer than a one-year contract. The drug test matter had been deemed by an arbitrator to be open for collective bargaining. But ownership and the players association have been log jammed about the drug issue because the association is firmly against drug testing.

During a season in which Smith blasted reporters, suspended Gossage, ripped Kevin McReynolds for his work habits and banned beer from the locker room, Smith's diatribe about Raines' drug problem was another in a long series of public relation nightmares. Smith quickly decided he had erred and sent a letter to Raines apologizing for using him as a platform for his comments. Raines, who has commissioner-ordered drug testing in his contract, obviously accepted that apology. But in the end, Raines' drug problem would weigh heavily on an organization whose owner had taken such a keen personal interest in alcohol and drug rehabilitation.

When the season ended, Raines filed for free agency and eventually shunned a three-year, $4.8 million ($5.5 million Canadian) offer from the Expos that he termed an insult. Raines had earned $1.5 million in 1986 and viewed the raise as paltry. Deciding to forego salary arbitration, Raines stated publicly that he would rather sit out the coming season than return to Montreal. He became one of several premier free agents who did not sign with their originating clubs prior to a magical January 8 cutoff date. According to the basic agreement, that meant Raines could neither negotiate nor return to Montreal until May 1. Raines then issued a list of teams he would prefer to play for—the Los Angeles Dodgers and the Padres were at the top of the list. The Dodgers, despite pressure from the players within their own organization, resisted negotiating with Raines. In late January, Smith tendered an offer of $1.1 million a year for two years to Reich for Raines' service. The offer, $400,000 below what Raines had earned in 1986, was rejected. Smith left that offer on the table and advised Reich to get back to him once he had tested the waters throughout the league.

Those waters proved to be frigid.

The Padres had elected to play an interesting game which was atypical of the boom years of free agency. Rather than negotiating, they intended to try and steal Raines with a lowball figure. Around the rest of the league other free agents were suffering through similar experiences. Detroit pitcher Jack Morris, for instance, could not sell himself to the four teams of his choice and thus opted to go to arbitration with the Tigers. Another Montreal free agent, Andre Dawson, eventually had to offer his services to the Cubs via a blank contract. Terming the affair a "dog and pony show," Cubs president Dallas Green signed Dawson for $500,000 and $300,000 worth of incentives. Former Detroit catcher Lance Parrish finally signed with the Philadelphia Phillies after a controversy about his threat to sue the owners. Both Dawson and Parrish signed at a rate well below what their original teams had offered.

Smith was banking on Raines making the same type of concession. And as the beginning of spring training grew closer, Raines was becoming edgy. Through Tony Gwynn, Raines made it known to Padres management that he might now be willing to come in closer to the original San Diego figure. Based on that conversation, Smith decided to contact Reich again several days after the Padres opened camp.

"He's won the battle over the new proposal," Smith had said several days earlier. "I'm going to make it. I got the point during the conversation that the guy who was going to make the new proposal was me . . . . The ballclub has to proceed like we're not going to get him. Because the fact is, we're not even close. But we'll keep trying to pursue him as long as he's available. You're always trying to improve your ballclub. It's tough when a guy is offered all that money for three years by Montreal, but I can't be embarrassed when I make somebody a $1.1 million offer like I made him."

But as the week went on, Smith attended to other business interests and his own personal problems. The new offer was never made. Through his conversations with Reich, Smith became convinced that even a sweetener of $200,000 per year to $1.3 million per would not be enough to satisfy Raines, who continued to make public statements posturing that he would not sign a contract for less than $1.5 million a year and that he was not about to return to Montreal.

And finally, Smith made this sweeping conclusion: "I'm not convinced adding Tim Raines would make us a winner. Montreal hasn't had overwhelming success with Raines playing for them. It takes 24 guys."

Smith's opinion was not shared by the baseball people in the organization—Bowa and McKeon—who were not intent on letting the Raines "lack of negotiations" die. Of one thing it is certain. The specter of Raines was complicating a camp in which little progress was occurring at all levels.

WEDNESDAY, MAR. 11, 1987 ◆ MESA, AZ

T he toughest thing about my first spring training as a big-league manager, to be honest with you, is knowing these guys' personalities. Like Stanley Jefferson, he's scared of me. He's told coaches, "I don't know where the man is coming from." He thinks I'm crazy. I've pulled him aside and told him, "I talk loud, you talk soft. I'm emotional, you're not emotional. When you listen to me, don't listen to my voice, just listen to the words I say." I'm tryin' to go slow with this kid. Hey, you don't want to lose him. You try to back off. He's very low-key. It's hard. Guys like Benny, you know, Benito Santiago, guys I had last year in Vegas, you scream at him and he laughs. He listens, you know, but the next day . . . He thinks it's funny . . . Gary Green knows me.

I wanted to make sure that I came across, not as a tough guy, but I'm not gonna put up with any crap. And I think I made that clear. The way guys have reacted, I think that's established. It's just a matter of stayin' consistent. Like today, I had to fine Shane Mack. Here's a kid that's probably not even going to make the club and I've got to take a hundred bucks. But I've got to do it. You know. I've got to take his hundred bucks. Here's one guy I don't want to fine because he's going down. But hell, it's got to be done. You've got to make 'em aware. It's like Marvell Wynne today. He's sitting on the bench with Amos Otis, one of our minor-league instructors. Amos said he didn't miss a sign all day and he didn't. And here's a guy who had trouble all last year with signs. But I've got to fine 'em. For missing signs, on bunts, steals and hit and runs. For coming in late. For staying out too late. You want to treat these guys like men. But they've got to know you bleepin' mean business.

It's like Kevin Mitchell. I think he would be a real problem if you let things slide. You say, "Hey, Mitch, you don't come in 10 minutes before you're supposed to be dressed." I thought I was going to have an incident with him the other night. Mitch came in. He was sick. He came in like at a quarter of four. You know, I told him, "Hey, if you've been sick all day, there are telephones. All you have to do is call the trainer and he'll give you some medicine." I've been trying to stick up for Mitchell, but I don't know what the story is. He's drivin' back and forth from Yuma to San Diego. Back and forth. I don't know what the hell he's doin'. God knows. He'll call up and say that he has to go to a dentist in San Diego. That makes a lot of sense. Like there's no dentist in Yuma. He's asleep in the chair in the clubhouse because he didn't sleep in San Diego. I guess he has all kinds of family there and he's trying to entertain them. At least I hope that's what the bleep it is.

All the guys we got from the Mets in the McReynolds deal—Mitchell, Jefferson and Shawn Abner—to me, there's no discipline instilled in them at all. Their philosophy when they were younger was you throw the ball out there and hit .300. That's the magic thing. Do that and you'll be in the big leagues. Some of these guys, you try to talk with them about a little inside baseball and they look at you like you're nuts. You know, like the guy in front of you walks on four pitches that aren't even close, go up there and wait for a strike. One of these guys will look at you like, "What do you mean, a strike?"

Today, something happened that just ticked me off. One of our rookies, Jimmy Steels, a guy that played with me last year, is hitting with a two-ball count and he swings at a pitch up by his eyes and pops up. It's not the fact that he popped up that ticked me off, but the fact that he swung at a screwed up pitch. You know, he should be looking in the strike zone. If the guy throws you a bitch pitch, it's still 2-and-1. You don't say anything to them in that situation because it is a physical mistake. But the point I'm trying to make, tomorrow, I'll tell him, "Steely, you probably could have been a little more selective, couldn't you?" And I know the first thing he's going to say is, "Yes, the ball was over my head." He knows he screwed up.

There are guys you've got to ride. Like Benny. You've got to stay on Benny. You've got to stay on Gary Green. Last year, I made a special project of Gary Green. Not because he's a shortstop like I was, but because I watched him and he was doing the minimum to get by. I'd say, "Get your ground balls." He'd take 10 or 15. "Take BP." He'd take one round. He'd do everything I told him, but it would be the bare minimum. Maybe it was because this kid was the shortstop on the '84 United States Olympic baseball team, I don't know. Maybe it was because he had it easy. One day, I just called him into my office and said, "You're hittin' .210. You've got to be kiddin' me. You're missing balls, you're missing pop flies. You're not getting ground balls you should get to. I want you out there taking fifty to a hundred ground balls, taking extra batting practice every day."

So for three weeks, he went out every single day. He hit extra. He took ground balls. We hit him pop flies. And all of a sudden, everything started clicking. He started making plays. He started getting big hits. He started playing with confidence. He wanted the ball hit to him. At the end of the season, the greatest thing that happened to me all year, he came to me and said, "I want to thank you."

I said, "For what?"

He said, "You made me realize what it is to work and play at baseball."

And whether we won the pennant or not, that made my whole season. Because I know one guy turned it around. I watched him in April and he was a piece of crap. He had ability, but he was just lazy.

See, the reason I stress the mental so much is that I had to have both. If I had just gone on the physical, I'd have been looking for a job. I would have been managing a little-league team or something. Because I just couldn't do it on physical ability. I had to do everything. I had to use my head. I had to use the knowledge I had of hitters. I went over the charts every day. I'd take 'em home at night. Teams we were playing, I'd look at where they hit the ball. What the count was. I mean, I was obsessed with it. I know nobody does that. I'm not telling people to do what I did. But there is a fine line. A happy medium. You can do a little bit of what I did.

You know, like maybe before the game starts, come and look at the charts, the defensive tendencies. The last time Eric Show pitched, this guy hit two ground balls right here. Right over the bag. Managing is just a game of percentages. To me, you use every edge you can. And that's how I played. I used to study this thing until two, three in the morning. But I'd know exactly where I would play in the game. I wouldn't be out of position. If a guy got a base hit, it would be one of those check-swing deals where he never hits the ball. Stuff like that. Most of these guys, they get their scouting reports, they don't even look at 'em. But see, what I did is, whoever was playing second next to me, I'd use the reports this way, too: I'd say, "Let's go read these." And we'd read 'em together. I remember the 1980 World Series when I was with the Phillies. I'd study those suckers on the Royals until I was blue in the face. I knew where Amos Otis hit the ball. I knew where Frank White hit the ball. I think I tied or broke a major-league record for double plays in that series. I was in the right place at the right time. It just wasn't coincidental. I looked at the stuff the scout scouted for us. He scouted Kansas City from the end of August on. I had papers stacked up that big. But they don't play the game like that anymore. That's what ticked me off. Because these guys are better athletes. They're stronger. They're faster. They're quicker. They throw better.

I'm trying to instill it, but it's like talkin' to a bleepin' wall. Some of these guys, it goes in one ear and out the other. You know the attitude. Like, "Bleep off! I'm tired of listening to this shit." You keep having to tell somebody the same thing day in and day out, I get tired of it. But I've still got to do it. That's my job. I can't stand saying, "Hit the cutoff man. Hit the bleepin' cutoff man." I'm getting sick of it and they still miss 'em. I keep them after games. For longer practices. And they still miss 'em. It's hard to believe. It gets frustrating. I know when I tell my little girl Tori, who is four years old, not to touch something, she doesn't touch it. She might touch it until she gets a shock or something, but she won't touch it again.

And that's why I try to tell these guys: "If you look at the scoreboard and study the scoreboard and study the inning you're in and the score, it dictates to you whether you take chances, it dictates to you whether you play it safe. It's common sense that when you're behind 5-0 in the seventh inning, you don't go from first to third on a single unless you are sure you can make it. If it's 90 percent, you don't go, because there's that 10 percent chance you're gonna get thrown out. So why even think about that? Now if you're ahead four or 5-0, take a chance. He might throw the ball in the dugout. But we have room for error there because we're ahead 5-0."

I can't get some guys to think about the score. To think about the inning. To think about the situation. That's the hardest thing I'm having trouble with and I don't understand why, because it's common sense.

Like the other day with Jefferson. Sandy Alomar, our first base coach, went up to him and said, "You are running. The count is 3-and-1 and you are running." He didn't run. Afterward I went up to him and said, "Maybe I'm wrong, but did Sandy tell you to run?"

He said, "Yes."

The count was 3-and-1, they know we run automatically on 3-and-1 in spring training. I told him, "Everybody runs unless we say no. We didn't say no. Why didn't you run?"

He said, "I got my lead. I said, I'm running, I'm running. Before I knew it, the pitch was across homeplate."

What am I going to say to that? That's why it's costing them all a hundred bucks if they miss a sign. If I have to treat them like bleepin' babies, I will. Jefferson is afraid right now to make a mistake. He's getting confused between mental mistakes and physical mistakes. He thinks that if he gets picked off that I'm going to jump on him. But I'm not going to jump on him. I told him. I said, "If you try to steal 20 bases and you're picked off first 10 times and thrown out at second 10 times, I'm not gonna say a word to you. The only thing I will do, you won't be on your own anymore. I'll tell you when to steal." I mean, I can't make it any more simpler than that. But he's still afraid to go out and try it. A good base runner is a gambler. A good base runner is aggressive, daring. He's got a certain air about him. Like, "He might throw me out, but I don't give a damn." Stanley Jefferson doesn't have that yet. I hope he will have it. I wasn't a great base stealer, but I stole over 300 bases. I knew when to go. I knew the pitcher. I knew his faults. I studied everything.

Like today in the dugout, Joey Cora is not playing. I told him, "You'll probably make the team. We'll give you the day off to watch the game." He's all excited. I look over there. The Cubs are hitting and he's got his back to the field talking to Carmelo Martinez. I said, "Joey, what the hell are you doing? Do you think it might help to watch how we're playing these Cubs hitters? Because we're going to go into Wrigley Field and you may be the second baseman." After that, he watched the whole game. But I'm just saying, what was he thinking about? Here's a kid who is pretty intelligent. I'm saying to myself, if that was me, I'd be watching every hitter. What kind of pitch he hit. Where he hit it. Who was hit and running. Until I told him, he had no idea. That's discouraging. Someone told me I'm expecting too much from these kids. Maybe I am, maybe I am. But that's how I was taught to do it. And if I was taught to do it this way, and I was successful, I've got to put some credence into what I think is right.

Yeah, a couple of my coaches told me that I'm too hard on them. They're worried that I might lose some of them. How can I lose someone if I've given him the job? I've all but handed Jefferson the damned job in center field. I've already told him not to worry about physical mistakes. But I'm losing him because I'm screaming at him.

My philosophy is, if I push them to the point where they become overachievers, they're going to be better players. That's what I'm trying to do. I'm not trying to push them over the brink or make 'em say, "Screw him. Let me get away from this guy. He's driving me crazy." I don't want to do that. I want to push them to the point where they're going to play to their max. Once the game is over, they can sit down and take it easy. See, every guy who plays nine innings should be dead bleepin' tired after the game is over. Whether it be mentally tired, physically tired or whatever. If you're not tired either mentally or physically, then you didn't do what you're supposed to do. I'm worn out and I didn't even catch a ground ball. I'm worn out. When I go home, I'll go right to bed. I may not sleep, but I'm tired. I'm bleepin' drained. And I haven't played one game that counts. Spring training is all for fun. It's going to get worse.

Greg Riddoch, the only coach I had a chance to bring in here, made the point. He said, "I've never seen anybody as intense as you are." Like he says something to me during a game and I don't even hear him. He told me today, "Do you want me to say something to you?" I said, "Yes." And he said, "Well, you act like you don't hear me." And I said, "Hey, I don't. When I'm looking at something, don't be coming to me. Wait until between innings or when the side is out." He can't understand why I get so involved.

See, these guys don't know how to take me because I scream and holler at them out on the field and in the clubhouse I bullshit with them. That's why they should know I care about them. Because if I didn't care, I'd tell 'em to get the bleep out of here. I don't want to talk to you. I kid around with Jefferson and he's scared of me. The man is scared of me and I hate that. I don't want that. But I'm still going to stay on them about not making mental mistakes on the field. What I did in Vegas, I wore them down. They all thought, "He'll forget about it." But I won't forget about it. I'm going to keep after them. I did it in August. I did it in April. I did it in September. I will stay on it. Do it again. Do it again. It gets old. I get tired. I get worn out. When I get home at night, I'm tired. I haven't picked up a ball. But I'm tired because I have to do all the thinking for some of them.

Monday, Mar. 16, 1987 ♦ Scottsdale, AZ

By the time the Padres team bus had pulled into the parking lot of the Ramada Valley Ho, the club's hotel headquarters in the Phoenix area, the news had already broken all over San Diego. Tim Raines, who had his bags packed and was ready to travel west, would not sign with the Padres.

Players, writers, radio announcers and front office personnel were handed this brief statement from club president Ballard Smith: "After reviewing this latest proposal, it became clear to me that we are not going to reach an agreement with Tim Raines."

This time it was really over. And with one round-house upper cut from a deft opponent, the already staggering Padres were leveled by a blow that would have lasting implications for months.

Raines and the Padres, TKOed in round three.

"Jack McKeon and I had a long talk about it," Bowa said months later. "And he thinks the day we said we were done with Tim Raines, that was like letting the air out of the balloon. He said, 'Even though we had let people know it was over, I guess the players still thought there was a chance. And when we finally said we can't get him, it took awhile for them to believe it was over with.' He keeps telling me that on that day he saw a big change."

Certainly, it made everyone look at the Padres situation more realistically. Both the players and the baseball people in management took a look at the potential lineup for opening day, now less than a month away in San Francisco, and were horrified. They saw a team with little experience up the middle. A rookie catcher with tremendous potential, a rookie center fielder with a growing reputation of having a low pain tolerance, and a rookie second baseman who had never played a game above the double-A level and had missed a good portion of the 1986 season after he was felled by a knife wound during a post-game fight.

"Bleep it," Bowa said when he heard the news. "We might as well just go with all our kids."

In San Diego, fans felt a sense of betrayal. A local radio station even held a charity drive to help raise the money so the Padres could sign Raines. A drive-in window was set up at the station so people could quickly drop off their contributions. During the day, a limousine pulled up to the window and the driver deposited a check for a thousand dollars. The check was signed by Joan Kroc. But the fans and media did not take this decision with such good humor. Penned executive sports editor Tom Cushman in the *San Diego Tribune*:

> Whatever dictated the decision to pass on Tim Raines, we now can await the trickle down effect, which—in this instance—may be more in the nature of a hemorrhage. Teams, after all, tend to reflect the attitude of ownership; when there is no real commitment to winning at the penthouse level, that attitude is usually mirrored by the men who inhabit the dugout.
>
> Under these circumstances, the players are more likely to reject a martinet like Larry Bowa. Bowa himself—a man driven to succeed—has little patience with those interested in being anything but the very best....
>
> This is not the sort of team portrait one usually paints in the early spring...but then, I'm not the guy holding the brush. Have a lovely season.

The nagging question that still remains more than a year later is why did the Padres let this happen? Why had they begun a course of wooing Raines if they really had no intention of signing him on anything but their own narrow terms? And how could they have so badly misread the mood of the fans?

"I never thought there was going to be that type of backlash," one high-ranking Padres official said about the decision. "If I did, I never would have gotten involved in it. I knew that signing him was a longshot right from the beginning. He just wasn't going to come in on our terms. It's the worst situation I've ever been involved in. It's too bad that people will remember that about Ballard more than anything else. It wasn't the way he wanted to go out as president. I think he did a pretty good job. The '84 team was put together by his people and he had a lot to do with it. They can never take that away from him."

Smith might have escaped the rancor on this one had Raines not gone on the offensive in the days preceding Smith's ultimate decision. Tiring of working out in isolation at his home in Palm Beach Gardens, Florida, Raines tried to make headway with four National League West clubs—Los Angeles, Atlanta, Houston and the Padres. When negotiations stalled on all fronts, Raines made a decision that he might have to take less money to go to the most desirable club. The Dodgers simply refused to negotiate, which engendered more than enough anger from their players and fans.

Even president Peter O'Malley, long a paragon of baseball tradition, came out looking foolish when several Dodgers players implored him to bring in Raines as the club's center fielder. O'Malley informed everyone that the Dodgers had no need of a center fielder since they already possessed Ken Landreaux, who at the same time was being mentioned in trade rumors. The Dodgers, obviously, had no intention of becoming involved in the Raines situation.

Frustrated with the proceedings, Raines, who had been incommunicado for months, suddenly made himself available to the San Diego media. On the Thursday prior to the final decision, Raines told this reporter in a phone interview: "At this point, I may not go to the team that gives me the best offer. I'm going to go to the place that's right for me. And San Diego is right on top. I've told people that I don't want to play for any less than I made last year, but there are a number of ways to do this. We can come in under $1.5 million, if they would just give me the opportunity to make it up."

Sounding like a man who was about to face his own execution, Smith said simply, "That's nice to know," when contacted about Raines' latest comment.

That set round three in motion. Bill Landman, a representative for Tom Reich, contacted Jack McKeon at the Valley Ho. McKeon put Landman in touch with Smith in San Diego. McKeon, who put in his best pitch, had gone to his own limit within the power structure of the organization. That left it up to Smith and all weekend Smith played hard to get. Smith even maintained that he had received no contact from any of Raines' representatives, which isn't what Reich was saying. Reich said Landman had contacted McKeon on Friday and that Smith was reached at his home on Sunday. Why was Smith being so evasive?

"I don't know," said Reich. "All I can tell you is that the facts I'm laying out are correct. That's the way it happened."

Smith's explanation was that he was going to "try very, very hard not to negotiate in the papers."

Strangely, there really had been no negotiations. Just a series of one-sided proposals. By early on this particular day, when Smith arrived at the Padres offices at Jack Murphy Stadium in San Diego, he had Raines' final proposal in hand. A $1.2 million, one-year package with $300,000 worth of incentives that would have given Raines the chance to reach his goal of $1.5 million. Raines' message was clear: Accept this offer and I'll be in Arizona tomorrow. Bowa's shot at a successful first season was just one phone call away. The phone call never came. Smith, despite theories to the contrary, was the man who ultimately made that decision.

"The proposal was for far less than Raines made last year," Reich said. "We showed that we were willing to do that. If that doesn't get it, what can I tell you? This is only Tim Raines. Nothing serious."

Since then, sources high within the Padres organization have countered that assertion. The sources say that the incentives were so attainable, it made the proposal ludicrous. "The way they were structuring it, the contract was virtually for $1.5 million," said the source.

But wasn't that worth the price of admission? Wouldn't two sellouts at Jack Murphy Stadium have paid the balance of that contract?

"There were several reasons that we didn't sign him," said the source. "First of all, it would have thrown off the economic balance of our player payroll structure. Secondly, we had a slim chance of winning the pennant, so why escalate the payroll? And finally, right or wrong, his drug problems had a lot to do with it. Hopefully he'll continue to stay healthy, but as we've found out, a drug problem is a lifelong problem. We didn't want to get into that."

The decision ignited plenty of bitterness in the Padres clubhouse. The next day, Bowa held a meeting and told his team to get on with business. "I told them that I know we've had a lot of distractions the last few days," Bowa said. "But it's over. Let's forget about it. Let's go with what we've got."

Asked what kind of response he received, Bowa said, "Nobody said anything." They didn't have to. Bowa, himself, was in no mood for kindness. Earlier in the week Bowa had been livid at rookie Shawn Abner when he overran second base for the final out of an inning to cost his team a run. Bowa had to wait awhile to snap at Abner because, "The guy never came back to the dugout. Someone brought him his glove." When Abner did come back, Bowa let fly. "I just went bleepin' nuts," he said. "You can't be making the same stupid mistakes over and over again. We're already four weeks into spring training." During batting practice several days later, Bowa was miffed because Stanley Jefferson missed his scheduled time in the batting cage. "Where's Jefferson?" Bowa screamed. When Bowa was told that Jefferson was in the clubhouse having his ankles taped, he continued to rant and rave. "Like that isn't something he couldn't have done this morning," Bowa said.

These days had all the portent of a long dismal season. But at least Bowa was beginning to understand his own role in the club's fabric.

"I think the Raines thing sent me the message that I'm the manager of this team and I have to manage the players they give me," Bowa said. "In essence, the owner of a team has the right to sign or not to sign whomever he or she wants to sign. My job is manager of the San Diego Padres. Jack, Joan and Ballard give me 24 players and say, now, "You're the manager." Unless you're a Whitey Herzog or a Dick Williams, there aren't too many managers who have a say in who comes in or out of here. Jack asks me about players. What I think of this guy, what I think of that guy. Do you think this guy can help us? But I think when the decision is made, it's his. Like he says, 'I'll give you the players and you run the team.'

"The ideal situation would be to be able to go up to him and say, 'I'd like you to go out and get so and so.' But you have to get time in and more or less get established as a manager. The best thing would be to have a baseball man handle baseball business. Trades, signing free agents, moving players, releasing players. I think that's the best thing that could happen.

"I just don't think Ballard wanted to be the only owner to sign a free agent. I think they got permission for Andre Dawson to sign with the Cubs and Lance Parrish to sign with the Phillies. I don't think Ballard wanted to step on anybody's shoes. That's the big difference between being a baseball man and just a business man. A baseball man knows that a guy like Raines is going to make players like Jefferson and Joey Cora better just by being in the lineup. A business man must also look at the dollar signs and on occasion says, nah, it's too much money or it doesn't fit into our payroll structure."

At the time, Smith did not deny that the climate within baseball had also played heavily on his decision not to sign Raines.

"This is a war," he said candidly.

But in this battle, the Padres certainly were not the winners. Raines ultimately received his money. When all the smoke had settled, Charles Bronfman, the owner of the Montreal Expos, announced that his original offer was still on the table. Raines could come home on May 1 and he would not lose a dime. At that point, Raines' wife, Virginia, stepped into the picture and mused publicly that her husband was returning to Montreal. All resistance had dissolved. Raines would not buck the system. That fight was over.

On May 2, Raines played his first game of the year and helped wreck the New York Mets. He eventually took a club that was ticketed for the basement in the National League East to a third-place finish, just four games behind division-winning St. Louis. He was the Most Valuable Player of the All-Star game.

The results on all fronts made havoc of Smith's assessment that Raines might not have turned the Padres into a winner.

"When you look back on it, it might have been a bad decision, I don't know," Smith said.

It wasn't the first and surely, it would not be the last.

WEDNESDAY, MAR. 25, 1987 ◆
YUMA, AZ

W̱ith less than two weeks to go before the start of the regular season, I'm starting to get pretty uneasy. In my mind,
all the long hours of spring instruction are not paying off, particularly when it comes to our new kids. I had already gotten on
Storm Davis because he refused to take direction or make adjustments in his pitching motion. Here's a guy who had played the
first five years of his career in the American League where umpires give pitchers the benefit of the higher strike zone. Over
here, he can't seem to find his control.

He's gonna find out real quick that you can't pitch ball one,
ball two in the National League. If you do, you'll get killed. I'm
waiting for him to make some kind of adjustment. But I'm not
seeing it.

I guess I was really ready to snap, though, at Jimmy Jones, a
young right-hander of mine who's in a battle with Ed Wojna for
the fifth spot in the starting rotation. Ed's kind of a journeyman
right-hander who hasn't made it in several tries with the Padres.
The guy who can't cut it will be sent back to Las Vegas where I
had both players in 1986. You know, Jones was supposed to be a
whiz kid. He was so highly thought of by the Padres, they picked
Jones in the 1982 amateur draft ahead of the New York Mets
Dwight Gooden. Gooden has been winning major-league games
since 1983. And I guess Jones and the Padres have been under a
lot of pressure ever since. I wasn't there, but everybody has told
me about Jones' first major-league start last September when he
faced just 28 Houston batters and pitched a one-hitter in the Astrodome.

He figured because of that performance he had the job this

spring. That it was his alone to win or lose. But I nearly blew my top when Jones walked four Chicago Cubs and allowed four hits and three runs in four innings out there today. Some writer asked me about it and I told him, "I told those guys that whoever pitches the best gets the bleepin' job. And Jones' last two outings have been horsebleep. That's as simple as I can put it. And Eddie Wojna is getting people out and throwing strikes."

Then the same writer tells me that Jones had felt pressure going out for what he considered to be a critical game. It was sort of make it or break it. He was nervous. That's why Jones opened up the game by walking the first two batters and allowed two runs in the first inning? I know Stanley Jefferson made an error in center field and that didn't help him. I know he's 22 years old. But you've got to be kidding me?

Jones tells the reporters: "All week I've been thinking, 'OK, it's a do or die game.' But it's no big deal. It's not really do or die. I just thought it was supposed to be a big game, and a couple of guys came up to me and said the same thing. I just almost talked my way out of a good game."

When I heard that, I exploded. I said:

"If he's this nervous with 4,000 people in the stands, then we'd better put him in a cage in front of 50,000 people. If you can't pitch in a spring game without being nervous, then something's wrong. I guess you're not mature enough to be in the big leagues. I don't know. I can't get inside the man's head.

"You guys talk about pressure. What the bleep? You've got pressure in this bleepin' game? You've got to be kidding me. There's no pressure out here. Pressure. Pressure is when you've got a $500 rent payment and you don't have any damn money. That's pressure. Or you've got a family and you can't provide any food. That's pressure. This isn't pressure. Maybe we'll ease the pressure and send him to Vegas. There's no pressure there, just slot machines."

I mean, man, for more than a year I've been trying to figure out this Jones mystery. And I'm not having too much success. I can't understand him. He's been inconsistent. One day he'll go out and look great. Then he'll give you two or three horsebleep outings in a row. Then, when you're just about ready to give up on him, he'll give you another great game. You figure him out.

He's probably got the best arm in camp. There's no doubt about it. He's got as good an arm as I've ever seen. But you know what? There are all kinds of guys with great arms who don't ever pitch in the big leagues. You keep making excuses—the pressure, the wind, the mound. You can do it for the next 10 years. And before you know it, you'll be 34, 35 years old, saying, "Bleep, I wonder why I can't pitch in the big leagues?" It's because you make excuses instead of correcting the problems or just going full-bore.

To me, I don't ever use the word gutless, but he has been sheltered. He was very spoiled by the organization because he was a No. 1 pick. And no one has really jumped on him about playing. Like, "Come on, let's go. It's been six years and you haven't made any progress." Last year was the first time he went through a whole year without getting hurt. But I threw his butt out there. A couple of times he said he couldn't pitch, but I said, "Bleep it. You're pitching." I never heard from him again. I don't know what happened before, but I guess because his arm was sore or tender they said, "OK, don't pitch. We'll put you on the disabled list."

When I know a guy has that type of personality, I don't ask them how they feel. I write out the lineup. Because I found out if you ask somebody how they feel, and they're neurotic, then you're giving them an out. So I don't ask them anymore. I remember, I went out there, I had measles. I had spots and bumps all over. I played with 103 temperature. I mean, if you don't have a temperature, I say, go out and play. You know, colds. That's all bull. It's all how you approach the season. You approach the season and say, I'm playing every game unless I have something broken on me or something. That's mental toughness. Tony Gwynn's got it. He wants to play every inning of every game. He hits extra every day. It's hard to teach somebody that. It has to come from inside. If you keep harping on them long enough, they'll get the message.

What I'm saying is, you can take a guy who has been real

timid and maybe not make him as aggressive as you want him, but he's going to be more aggressive than he was. If you just don't let it slide. I think differently than the organization. I think, when you get a No. 1 pick, you're harder on him than you are on anybody else in camp. Because if you start giving him leeway, then you start spoiling him. And before you know it, he'll take shortcuts. He'll start saying, "Well, they're not going to do anything to me because I'm the No. 1 pick. He's not going to make me go home because I'm the No. 1 pick." I say, screw it. I say, you treat 'em rough. Kick 'em in the butt every time he screws up.

The hardest thing for me as a manager is dealing with players who won't play as hard as I did. I'm having a real hard time right now with that. I'm trying to be patient with some of them. But how can I when things like this come up?

In the middle of this whole thing, Wojna has been inconsistent also. A couple of days ago Wojna told a writer that he felt his chances of making the team were slim and none. It was off the record, so the writer didn't print it. But I heard the story through the usual clubhouse grapevine talk. Man, was I burned. I found out about it from one of our play-by-play broadcasters, who was ticked himself because he thought I had given the writers some information about cuts without giving it to them.

You gotta understand that it has been one tough week for me. It's late in spring training anyway and tensions in the clubhouse are starting to get up there. With camp breaking here on Saturday, my veteran players are already edgy to go home and my marginals and rookies are waiting for the cutdown hammer to drop. I had already cut down 14 players during the last few days so I could get the roster down to the 24-man limit. Now, we're at 29. Let me tell you, it was no picnic. It has been the toughest thing yet I've had to do as a big-league manager. And my five toughest cuts are still left. And one of them is either going to be Wojna or Jones. I don't like telling a guy he's short or lacking in ability. That the guy in front of you is better than you. That you might as well go out and find another job.

I mean, it was bad enough having to call in Wojna to tell him he was acting like a little kid. I said, "Hey, I mean, you're 26 years old. Let's act like a man." I told him, "If you're thinking that negative, then why don't you get the bleep out of here? You make the cut. You did it yourself. Go on. Go to the other side right now. If that's how you feel, then what's the sense in staying around?"

And I admired him after that yesterday because he went out and pitched pretty good. He threw two innings after I aired his butt out. During that meeting, he started to talk and I told him that I didn't want to hear from him. "This is my meeting. I don't want to hear from you." So today, he came in and said, "Can I talk to you?" He told me, "I can pitch for you. I can make this team." And I said, "Well, I'm glad. Because I think you can help us."

And that's where we're at. These are some of the things I've had to deal with. He tells a writer the writing is on the wall . . . Well, the writer is not making the team. I'm making the team. Even if he believes that, he should keep his mouth shut.

Now he's got a real shot at making it. After the way Jones pitched today, I told the media that Jones was losing his next start.

"Let's let Wojna start," I said. "Let's give him a chance. Then if he has a bad outing, we'll sit down and talk about it. But if he goes out and does well, then he definitely wins the job as far as I'm concerned."

With the team going from here to Palm Springs on Sunday for the last few games, there's still plenty of spring training days left for me to change my mind on that account again.

THURSDAY, MAR. 26, 1987 ♦
YUMA, AZ

(T)he telephone in an apartment just a mile from the Ray
Kroc Complex rang at about ten-thirty in the morning,
mountain standard time. It was *San Diego Tribune* sports editor
Bill Pinella on the line. "The Padres have a new owner," said the
man who is known around the office simply as "Sweet." "George
Argyros of Seattle."

Those four words, "George Argyros of Seattle," would give
many people a sinking feeling in the heart. What was Joan Kroc
doing? How could we be exchanging benevolent Joan for
George Argyros? Wasn't she the woman who had contributed a
huge sum of money to the survivor's fund for the poor souls who
were murdered at a McDonald's restaurant in San Ysidro several
years earlier; the woman who had once spearheaded Operation
Cork because she was so concerned about people's dependency
on alcohol and drugs; the woman who had funded and actually
went on food and clothing runs to poor neighborhoods in Ti-
juana each winter; the woman who would donate a million dollars to the Democratic Party and a million more for AIDS
research? How could we be trading off Joan Kroc for George
Argyros, a man who had just made a killing by selling off Air California to American Airlines, a man who was known as a ruth-
less business man?

And anyway, didn't Argyros already own the Seattle Mariners? Wasn't he shunned by American League owners and hated
by King County officials in Washington State where he had been
bartering the threat of a move in exchange for countless financial concessions from the local government? Wasn't this a man
who hadn't paid a cent in rental money on the Kingdome in sev-

eral years because the Mariners had never shown a profit? And wasn't this the same man who had agreed to put millions of dollars into the team to make it a viable product only to renege on the promise?

The deal seemed to be a godsend for Seattle. Wrote Steve Kelley in the *Seattle Times:*

> Seattle gave George Argyros everything. Yesterday Argyros gave it the bird...Never once did Argyros thank the city for its support or apologize for the losers on the field. He was too busy plotting his exit...He promised us Macy's and gave us K-Mart...I think George Argyros choked the life out of baseball in Seattle yesterday. He left it with a lame duck team and a lame duck season....

Well, you get the picture.

For the second time in little more than a year, the Padres would be held in limbo in the Arizona desert while a press conference that had dramatic implications on everyone's life—from the bullpen catcher to the assistant publicity director—would be taking place 175 miles away in San Diego. Argyros, a man who ran a streamlined operation in Seattle, had established a first in baseball history. Minority owners in one club had purchased majority interest in another. But never had a majority owner in one club agreed to buy majority ownership in another. And this deal involved the two leagues. There were certainly questions of propriety. Who would run the Mariners while Argyros went about the business of purchasing the Padres in what was rumored as a $50 million deal? Argyros offered to put the Mariners into a blind trust where the club could be run by the present staff without interference from Argyros until the date of sale.

He told a press gathering in the Stadium Club: "My objective, my goal is to win here. Ray Kroc bought this franchise and saved it from being moved to another city. He nurtured and loved the community. I too am committed to excellence on and off the field. I have a great love for America's game. I am strongly committed to the role model baseball represents...I will have no control over the club until the approval of major-league baseball of the transaction. As an outside date, I've been told by the commissioner's office that the deal should be done within 90 days. I hope to have it done sooner than that, but it's out of my control."

About Seattle, he said: "I, frankly, am very proud of the condition the franchise is in. And I think it has a good chance there to do well...It's poised now to be stable and economically viable...What it needs now is some local ownership."

The announcement was met with a great deal of shock and skepticism by those who knew Argyros' background. And well it should have been. A cursory view of an audit provided by officials of King County noted the stunning fact that the corporation which owned the Mariners was perilously close to bankruptcy. According to the county attorney, Argyros had only recently been threatening again to bankrupt the team if officials did not come up with more financial concessions. In San Diego, many people felt an Argyros ownership was not what the Padres franchise needed as a substitute for the consistent turbulence that had plagued so much of Joan Kroc's recent past. Almost immediately, Kroc went from the villain who had botched up the Dick Williams situation and who was so anti-drug that she had not allowed the signing of Tim Raines, to the personification of the beloved savior.

Said one highly placed member of the Padres organization, who preferred to remain nameless: "When you've dealt a little bit with this guy, you're going to wish you had us back."

Some folks were already wishing.

The San Diego City Council, currently negotiating a new lease agreement with the Padres, was chilled to the bone about the prospect of Argyros wheeling and dealing heavy financial concessions under threat of moving the team. Not only that, front office personnel began to fear for their jobs in what they figured would be an Argyros austerity campaign. But they had little to worry about yet.

Argyros needed just a majority vote of the American League owners to allow him to sell the Mariners—a vote that few people viewed as anything but a rubber stamp. His cronies in the American League would be glad to shed him. But Argyros needed a three-fourths vote to be accepted into the National League. This meant that four negative votes out of 12 owners would blackball him. And that vote would be difficult to obtain. Finally, the logistics of the transaction would be a lot more complicated than anyone was led to believe.

To help still the fear that already was spreading among front office staff members, Argyros spoke to them in San Diego. He flew east for a similar appearance in Yuma a day later. Argyros claimed there would be no front office slashes. The general opinion about that promise was almost unanimous disbelief.

On the day of Argyros' Yuma arrival, new National League president A. Bartlett Giamatti was watching the game at Desert Sun Stadium as part of his initial Cactus League tour. It was at a press conference in Yuma just after the two men had met for the first time, that Giamatti cast the initial doubt this particular transaction would ever transpire.

Asked what he had told Argyros at the meeting, Giamatti said: "I told him I had the honor of talking with the owner of the Seattle club of the American League. He owns Seattle. He's declared his intent to buy San Diego. But all of this is going to take a great deal of time. . . I think there's some question; I told George this and he doesn't disagree. I think the commissioner is going to have to take the view—because it involves both leagues—as to what the sequence of events will be.

"No, this is going to take some time. At least 60 to 90 days. You've got a lot of processes to go through in both league offices and in the commissioner's office. And that's assuming some other things get clarified. I don't know if I foresee any problems, but it is a difficult situation. . . I don't want to forecast problems and I don't want to forecast a routine event. Because by definition this is not routine. As far as clarifications go, I want to find out myself just what the proper sequence is. My impression is, unless I'm told differently, there has to be some clarification of George's non-involvement in the Seattle situation before his San Diego involvement is construed. Otherwise, you have a situation that might be difficult.

"He's not a stranger, but he's not an owner in the National League, either."

That clarification came swiftly. Commissioner Peter Ueberroth, who it was later learned was a strong advocate of the Argyros deal and had counseled Joan Kroc on the matter, laid down this law: Except for certain pre-approved accounting matters and analysis of books that is essential to any such deal, Argyros was to have no contact with the Padres until the transaction was final.

It didn't take long for Argyros to prove he couldn't handle that stipulation. As of now, though, he was still making light of the entire matter. "In a lot of ways, this is like being traded for a player to be named later," Argyros said. "I don't know if this has ever happened to an owner before. . . What I just told the players is the same thing I've already been saying. I'm committed to winning. I'm committed to carrying on the commitment to excellence that Ray Kroc started with this franchise. I have an open door policy. My job is really to give them all the help they can stand."

The baseball people, though, were outwardly cautious. Larry Bowa and Jack McKeon were drinking coffee and telling stories with a group of people in Bowa's bright Yuma office at about nine-thirty when they heard the news. Randy Smith, who works in minor-league development and is the son of baseball executive Tal Smith, came bursting into the room. "There's about to be a staff meeting at our offices in San Diego," a breathless Smith said.

"When he said that everyone was required to attend, I figured it had to be to announce the sale," said McKeon.

Five minutes later, traveling secretary Doc Mattei paged McKeon in his gravelly, baritone voice for a telephone call from club president Ballard Smith. Ten minutes later, McKeon was in his car, racing back to San Diego. Asked upon his return later that night for his impressions of Argyros, McKeon said: "It's hard to tell. I only had about 10 minutes with him before the press conference. I think it shocked the hell out of everyone."

But wasn't it still business as usual on the baseball diamond? That night, Eric Show proved that his elbow problems were indeed behind him as he pitched five innings, allowed two hits and struck out nine Milwaukee Brewers in a 4-0 Padres win. It was certainly ironic that the next day, when Argyros met the team and Giamatti, the Padres would win their final game of the spring. Kevin Mitchell chose the occasion to miss the night game completely without informing anyone.

"He just had a dentist appointment that went a little longer than it should have," Bowa said, trying to cover for Mitchell. Said Mitchell, pointing to a crown in his mouth: "It was nothing. I was here." Concerned privately about the change in ownership and worried about the state of his club with the season quickly approaching, Bowa elected to remain noncommittal as far as Argyros was concerned.

"Nobody said it would be easy," said Bowa, trying to remain philosophical. He should have been used to it. Nothing had come easy for Bowa throughout his career.

JAN. 27, 1982 ◆
PHILADELPHIA, PA

his is how I forced the Phillies to trade me to the Cubs and even got Ryne Sandberg thrown into the deal.

When Ruly Carpenter sold the Phillies back in 1981, he called me in before the sale to talk contract. I always did my contracts face to face with him. Hell, I didn't even have an agent in my early years. He was firm, but he'd listen. I'd go up there and say, "This is what I want." He'd say, "Get out of here, man." Sometimes it would go on for a couple of months. Then he'd call my wife. He'd say, "Sheena, why don't you come up here for lunch and we'll get this contract hammered out." I'd get on the line and laugh, "Sheena's not negotiating this contract." He'd say, "If I can get your wife in here, we'll have this thing settled in a second."

I mean, he would always work it out with me. Once, I had a contract where on paper it showed I was making $200,000, but he paid for a $250,000 house in cash. He did things like that. He'd say I was asking for too much money. And I'd say, "Well, let's do it another way. Buy my house for me." He was loaded. It was nothing to him. He used to have parties. I mean, you never see owners having parties. He was the most down to earth person I've ever seen in my life. Always talked to the wives, to the kids. He kept everything in proper perspective. If you looked at him walking through a hotel lobby, you'd say, "I wonder who he is? He must be a salesman for some men's store or something." That's how down to earth the man is.

That all changed when that Bill Giles group bought the club. In the old days the Phillies were like a big family. We did everything on trust and a handshake. I found out pretty quick that times had certainly changed when Giles took over. I was devastated with Ruly Carpenter after we won the World Series in 1980. It was the opening of our next spring training and he called everybody together and said, "We're putting the team up for sale." I said, "Ah bleep, what's he doin'?" The straw that broke the camel's back is when Claudell Washington signed that big contract with the Atlanta Braves. Ruly said, "This is it. He's comin' off all those mediocre years. That's an unbelievable amount of money Ted Turner gave him." He said, "I'm outa here."

He got out of baseball because of free agency and everything going to court. He loves the game, watchin' the game. He'll go watch minor-league games. But he said, "When you start dealing with lawyers and agents instead of balls and strikes, I don't need it." Just recently I spoke to him. I asked him, "Do you miss it?" He said, "Not one bit. I still see my baseball." I was joking around with him. I said, "The next big league team up for sale, why don't you get it and I'll be your general manager?" He said, "You've got to be kiddin' me." So just before Ruly sells the club to Giles, he calls me in and says, "I'm going to sign you to a three-year contract. If I don't, you can ask to be traded." I was a five and ten year player with five straight years on one team and 10 years in the major leagues. I had the right to turn down a trade to anywhere I didn't want to go. So I told Ruly, "That's fair."

Now the team goes up for sale and the Giles group gets it. So my contract is up and Giles wants to give me a one-year contract. I say, "No way. The deal was, I get a three-year contract or you trade me."

He said, "We're not trading you."

I said, "That's the deal. You guys are trying to renege on the deal."

So I had to get ahold of Ruly, who was out of it. And Ruly literally told Giles that that was the agreement. Giles came back and they started making all kinds of things up because it was getting close to spring training and I still hadn't signed. I was ticked. I'd had it up to here. So I ripped Giles. And that's the way it came out in the paper. They asked me about all this crap and I said, "Well, Bill Giles is a liar." That's the way the headlines read: "Bowa Calls Giles Liar." I said, "They're going to have to trade me or there is going to be a problem here." Because it was a verbal commitment that Ruly Carpenter gave me. In fact, everything I did with him was verbal. I mean, he'd say, "You're going to sign a two-year contract a month from now. Let's do it." And it was always done. He was always fair with me. I was coming off a five-year contract. And he paid me $500,000, the most I ever made in baseball for one year. He was as good an owner as I've ever met in my life. But he was from that old owner's school where it was family. Now it's corporations and conglomerates. You're not going to get that feeling.

I think Giles wanted to prove to everybody how strong he was going to be as the new owner. You know, "I'm going to stick to my guns. I'm going to do it my way." We bantered back and forth in the papers for a month. He'd say, "He can't play anymore. He's at the end of his career." I'd keep calling him a liar. So finally, Lee Elia, who used to be a coach for us when Dallas Green was the manager, got the job as Cubs manager under Dallas. It was kind of funny in a way. We had been knocked out of the playoffs by Montreal in 1981. And it seemed like the very next day, Dallas quit as manager and took over as general manager of the Cubs. I know Dallas wanted to be the Phillies general manager bad. But the way they were set up and the way it turned out with Ruly leaving anyway, it never would have happened. So, of course, he takes Elia with him. So Lee and I are playing golf together and I said, "Why don't you talk to Dallas and get me out of here, man. I can help you guys out."

He said, "Hell, they ain't gonna give you up."

I said, "Hey, they've got to give me up. They've got to trade me or they've got to give me three years. And they're not going to give me a three year." So I kept getting on Giles in the paper and everything. Then Dallas called me. He said, "Would you be interested in coming to Chicago?"

I said, "Yeah. But I want a three-year contract."

He says, "I've got no problem with that."

I said, "Hell, this is great."

So then they had a big deal about who they were going to trade for me. And Green knew he had Giles by the throat. He knew I didn't want to play for him and he knew I wanted to get the bleep out of there. And Giles knew that. So they started throwing names around. I told Lee, "Hey, get Sandberg in that trade." And Lee, who managed Sandberg in the minor leagues, gave me that, "Ahhhhhh, I don't know." I said, "I'm tellin' you, he's gonna be a player." I know his work habits at that time were considered lazy. Very, very low key.

So they finally put the deal together that included Sandberg in the trade along with me for Ivan DeJesus. I guess Giles wanted another shortstop because he was trading a shortstop. So the Chicago writers call me up. They said, "It's nice to have you. Dah, dah, dah." And I didn't know the final trade yet. So I said, "Who was the guy they threw in?" When they said Sandberg, I told them, "Well then, I was the guy they threw in because Sandberg is going to be a great player." And the guy says, "Come on." I said, "I'm tellin' you. He's going to be an unbelievable player."

They traded me and Sandberg for Ivan DeJesus. That has to be one of the all-timers. And to this day, Giles will never give me any credit. I get along good with him now, but he never wants to admit he made a mistake. And it wasn't so much that he made a mistake. He just wanted to show people, "I'm the new owner and this is the way it's gonna be." And I guess I was the guy he wanted to set the example with. I had been in the organization a long time and I was the outspoken guy on the ballclub. A lot of people think he's done a bad job with the Phillies and maybe he has. But I think he's done a lot better now than when he started. I'll never forget this banquet I went to with him when I was still playing for the Phillies. Bill was in charge of community relations. He was in charge of putting people in the ballpark. He was in charge of ticket sales and promotions. So we had to go to a banquet together and I'll never forget this night in Philadelphia. It was a real nasty night.

He said, "I'll tell you what. I'll pick you up and we'll go to the banquet together." And I said, "You don't have to do that. I know a hotel. I'll meet you in the parking lot. I'll park my car and we'll drive up together." We were living in South Jersey at the time. So we started talkin' and this sticks out in my mind so bad: I said,

"What would you like to do, Bill?" He said, "I'd really like to own a baseball team. That's my long-range goal."

I said, "What intrigues you about that?"

He says, "I'd just like the feeling of being able to trade somebody anytime I wanted to. I'd like to have the power to get rid of people if I didn't think they were doing the job."

And I'm saying to myself, "Oh hell, what does this guy know about player personnel? He's in promotions. It doesn't work like that."

As I look back on that conversation, it stands out so clear. And when it happened to me, I said, "He got his wish." And to this day he still likes to make trades. But I think he's much more conservative. He doesn't take any chances now. It's like, "Let's wait." He just won't jump in and make trades now. But when he first took over, boy, he'd say, "Let's do it."

It's too bad things had to work out that way. It's too bad there was such a big deal. He wanted to do it his way and I was promised something by the previous owner. I still don't think it was the smartest way of making his point.

SUNDAY, APR. 5, 1987 ◆ DENVER, CO

Eight losses in a row.

Larry Bowa couldn't believe it, even if the streak was simply closing the exhibition schedule. The season was set to open the next day against the Giants in San Francisco. And all Bowa knew was that he would have a healthy Eric Show on the mound. The rest was a crap shoot. After a spring full of controversy and fundamentals, Bowa's clearest assessment was that his club was nowhere near ready.

He would start the season without reliever Rich Gossage, who had torn some cartilage in his rib cage the past week pitching against the California Angels in Palm Springs. Center fielder Stanley Jefferson, who had twisted his ankle severely against the Angels, was back in Bowa's doghouse and would not be in the opening day lineup.

Asked if he needed more time to ready his team for the season, Bowa said: "Yeah, I could use another month." If he had said two months he might now be viewed as a mystic based on the muddy road that Bowa later found stretched before him. By Bowa's own admission, he was a little bit scared and quite a bit irate after the Padres ended his first preseason by dropping a pair of games to the Chicago Cubs in the 44-degree weather at Denver's Mile High Stadium. Seated in a dank, tiled office, Bowa pointed his finger at everyone.

"They think they can just turn on a switch and play well when the season starts," Bowa said. "Why don't you ask them what the bleep is wrong? They're the ones that are out there playing. I'd go to every damn locker and ask 'em. Ask them what they're thinking about. Maybe I should say we're playing great.

We're making great pitches, we're catchin' the ball and we're all hitting over .300. They don't like criticism, so maybe we'll praise them. They're playing great. Just stay right where they are.

"We're not supposed to rip anybody because we might hurt their feelings. But it's OK for us to go out and get our butts kicked every day."

Bowa had finally let loose on Jefferson, who was beside himself in the post-game locker room. The 24-year-old, who had grown up in New York City—the Co-Op City section of the Bronx—was questioned by Bowa about his pain tolerance throughout the course of training camp. First, Jefferson had arrived with a badly sprained wrist he sustained during his cross-country trip from the East Coast. Jefferson said he had parked his car at a scenic viewpoint and, slipping on the snow, jammed the wrist while breaking his fall. Jefferson wore a fiberglass cast on that one for awhile, although the team reported that X-rays and bone scans had proven negative.

In his angst today, Jefferson confided that he thought he was playing with a hairline fracture of the wrist, but was scared to sit out of the lineup because Bowa might think he was faking it. During the middle of spring training, Jefferson was hit on the head by a pick off throw as he slid back into second base. The throw split Jefferson's helmet and sent him back to the hospital for more X-rays.

There were various other nagging leg and shoulder injuries, but the *coup de gras* was Jefferson's ankle injury. Nearly a week ago, Jefferson led off a game at Palm Springs with a line shot to left that appeared to be a double. As he rounded first base, his left foot hit the bag wrong and Jefferson collapsed several feet up the line as if he had been felled by a sniper.

"I never saw anything like that before," Bowa said. "I thought he had broken his leg in six places."

Jefferson, who could be found later stretched out on a training table with ice wrapped around his foot, had merely twisted the ankle. But evidently, he had sustained a nasty sprain. Jefferson was advised not to play until team doctors gave him clearance. The club, which played an exhibition game in San Diego on Friday night, then traveled to Denver for the two games where, evidently, Bowa expected Jefferson to play.

It was cold enough Saturday that Jefferson was excused from his fifth straight game. But several hours before today's contest, Bowa asked Jefferson if he could play. The rookie gave an affirmative nod. Everything was fine until Jefferson took a few flies in the outfield and realized that his foot would not loosen up. He then went to trainer Dick Dent and told him that he couldn't go. "Go tell the manager," Dent evidently told Jefferson. Jefferson, still in the process of learning clubhouse protocol, did just that. And predictably, Bowa erupted.

"That was my big mistake," Jefferson said. "I was told by a couple of players I should never go to the manager and tell him I can't play. I'll never make that mistake again."

But for this day, the damage had already been done. Jefferson was yanked out of the exhibition game lineup and reporters covering the team were also informed that he would not start on opening day. "If I was a kid, I'd want to be in the opening day lineup if it was my first year in the big leagues," Bowa said. "I've got to talk to Jack McKeon about it. Jefferson's just a body right now. If he is hurt maybe he's better off going to triple-A."

Jefferson remained with the team. The next morning, Jefferson went to Bowa's hotel room to talk over the situation with the manager. He had been told by a number of people that he had to open up lines of communication with Bowa. Jefferson, a quiet man who does not like to talk about his problems, had become a whipping boy for Bowa's verbal attacks. He could not deal with them then but he made some progress during the season.

Assistant publicity director Mike Swanson told Jefferson that Bowa was not as bad as he seemed. "You can talk with him," said Swanson. "Really, his bark is worse than his bite."

The result of the talk might have been encouraging for the short term. "I had a long talk with him," Bowa said. "He knows now that everything is OK. Too many guys were telling him what to do. When too many guys are pulling your chain you don't know what to do."

Jefferson agreed to go back in the lineup for the second

game of the season despite the painful ankle. That decision might have made Bowa happy for the moment, but it would turn out to be his first major mistake. "It was a combination of me not knowing him and him not knowing me," Bowa would say about the early phases of his strained relationship with Jefferson. "I'll take the blame for that. He's the kind of guy that if you watch him on the baseball field, just watch his mannerisms, you'd say he's not givin' everything he's got. But that's just his mannerisms and it took me awhile to find that out. Another thing that I found out is you've got to understand that everybody's tolerance for pain is different. Just because I can play on something, doesn't mean another guy can. I'll be the first to admit I made a lot of mistakes handling different personalities. But I tried like hell with Jefferson and couldn't figure him out.

"I told him, 'You're never going to be like me. I'm never going to be like you. You're low key. I'm high strung. You're quiet. I'm loud. But we both have the same goal. That is to win. No matter what we do, we have to win and we have to play hard. Do you agree with that?' When he said, yes, I said, 'Then, when I yell at you or scream, don't think I'm trying to embarrass you.' When I talk to him, usually we're alone. I'll say, 'Damn Stanley, what the hell is going through your mind?' And right away he'll put his guard up. I know right now he's playing scared. He's afraid to make mistakes.

"I think some guys think about me, that, 'Hey, he never made a mistake when he was playing?' That's not the point I'm trying to get across. The point I'm trying to get across is that I could probably count on one hand the amount of mental mistakes I made. Physical mistakes, I made a lot of them. Everyone does. I just wish I had a manager who pushed and prodded like I'm doing. Because I wouldn't make any bleepin' mistakes— mentally. I had low-keyed managers. I had Frank Lucchesi. I had Paul Owens, Danny Ozark. Jim Frey was pretty low-keyed. The one guy who was emotional was Dallas Green. That one was extreme. And it won us the World Series. I'm not saying it was because he was emotional. It was because he let people know when they bleeped up. Not physically—mentally. Mentally you just weren't ready to play this game.

"Guys come out, there's a game. They don't take batting practice, they don't take infield. You're going to tell me that you're mentally ready to play the game? No bleepin' way. No way at all. I can't buy that. They go out and do five sprints, OK, let's play. There are going to be times when you have to play the game that way. When there's a tarp on the field. When it's raining. But I'll tell you what, if you have that approach, you'll get buried."

Jefferson wasn't Bowa's only dilemma. During the last few days, Bowa had elected to send pitcher Jimmy Jones to the minor leagues after his third straight poor performance—two walks, eight hits and four runs in four innings against the Angels. Ed Wojna was given the job, at least temporarily, as fifth starter. Tom Gorman, a journeyman middle-inning reliever, was given the last slot in the bullpen. To Bowa's displeasure, Storm Davis had completed the spring with an earned run average six times higher than his better than average IQ. Left-hander Dave Dravecky, who unlike Show, had not shown significant recovery from his 1986 arm problems, was also placed in the bullpen.

And Steve Garvey, who had not shown signs of hitting, was disgruntled because his attempt to buy the team had been shelved in favor of George Argyros. Not only was an offer by a Garvey group rebuffed, the Padres went to great lengths to downplay that offer when Garvey complained that his group wasn't given a fair chance.

Said Beth Benes, the Padres' attorney: "I want you to know that Garvey didn't call us until 10 days before the sale. By that time, I told him it was probably too late."

Garvey, who had plotted purchasing the Padres all winter, told another story. "I guess they were just trying to discredit any efforts I made," Garvey said. "They can't deny that an initial attempt was made to contact them back in January by Alan Rothenberg, our representative. It was made without any success for about six or eight weeks. They just wouldn't return our calls.

That's why I finally had to get in touch with them personally. To get the whole thing in motion. I just wish we had been given a chance to begin the process a lot earlier. That's all."

And so, the Padres were going into the season with a veteran at first base, who wasn't hitting, a double-A second baseman, a shortstop with tender knees, a third baseman, who had spent more time on the road this spring than on the field, a catcher, who had caught 17 big-league games, a plodding left-fielder, a center fielder in the manager's doghouse, a pitching staff in chaos, and Tony Gwynn.

No wonder this was Bowa's final assessment of the spring: "I'd have to say that at this point, our triple-A team at Las Vegas was better at the end of last season than this team is right now. We didn't make that many mental and physical errors at triple-A all season. If we keep playing the way we are right now, we'll come home oh-and-six. Cincinnati and San Francisco are going to kick our butts. They have a lot more talent than we have. They're the two teams that are picked to win our division."

And so, as the baseball turns. The season was only one day away.

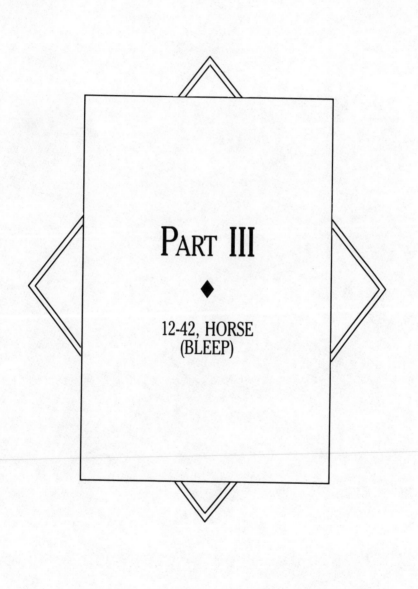

PART III

◆

12-42, HORSE
(BLEEP)

Oct. 12, 1965 ♦
Sacramento, CA

E ddie Bockman sat in front of the Bowa household on the south side of Sacramento in his late model car. He held a copy of the contract that Paul Bowa and his son, Larry, were studying inside the bright ranchstyle house. To Larry, the important matter was the contract. To Paul, the numbers that jumped off the page in black and white were even more significant: Two thousand dollars. A scout for the Philadelphia Phillies wanted to sign his son for a measly $2,000. Larry was ready to go. To his chagrin, he had not been selected in baseball's first draft of amateur players. Not even in the last round. The contract meant redemption. A chance at the big leagues. All the younger Bowa wanted was a chance. He'd take it from there. Paul was counseling Larry to hold out for more money. He had talked to some friends involved in American Legion ball in the city and they had told Paul that there were other major league teams interested. That Larry was worth more.

"I didn't want him to sign," Paul, 67 now, said recently. "I think he could have gotten more. But if he didn't, I didn't want to be the one to kill Larry's chances of playing in the major leagues."

Recalled Bowa: "I didn't care about the money. All I wanted to do was play ball. That's all I had wanted to do for as long as I can remember."

That insatiable desire was what Bockman had counted on. The Northern California area scout for the Phillies had seen the wiry kid play on a consistent basis. Once, he had journeyed the ninety miles from his home on the San Francisco Peninsula to Sacramento to watch Bowa play shortstop for Sacramento City

College. But Bowa was ejected during the first inning of both games of a double-header.

In the first game, Bowa walked to lead off the inning and tried to steal second. When he was called out by the second base umpire, he came up jawing and was immediately sent to the bench.

"In junior college games they only use two umpires," Bockman recalled. "I don't think Larry realized that the umpire who had thrown him out of the first game was behind the plate in the second game."

Bowa led off and was rung up by the same umpire on four pitches. Before he knew it, he was thrown out again.

"I'm sure I deserved to be kicked out, but he carried a grudge into the second game," Bowa said. "And I was boxed that game, too."

So much for Bockman's scouting trip.

"I caught him as he was going over to the bus," Bockman said. "He was still upset. You know him—throwing helmets, trashing bats. I told him, 'I'll be back to see you. You'll be a pretty good player if you can stay in the game.' He asked me who I was. When I told him, that pretty much quieted him down."

In so many ways, one can't help to be taken aback by Paul Bowa's resemblance to his son. He is a craggy version of Larry, who is 26 years his junior. He is similar in size—five-feet-ten inches, 160 pounds. He has that same protruding jaw that seems to beckon all challengers. He has those same squinty eyes.

"We're clones," Bowa said.

They are also like one in personality. If anyone is seeking clues about the genesis of Larry's infamous explosive streak, one need go no further than his father. Paul and his wife Mary are Sacramento natives. Their bloodlines date back to the days of the great gold rush when fortune seekers and frontiersmen panned the basins of the Delta region. Like his son a generation later, Paul was the type of gritty baseball player who would just as easily run over you as around you.

Battle umpires? Paul was the scourge of the minor leagues with his temper—a trait he handed over to his son along with that dogged determination. "There was nothing I wanted to do more when I was a kid than play major-league baseball," Paul says.

He never earned the chance. Paul, a scrappy third baseman, found himself bouncing around the St. Louis Cardinals organization. During the 1940s he was the player-manager of the low level minor-league club in Duluth, Minnesota. Little did he know at the time that he had embarked on his final professional baseball season. Just having recovered from the sudden debilitation of an appendectomy, Paul dug in at home plate. In a microsecond he was slammed in the head by a fastball. Paul was protected only by his woolen baseball cap—in effect, no protection at all. When he awoke three days later, Mary was standing by his side. A priest had read Paul Bowa his last rites.

"I can remember some of it," Bowa said. "I remember riding a train with my mom. That's how they used to travel. And all the players who played for my dad used to come and pick me up and take me down through the cars and all that. I remember all that stuff. I remember him going on a road trip in Duluth. Poor old mom was holding me. We were looking out the window. Talk about a blizzard. And my mom was depressed. I remember things like that. I don't remember him getting hit in the head. I know they brought a priest. He'd still be in baseball somewhere if it wasn't for my mom. I mean, I'm not sayin' now, but he would have stayed in baseball. She was just tired of all the travel, bein' away from home."

Mary Bowa was also scared. The beaning incident was more than she could handle. "I didn't think I could go through something like that again," Mary, 65, said last winter.

It was then that Paul Bowa came to the crossroads faced by so many professional players who had not been able to make the grade after an extended period of time—go back for another season in the bushes or return home for good. Mary pushed hard for the return to Sacramento, even threatening what remained of their matrimonial bliss. She was tired of boarding houses, cheap hotels and long periods alone in strange little towns, caring for her young child. So Paul left his baseball dream behind—a decision he still laments today. "I think he does," says Mary, who gave birth to a daughter named Paula shortly thereafter.

"I wanted to go back for one more season on my own. Give it one more shot as a manager. Leave them at home," said Paul.

Added Bowa: "I think what's in his mind is, if he wasn't pushed out by mom, could he have been a successful manager in the big leagues? He loved it. He knew the game of baseball. They finally got cable and he watches our games. He calls me up sometimes and asks me why I do things. He tries to watch all the games. He's from that old school: Don't take any crap from anybody. If they don't like it bleep 'em."

And so, Larry was left as the standard bearer of the dream. The elder Bowa drove a beer truck, ran a bar, and worked on a printing press. He eventually retired with emphysema, because he worked continuously with certain chemicals, he believes. He continued to manage and play America Legion ball on weekends, becoming a local legend because of his confrontations with umpires and other managers. Paul believes that Larry was short-changed at McClatchy High School because of a long-time feud between the elder Bowa and Bill Whiteneck, then the baseball coach.

Larry never played high school baseball, ostensibly, Whiteneck told him, because it conflicted with his position on the basketball team. How would you like to be remembered for having made that decision? List Whiteneck up there with the editor who once told F. Scott Fitzgerald that he'd never be a major American writer. Of course, there are different versions of what happened in that sticky situation.

Paul Bowa: "We had gotten into some arguments when we were managing against each other, so he took it out on Larry."

Larry: "I don't know if they feuded. That might have been the reason. But in my mind, I really believe he thought I was too small. He was a big guy. He was one of those guys who lifted weights. He was a pretty good physical specimen. That's my opinion. My dad probably had his own opinion. I mean, I was cut three years in a row. That was the worst. I don't know, I can't tell you what death is like, but I didn't feel like doing bleep. I was so depressed. I got home that day, I mean the first time I was cut, I was so embarrassed I didn't even tell my dad. Every day, they would pick me up at five-thirty, or something. So for two days, I would just hang around school and pretend that I practiced.

"And then, a friend of my dad, who knew the coach, saw my dad at the park and said, 'It's a shame Larry got cut.' He said, 'He what?' 'Yeah, he got cut a couple of days ago.' So I went home that night and my dad says to me, 'Sit down, I want to talk to you. How's practice going?' I went, 'It's doin' alright.' He says, 'Why are you lyin' to me? You got cut, didn't you?' And it was just like. . .I said, 'Yeah, I got cut.' He said, 'That doesn't mean anything. You got cut? So you got cut. It's just one man's opinion. What was the reason he gave you?' I said, 'Well, he said I was too small. The guy they were going with, they felt he was going to be a better player.' So my dad says, 'Well, you can go do one of two things. You can quit or you can go out for the legion team.' "

On his father's advice, Bowa played legion ball and eventually made his college team. According to Bowa, he was named all conference both years he played at Sac City.

Despite his size—peewee at that time—Bowa also was a pretty fair basketball player in high school, attacking that sport with the same zeal he attacked baseball. "I played basketball for the B team because I was too small," he said. "I averaged 20 points a game. I could shoot. I'd go out in the backyard at home. My dad put up a basket. During the basketball season, I'd shoot until nine-thirty, ten o'clock every night. We'd have a big spotlight on the basket."

Bowa is clear about who had the greatest influence on the early stages of his life: His father. Paul would take Larry out to Land Park during his little-league days and riddle him with fundamentals. When his father was at work and there was no one around for a game, Bowa used to bounce a hardball off the whitewashed wall of Holy Spirit Catholic school close to home until his father would fetch him and bring the boy home for dinner. "He'd just play there all day with a hardball and a glove,"

Paul recalled, allowing the memory to stream through his mind. "The cover'd come off the old ball and he'd tape it up and go out there the very next day."

Said Bowa: "See, even then, I did the little things. We went out and bunted. You know how your dad goes out and throws to you and you hit? We bunted for a half hour. He'd throw 'em, then we'd pick 'em all up. Then he'd say, 'Now we're gonna hit.' Just him and me. Then we'd go out and pick up everything. It was unbelievable. But the one thing my dad never did. He never said, 'You're going to the park. Let's go.' I always had to say to him, 'Come on, let's go. I want to work on a couple of things.' Even though there were balls and things around, he never said, 'You have to play baseball.' In fact, he tried to talk me out of playing baseball because I was too small. He thought I'd be in the minors for 10 years.

"He's still hyper. He still has to get up and go. I think the proudest he ever was was at the World Series. That was the ultimate, I think. He came down to the locker room when we were celebrating. He was in hog heaven. He was a ballplayer who found out how tough it was to get a job. He always preached getting a college degree and all that. I used to say, 'Yeah, OK, dad,' because I hated school. I kept tellin' him, 'I'm gonna make it. I'm gonna make it.' He said, 'I'm tellin' ya, the odds are against ya.'"

By the time Bowa went out for legion ball, a full-grown rivalry had developed between the two men. The young Bowa, maniacal on the one hand—"I was obsessed with it"—and the elder Bowa still charged with that incredible will to win. Bowa had become so much like his father in on-field temperament that his parents ultimately decided to watch the ballgames from beyond right field. Both parents, of course, had their different reasons. Mary didn't like to hear her son's gutter language. "The Larry who comes home is not the same person I read about in the papers," she says. "I've never heard a foul word out of his mouth in this home." Paul didn't want his presence to influence the umpires against Larry, who had learned to create enough trouble for himself.

"Umpires," said Bowa. "When I started to play winter ball,

there were the same umpires as when he played. He got kicked out of so many games, they started baiting me. My dad sitting there would probably infuriate the umpire even more. My mom would get embarrassed."

But when the two men were on the field at the same time, it became even more heated.

"It became so bad in American Legion," Bowa said. "He was manager of a team called Fort Sutter and I played for Post 61. You talk about tension at the breakfast table and before we'd go to the park . . . My mom hated it. It was unbelievable. I mean, we literally didn't talk. They'd beat us and we'd come back and beat them. That particular year, his team won it. But when they played us, I tried to do anything to beat his butt. Mom was like the mediator. The first thing we used to do when we sat down at the table, and I'm talkin' about from little league on, was to establish one rule—no baseball talk at the dinner table. But inevitably, it seemed like every single night there would be a fight at the dinner table. I mean, people would get up without finishing their meal. To this day, my mom is obsessed with sitting down because something would always happen. He'd say something about baseball. I'd say, 'No, that's not right. I didn't do that.' Before you know it, he's yelling at me. I'm jumpin' up. I'm walkin' off to my room. My mom's leapin' up. She's just cooked a meal. It would happen every day.

"I always felt sorry for my mom and younger sister. My sister, all the way through high school until I signed, she thought she was left out. I used to get all the headlines playing ball. She says she felt like the outsider. Which was understandable. She was raised around sports and she loves sports. She has two boys, Joe and Nick, who are going to be pretty good athletes. We always got along great because of our ages. She's six years younger than me. There was no problem with her. But when we set up vacations during the summer, it was always around me. As you look back on it, it probably wasn't fair.

"One thing that stands out in my mind as I look back on my teenage years: Guys used to always go out and get drunk. The big thing in high school then was to go out and get a six-pack of beer. I never did that. It wasn't that I was afraid of my mom or dad, although I always was told that you were not supposed to do that stuff. When I see kids now who drink or do drugs and say it's because of peer pressure, it's hard for me to relate to that. There was plenty of peer pressure when I was in high school. It was just as prevalent then as it is now. When guys do cocaine now and blame it on their buddies for doing it, that's hard for me to relate to.

"That's personal makeup, I guess. I've never had trouble disciplining myself. Maybe it was because of the army. But even before I went in the reserves, I had a schedule I used to adhere to. If I told the guys I would meet them at the park at eight-thirty, I'd be there at eight-thirty. I know I got that from my dad. He hates being late. I can't tell you how much I respect him.

"You know, we were never what you'd call, well off. But me and my sister always had what we wanted. He found a way. By workin' hard. Gettin' extra jobs. At Christmas time, you know, kids rattle off about eight or nine things they want. We used to get everything we wanted. As I look back now, I know that they couldn't afford a lot. He just found a way to provide. Yeah, my dad taught me how to play the game. How you were supposed to play it. When you're in the field, don't worry about hittin'. When you're hitting, don't worry about the field. Never quit. No matter how tough things go. Never quit."

That last piece of advice, whether it was inborn in Bowa or drummed in by his father, was perhaps the single reason why he was able to carve a professional baseball career. That, and the ability finally to control the legendary Bowa temper. In college and legion ball, Bowa developed such bad blood between himself and the umpires that he was consistently ejected from ballgames. His father began to realize that Larry needed another venue. He had to whisk Larry out of the area.

"If I didn't do that, Larry would've never made it," Paul said. "The kid had to get a chance to play."

That's when Eddie Bockman stepped in. After Bockman's promise at the double-header debacle—I'll be back to see you—

months went by. The scout, who at 67, is now the Western Regional crosschecker for the Phillies, never made it back to the Delta. As fortune would have it, though, Bowa was invited to a Phillies tryout camp where he impressed Bockman with his pugnacious play. Bockman managed a winter-league team the Phillies sponsored on the San Francisco Bay Peninsula. Bowa was invited to play shortstop on that team with one stipulation:

"If he started throwing any helmets and bats or abused any umpires, he was through," said Bockman.

Said Bowa: "Every weekend we got up at seven o'clock in the morning and drove to San Francisco or San Mateo, all those small towns in the Peninsula League."

Added Bockman: "He behaved himself and he played like hell."

It just so happened that the World Series that year featured the Minnesota Twins and the Los Angeles Dodgers. Bockman was scheduled to join the Phillies brass for an organizational meeting when the series shifted from Minneapolis to L.A. for Game 3. Among the treasures Bockman took with him on the one-hour flight south from the Bay Area was an eight-millimeter film documenting the talents of one 19-year-old named Lawrence Robert Bowa.

"We were in the rebuilding process," said Bockman. "It was just after that disaster of 1964. You remember, when the Phillies blew a four and a half game lead with six games left to play? We were looking at everybody. I was talking to Paul Owens, who was the player personnel director at the time, and I brought up Larry. I asked him if he was interested in taking a look at the film. He said, 'Sure.' "

And so in a major hotel in Los Angeles, where the movie industry may be second only to the used car business, Owens and Bockman set out to find an eight-millimeter motion picture camera. A bellman located one in storage and set it up in Owens' room.

"Paul jerked the sheet off the bed, hung it up on the wall and we watched the film," Bockman said. "It was a little fuzzy, but you could get the picture. Larry was a speedy kid at the time with good instincts in the field. The question was whether or not he could hit."

Owens had this reaction to Bowa's speed: "Slow the film down," he told Bockman. "It looks like a silent movie." Bockman informed his boss that the film was running at the right speed.

"Paul asked me how much money he wanted," Bockman recalled. " 'Money,' I said. 'He doesn't want any money. All he wants is a chance to play. So Paul told me to sign him if it didn't cost too much. I gave him $2,000, but I didn't have to give him anything. After that, it was up to Larry. He made himself into everything he is today."

WEDNESDAY, APR. 8, 1987 ◆ SAN FRANCISCO, CA

The Padres had just opened the season by enduring three one-run losses to the San Francisco Giants in windy Candlestick Park. And that seemed to be more than Larry Bowa could handle—three losses in Bowa's first three games as a major-league manager. If you're looking for a glimpse at this man's delicate psyche, you may want to note that it was nearly a month ago in Yuma, when, after losing the first two exhibition games to the California Angels, Bowa confided in candid tones:

"I need a W!"

He wasn't kidding either. And that was the preseason. Those were games that Bowa himself termed, "fun." Some fun. It hadn't helped exactly that the Padres had lost eight straight exhibition games to close spring training, making it a nice, neat 11 in a row. So what if only three counted? The Padres hadn't won since March 27. It was enough to lead to Bowa's first major snap of the year.

Bowa had already turned a few neat phrases. In fact, he was quickly becoming the master of the expletive and the malaprop. During the spring, he had noted to *San Diego Union* beat writer Mark Kreidler that the Padres had spent more time on fundamentals than ever before.

"If we keep messing up, we'll keep going out and practicing. That's all I can do," Bowa said. "You can't, uh, beat a dead horse in the mouth. But you can't just sweep it under the rug." The comment was excerpted by the *New Yorker* magazine, whose editors concluded the passage with the comment:

"Casey Stengel lives!"

He certainly did. Later on in the ghastly season, Bowa would remark that he didn't want to "hedge around the bush" about one particular subject. And about his enigmatic young pitcher Jimmy Jones, whom Bowa could never quite comprehend, Bowa once said: "We thought he was over the hump, but maybe we've just got to go back to the drawing board." Bowa was a dream for writers. In his constantly flowing controversial and colorful comments, his true feelings nearly always ruled the day. He shunned the usual sentiment of baseball and politics that DIShonesty is the best policy. To players and management, Bowa was often too honest for his own good. "He wears his heart on his sleeve," said coach Greg Riddoch, a postgraduate with a master's degree in education, who turned out to be Bowa's closest friend and confidant on the team.

On this day, after a 2-1 loss in which right-hander Andy Hawkins had allowed a two-run homer to Chris Brown on an 0-and-2 pitch, Bowa was wearing his heart on his sleeve and certainly was not hedging around the bush when he stomped through the postgame clubhouse. For days he had been a caldron ready to blow a la Mount St. Helens. After Brown's homer, you could see the lava begin pouring out of his ears.

"Don't you guys bleepin' get used to it," Bowa growled as he stomped across the locker room to his office. " 'Cause I'm not going to get used to it."

Inside the office, these fateful words came rolling off his tongue like so much hot liquid:

"Good teams create things. Horseshit teams just wait to get beat. And that's just what we are now—horseshit. Oh and three, horseshit. The manager is horseshit. The coaches are horseshit. The players are horseshit. We're all horseshit. Everybody. We're horseshit because we're 0-3. And you can dissect that up any way you want."

In papers across the Southland, the comment was transposed to read: "The manager is horse(bleep). The coaches are horse(bleep). The players are horse(bleep). We're all horse(bleep)."

It became the hallmark of Bowa's first season: "BLEEP!"

For anyone, this would have been a bad week. After concluding spring training on such a sour note—eight straight losses—and after having had to negotiate a peace settlement of sorts with rookie center fielder Stanley Jefferson, Bowa's phone in his suite at the Westin St. Francis on Union Square rang early Monday morning. It was his father with news that no one would want to hear on an uneventful day, let alone the opening day of the season, and the opening day of a new career. His mother had been stricken overnight and rushed to the hospital. Her blood pressure was very low and her vital signs were failing. For a 65-year-old woman this was a clear emergency.

Bowa's parents would not be in Candlestick Park that day—the first time since Bowa ascended to the major leagues with the Philadelphia Phillies in 1970 that Paul and Mary would miss a Larry Bowa game in San Francisco.

"That was a big thing, not having them there," Bowa said. "You know, just looking up in the stands for them and not seeing them where they usually sit. In all my minor-league years, even in the big leagues, no matter where I was, they'd take their vacation. Two weeks, three weeks. My first year in pro ball, the Phillies sent me to their single-A club in Spartanburg, South Carolina. It was unbearable. I missed home. I was homesick. They weren't travelers, so to speak. Once my dad got done playing baseball, they just stayed in Sacramento. But they got on an airplane. They even flew to Spartanburg."

Bowa, who is a master at blocking extraneous matters out of his mind while a game is in progress, could not stop thinking about his mother's illness. When the game was over, Bowa drove the 180-mile round trip to Sacramento from the Bay Area. But first there was the game and that was painful. The Padres played well enough in front of 52,020 fans. For eight innings, all the prophecies of doom and gloom seemed premature. The Padres led 3-0 with Eric Show pitching well in his first start after returning from his 1986 elbow injury. But he began to crumble during the eighth inning.

Chris Brown knocked in the first run with a line double down the right-field line that landed just inside the foul line. That chased Show. A young right-hander named Lance McCullers stomped out of the bullpen instead of the injured Rich Gossage, who was still nursing that rib problem. Candy Maldonado drove in two more runs with a double in almost exactly the same spot. Dumb luck. Two inches to the right on two line drives and Larry Bowa's first season would have begun in a completely different fashion. But it wasn't to be. The Giants prevailed 4-3 in 12 innings.

"A couple of bleeders," Bowa lamented before he rushed off to see his mom. His mother's improving condition turned out to be the best news of the week, if not the season. The source of her problem was kidney failure and to this day she is still undergoing the psychological and physical strain of dialysis three times a week. By the time Bowa reached Sacramento, doctors had already stabilized her blood pressure. The immediate danger seemed to be over.

That brought Bowa back to the Stick for a Tuesday night game in which the well-documented wind that sweeps across Candlestick Point from the bay on the city's southern extremities ate up another young outfielder. This time, it was Stanley Jefferson, who probably shouldn't have been out there on a weak left ankle in the first place. During the first inning, Jeffrey Leonard hit a drive to center field that simply kept carrying. Jefferson didn't have a chance. The double scored two runs and sent the Giants on their way to another 4-3 win. "I learned later that when the ball is hit on a fly here, it dies," Jefferson said. "When it's hit on a line, it takes off. That one was hit on a line.... You just can't take your eyes off the ball. Everything after that first one was easy, but you've just got to watch the ball." Worse still, rookie second baseman Joey Cora, who at five-feet-eight inches seems tiny in comparison to Bowa, was charged with two errors. The first came when Cora crossed second base too early on a doubleplay pivot throw and didn't get the call from the second base umpire.

"I was told that young guys don't get too many calls," said the native of Puerto Rico within earshot of veteran shortstop Garry Templeton. "They would have given that call to you."

Said Templeton: "You're right, but I probably wouldn't have cheated that much."

The second error came when Cora's underhanded toss to first base on a Leonard dribbler sailed well over Steve Garvey's head. Garvey couldn't have caught that one if he was sitting on Kareem Abdul-Jabbar's shoulders. "It was pretty funny," said Garvey. "There haven't been too many times in my career when I didn't even attempt a vertical leap."

Except Bowa wasn't laughing. He had watched his young catcher Benito Santiago fail to block one Ed Whitson pitch that turned out to be his first passed ball in a half-season chocked with errors and passed balls. Santiago, who hit his first homer of the year in this game, was later caught napping off second base when he was doubled up on a soft line drive. The worst of Bowa's fears had taken place. His three youngsters up the middle had already combined to lose one game. And though Bowa was strangely silent afterward, he was ready to rock after the 2-1 loss when he promised big lineup changes for the next game on Friday night against manager Pete Rose's Reds in Cincinnati.

"I don't like to lose," Bowa said, warming up to the occasion. "I'm changing the lineup. You guys can figure it out. It'll be up Friday night. There will be guys mad and I don't give a damn. All I hear about is the bleepin' wind out there. The bleepin' elements. The Giants play in it. What the hell difference does it make? No one has said it to me. I just hear little statements running to positions, taking batting practice. Reading stuff in the papers. The mound is the same here. The bases are the same here.

"You just can't tell me that all the luck is going against us. I say you create your own damn luck. If you start feeling sorry for yourself, you're gonna get beat. If you wait around for something to happen, it'll happen. I don't buy that crap. You make your own breaks. All right, any other questions? Let's get this over with."

Outside Bowa's office in the locker room, general manager Jack McKeon, who had managed a few bad teams himself in a checkered career, was trying to be the symbol of calm strength compared to his rookie manager. It was too early, McKeon figured, to be that concerned about a season that had just begun its six-month roller coaster journey. "If we were oh-and-105, or oh-and-50, maybe I might be concerned," McKeon said. "You play 162 games. You don't change your ballclub just because you've lost three in a row.... It could be two months before you see any progress with a young team. You wish to hell it was something you could put your finger on."

Two months. Perhaps the ability to prognosticate was beginning to run in the Padres family.

SUNDAY, APR. 12, 1987 ◆
CINCINNATI, OH

Ⓕor three days Larry Bowa's old friend Pete Rose had watched his former teammate climb up the dugout wall at Riverfront Stadium. The Padres losing streak had grown to 13 in a row—five straight to open the season—and even Bowa's histrionics were losing their effect. After Friday night's loss, Bowa closed the clubhouse door, leaving the media outside to cool its heels for four seemingly endless minutes. Inside, Bowa held his first team thrashing of the season. He screamed, he yelled. He ranted, he raved. He even cracked a bat over his knee—no easy feat.

Later that night, Bowa was beside himself when he learned that four of his players had decided to stay out well past the unofficial 1 a.m. curfew. Those players—Goose Gossage, Andy Hawkins, Kevin Mitchell and James Steels—were all called in for private meetings and fined the obligatory hundred dollars. It left Bowa wondering what he could do. The lineup changes he had threatened in San Francisco never really materialized. And now he was losing his grip as an authority figure. These seemed like the darkest of days.

Rose was Bowa's teammate on the 1980 Philadelphia Phillies club that finally won the World Series. He had long since returned to Cincinnati to conclude his playing career and dabble in managing. Rose was well aware of Bowa's volatile personality. He had seen it as a player from both sides of the field. In several talks over a period of days, he had tried to counsel Bowa about curbing his temper.

"It's a little different here than it is managing in the minor leagues," Rose said. "I told him you can't have a meeting every time you lose. Meetings mean you're not playing well. His team wasn't playing that poorly as far as I could see. But they're not going to win if they play their best, then he chews them out and he tells them how shitty they are. I know his temperament. He's a lot like me. But some things you've got to change."

Rose wasn't the first experienced manager who attempted to counsel Bowa and he won't be the last. The parade included such noteworthies as the Dodgers Tommy Lasorda, the Braves Chuck Tanner, the Pirates Jimmy Leyland, and the Phillies Lee Elia. But Rose was the first in line. He was also first on the red clubhouse "hotline" telephone to congratulate Bowa after the Padres 5-2 victory, coming on the crest of Steve Garvey's first-inning, three-run homer, gave him his first win as a major-league manager.

Rose to Bowa: "Well, you finally got the monkey off your back."

Bowa to the media: "That was the president on the phone. . . . (laughter) I've spent some sleepless nights here, gentlemen. It's like a 10,000-pound weight off my back. Pete looked over to me with two out and he said, 'There's your first win.' I said that we still needed one more and he went. . ." Bowa made a downward motion with his hands that indicated Rose had told him to take it easy.

You'd figure Bowa would listen to Rose. It's hard to imagine that Bowa respected any single player more than Rose throughout his career. Rose was the epitome. A guy who came out to play hard every day and could match his intensity with his level of skill. His all-time career record 4,204 hits is enough to attest to that. Rose was simply a winner. The ultimate team player. In his illustrious 23-year playing career which seems to have finally ended in 1985, Rose set all kinds of records, but his most significant accomplishment may be that he played on seven division winners—five of them for Cincinnati before he signed with Philadelphia in 1979 as a free agent.

"Playing with Rose was great," Bowa said about his final Phillies years. "He's unbelievable. His intensity. . .I saw him go through a divorce. You know, when he had a hitting-streak going. He has a way of just putting everything out of his mind when he plays the game. That's how he releases all his anxiety and whatever is built up inside him. That's how he releases it. He concentrates better than any human being I've ever seen on every pitch. And he literally loves the game. He put us over the hump. We kept comin' close and comin' close before he got there. But he put us over it. He's got that cocky air about him. When you played against him, you hated him."

It may be just a coincidence that Rose played on the Phillies only world championship team, but it probably isn't. For most of the late 1970s, the Phillies club, with a nucleus of Bowa, Mike Schmidt, Bob Boone and Greg Luzinski, always seemed to creep to the precipice, but could not win the National League pennant. The Phillies lost the playoffs in 1976, 1977 and 1978, losing to Rose and the last of the Big Red Machine in 1976 and the Dodgers the next two seasons. Perhaps Game 3 of the 1977 National League Championship Series best illustrates the pathos of that particular Phillies team.

On Oct. 7, 1977, the Phillies, tied one game apiece with the Dodgers in the old best of five series, carried a 5-3 lead into the ninth inning at Veterans Stadium. They had gone ahead in the second inning, when, trailing that Dodgers team of Steve Garvey, Ron Cey, Davey Lopes and Billy Russell by a score of 2-0, pitcher Burt Hooton blew up. As 63,719 people in the Vet pounded their feet, shaking the stadium to its rafters, Hooton walked four straight men with the bases loaded to allow three Phillies runs. Bowa had drawn the final walk to give the Phillies the lead.

In the ninth inning, behind their ace reliever Gene Garber, the Phillies recorded the first two outs and with no Dodgers on base were just one out away from taking the series lead. Vic Davalillo pinch hit and beat out a drag bunt to second baseman Ted Sizemore. The knowledgeable but not always charitable Phillies fans held their collective breath as Manny Mota pinch hit. Mota hit a very catchable drive toward the warning track in the left-field corner. It probably would have been caught had manager Danny Ozark not left the lumbering Luzinski in left field.

"I never understood that," Bowa recalled. "All year long Danny is taking Bull out for a defensive replacement late in the game. Sure as hell, a fly ball goes out there that Jerry Martin just sucks up. If he's out there we win that game. Danny had some excuse about getting Bull another at bat in the ninth inning. But we weren't even going to bat in the ninth inning if we won."

It was a formidable mistake. Luzinski missed the ball. Mota had a double and Davalillo scored when the relay skipped through Sizemore for an error. Mota went to third. It was now 5-4 with Lopes coming to the plate. The next play would irrevocably change the season. Lopes smashed a grounder toward Schmidt at third which apparently hit a seam in the artificial surface and kicked up off Schmidt's glove. Bowa was right behind him in the hole to grab it with his bare hand. A remarkable heads-up play. In one fluid motion, Bowa caught the ball and threw it to Hebner. First base umpire Bruce Froemming spread his arms wide to signal Lopes safe in a call that seemed to be conjectured by every television replay angle. A huge argument ensued.

"I'll never forget that," Bowa said. "Man, Froemming anticipated that just because Schmitty didn't catch the ball, I couldn't throw Lopes out. I went crazy. That was the game. We win that game, we win that series."

As it turned out, the Dodgers won the game when Lopes went to second on Garber's errant pick off throw and scored on Russell's single. They won the series when Tommy John threw a seven-hitter in the pouring rain the very next night. The elements, a manager's decision and an umpire's call turned that series into a travesty. "That was the best team we had there," Bowa said. "It was better than the team we won with in '80. But in those years, it always seemed like we were one hit away. A guy busting it open. We couldn't get a big hit in a crucial time."

But unlike the 1977 team, the 1980 team had Rose at first base instead of Richie Hebner and the grumpy, stick-it-in-your-ear Dallas Green as manager instead of the kindly Ozark. It seemed to make the difference. The 1980 team had more guts than any of the earlier teams, which is evident by the Phillies one game victory in the National League East over Montreal, coming when Schmidt homered in the 11th inning off Stan Bahnsen on the next to the last day of the season at Olympic Stadium.

That was merely the appetizer for the Phils stunning playoff comeback in Houston to win their first pennant in 30 years. Trailing two games to one, the Phillies came from behind to win both Games 4 and 5 in 10 innings at the Astrodome.

"I'll never forget the final game," Bowa said. "We were down against Nolan Ryan, who never used to lose a lead in the late innings. Especially at home. Pete Rose came up to me and he said, 'If you get on, we're going to win this damn game.' And I didn't have much success against Ryan. My first game in pro ball, the Phillies send me to Spartanburg. The first bleepin' game, we're playin' in Greenville against the New York Mets team. I had had a real good spring training and I felt like a stud. The line on me was—this guy came from nowhere, he got $2,000, he's a prospect. First game we faced Nolan Ryan. Four punchouts. I had no prayer. I figured if this is what professional ball was going to be like, I had no chance.

"So here we are and Pete wants me to get on against Ryan in the eighth inning of the fifth game of the playoffs. I got a base hit over short. The next hitter was Bob Boone. He hits a ball to Ryan that goes off his glove. It would have been a sure doubleplay ball. That's first and second and it's all happening on first pitches. The next guy up, Greg Gross, drops a perfect bunt. We have the bases loaded with nobody out. They start warming somebody up. Pete ends up walking. That brought in a run. Before they could even get their relievers up, Ryan was on the ropes.

"Those playoffs and the World Series were amazing. The World Series, though, was the best. I had more fun in the World Series than I ever had playing baseball. The Houston series was draining. We bleepin' played our bleeps off. It was like, it doesn't matter what we do here. We just went out and had fun. First game, we were behind Kansas City 4-0 in the third inning. We were dead. We were just drained. We weren't doing anything. So I got a base hit off Dennis Leonard. I'll never forget the scenario.

I have the tape at home. They're saying on TV that Bowa isn't going to run here. 'They're down four runs and Bowa has to play it safe.'

"First pitch, I said, screw it. I'm gone. I'm on my own, but Dallas gave me a hold sign because we were down four runs. I said to hell with this crap. I thought I could get a jump. I thought I had a great jump, but it was a bang, bang play. I mean, boom, boom. I said to myself, hell, if I'm out, I might as well keep running. There was no way I wanted to go back to the dugout to face him. But I was safe. Boonie gets a double and knocks me in. We scored five runs and wound up winning 7-6. That turned the game around, being aggressive. Dallas didn't say a word to me, but I knew he was ticked. He was relieved that I made it, but I looked in the dugout. He had his arms folded and he gives you that look.

"We took a two games to nothing lead, and after they tied us up, we came home from Kansas City leading three games to two. I'll never forget how the sixth game ended. We're winning 4-1. They load the bases in the ninth inning with one out. Frank White is at bat. Around the rim of the field, are all those mounted horsemen and guard dogs and the people in the Vet are going crazy. It was some scene. White pops it up foul over near our dugout. Boonie and Pete converge. The ball pops out of Boonie's glove and Pete grabs it. That's when you knew we were gonna win. Willie Wilson struck out to end it.

"The unbelievable thing was going down Broad Street the next day. We must have had two million people at the parade. That place was packed. I mean, lined up the street past the Vet, the Spectrum and to John F. Kennedy Stadium, where the Army-Navy game is played. That's where we ended the parade. The place looked like the Army-Navy game was there. You never forget something like that. You look back on your career in baseball and through all the ups and downs, that's something that will never be replaced. It might be replaced if I ever got into the World Series as a manager. But as a player, it'll never be replaced."

Getting to the World Series as a manager might have been

the last thing on Bowa's mind seven years later as he reveled in his first win as a manager. Putting the whole season into sad perspective, the Padres 1-5 record would be their best of the season after a win. Their best overall record was 0-1. Rose couldn't predict how far reaching the disappointment might be for his friend. Neither could Bowa.

"Sleep, you can count the hours I've had during the last few days on one hand," Bowa said. "I've been watching CNN, Nightline, X-rated movies. I'm going all night. By the time I finally go to sleep, I wake up, it's four-thirty, a quarter to five, and I'm trying to make up another lineup."

Rose added this piece of advice for Bowa: "I never lose much sleep. Once I leave this clubhouse I forget about today's game. There's nothing I can do about today's loss. I mean, I can't do anything about it. Why should I beat my head against the wall or go home and beat up my wife and kid? This business is tough when you have a direct result in the outcome. When you screw up as a manager, that's when you lose sleep."

Though Bowa believed he was making all the right moves, the losing wasn't letting him sleep.

"These have been the most miserable days of my life," Bowa said. "I didn't think it was so hard to win a game. I mean, I knew it was hard to be successful, but I didn't think it would be that hard to win a single bleeping game."

Maybe he could already sense it then, but for Larry Bowa there would be many more such miserable days to come.

THURSDAY, APR. 16, 1987 ♦
SAN DIEGO, CA

As if things weren't tough enough for Larry Bowa in his first few weeks as manager... After finally winning his first game last weekend in Cincinnati, the club had returned to San Diego on Monday night for its home opener against the San Francisco Giants. The Padres set a major-league record by opening the game with consecutive homers by Marvell Wynne, Tony Gwynn and John Kruk, whose bats all were whisked away to the Hall of Fame. Bowa put on a show by being ejected from his first major-league game as a manager by second base umpire Bob Engel. "It's going to be a big ego thing, I guess. Who ran me first," Bowa said. "Now that's out of the way."

But the Padres lost 13-6 leading Tony Gwynn to note: "When you look up at the scoreboard and you have six runs and 12 hits and you're not even in the ballgame, well, danger signals are sounding off right now and it doesn't look good."

The week didn't get any better. As the losses continued to pile up, so did the injuries. During the home opener, Bowa had been told that reliever Goose Gossage, who had been nursing a rib cage problem for two weeks, would be available. The Goose was up and heating in the bullpen when he told pitching coach Galen Cisco that his ribs were still hurting and he couldn't pitch. Shortly thereafter, Gossage was placed on the disabled list. Center fielder Stanley Jefferson hadn't played all week because his already sore left ankle had swollen after a weekend series on the artificial surface in Cincinnati. Jefferson would be disabled as well. Bowa also lost backup catcher Bruce Bochy to a hand injury. Reliever Tom Gorman, who came on in the home opener to allow a Robby Thompson grand slam, was complaining about a

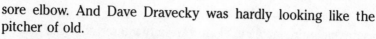

sore elbow. And Dave Dravecky was hardly looking like the pitcher of old.

Win No. 2 was no easy feat either. It came at home against the Dodgers when Tony Gwynn sailed around from first base on a Carmelo Martinez hit to score the winning run in the 10th inning. Gwynn, who had enjoyed the first 5-for-5 game of his career, stood in front of his locker laughing afterward because he had missed a hit and run sign on the play and was being nailed with a hundred dollar Bowa fine. The manager himself was in fine fettle. As he addressed reporters afterward, the phone rang.

"How ya doin', George," Bowa said into the receiver. "Thanks, thanks for calling."

When asked who had called, Bowa gave the simple question an honest two-word answer: "George Argyros." Bowa could hardly have known at the time how costly his remark would be.

"If I would have known it would've gotten him into trouble, I wouldn't have said anything," Bowa said. "Or I would have said it was my dad, or something. I guess it was my fault for saying what I did. Take the fine out of my salary."

When the media cleared out of Bowa's office an entourage descended. General manager Jack McKeon, vice president Dick Freeman and National League President Bart Giamatti constituted that particular group. It just happened to be Argyros' bad fortune that he had infringed on San Diego business on a day when Giamatti was attending a Padres game.

"Isn't this great?" Bowa told Giamatti. "I meet the new president and get a phone call from my new owner all in the same day."

Just trying to make sure he was hearing correctly, Giamatti asked Bowa specifically who had called. "George Argyros," Bowa said.

When Giamatti imparted this bit of news on the commissioner's office, Peter Ueberroth slapped a $10,000 fine on the wrists of George Argyros, who was still the owner of the Seattle Mariners and had been told specifically to stay out of Padres affairs until the sale of both clubs was approved. Bowa had become an unwitting pawn in Argyros' misplayed chess game.

When reached at his Orange County home, Argyros brushed aside the entire incident. "I am certainly interested in the Padres, but it wasn't a matter of my trying to use influence or anything else. It's rather silly, really. My intention was to be positive, not to be negative. I was just congratulating the guy for winning his second game, because I know the struggles that a manager goes through. If someone misunderstood that, I am sorry. The commissioner is entitled to do whatever he wants to do, and I will certainly live by any decision he makes."

The situation, though comical at the time, had ominous implications as far as Argyros' future ownership of the Padres was concerned. In Bowa's mind, he must have been wondering how an incoming owner might feel about a manager who had already inadvertently cost him $10,000. But the Argyros ownership was far from a fait accompli. Already, rumors were circulating around the National League that Argyros was not going to get the necessary 75 percent vote for approval. The Padres were 2-8 and counting. The Mariners were 4-6.

WEDNESDAY, APR. 22, 1987 ◆
SAN DIEGO, CA

L arry Bowa wasn't interested in any votes of confidence from general manager Jack McKeon. He was much more interested in why his pitching staff had given up a National League high 27 homers in just 15 games. And so, while McKeon was pontificating about Bowa and the Padres, Bowa was considering slicing open a number of baseballs to see just what was at the core of all his problems. After Tuesday night's third Padres win of the season—a knuckle-wrenching 3-2 victory over the Reds in which reliever Lance McCullers struck out pinch-hitter Paul O'Neill with runners on first and third to end the game—Bowa joked about some pregame McKeon remarks.

"I've heard those votes of confidence before," Bowa said. "I'd just as soon not have a vote of confidence. I've played for a lot of managers who've had that vote of confidence. The next day, they were saying, 'Have a good season, Larry.' I'd rather stay away from that."

McKeon's vote: "I think Bowa has done a good job managing the ballclub. Unfortunately, the wins are not there to justify what I said. As far as handling the ballclub, I don't see anything wrong with his moves. The only thing I see is that it's tough. It's very, very difficult on Larry. He's very intense. He wants to do well. Here you get a chance to come to the big leagues for the first time and your ballclub starts out 2-12. But as far as any pressure from upstairs, there's none. None whatsoever. We're 100 percent behind him."

The next day the Padres finally won two games in a row for the first time under Bowa's stewardship to bring their record to an inglorious 4-12. But that didn't mean Bowa was satisfied. He had to take his frustrations out on something. When he arrived at the ballpark hours before the game, Bowa sought out the help of clubhouse man Whitey Wietelmann, who is more of an institution in these parts than the franchise itself. Wietelmann, dubbed Mr. Indispensable, has been a Padre dating back to the long lost minor-league franchise of the same name. He is bald and of wide girth. In his seventies now, he waddles around the clubhouse like a penguin on flat feet and gnarled legs. But if one wants a strange task accomplished, Whitey is the man.

Bowa was simply wondering why baseballs were jumping out of the stadium in record numbers this season—25 homers in the first 10 home games. "I was watching those balls flying out of here in batting practice, so I figured, let's cut one open and see what's inside," Bowa said.

Wietelmann escorted Bowa into his inner sanctum and from within his desk produced baseballs from different eras: The old Spaulding baseball with the signature of former president Warren Giles on it. Vintage 1965. Another Spaulding ball of more recent corkage with the signature of just retired president Charles "Chub" Feeney etched on the cowhide. Last year's ball, produced by Rawlings, marked with the same Feeney signature. And finally the ball in question—the A. Bartlett Giamatti model, also from the Rawlings cellar.

Bowa's orders: "Slice away." Wietelmann hobbled into the workroom adjacent to his office and produced a hacksaw ripe for the occasion. Despite consistent denials from the Rawlings people that the latest balls certainly have not been juiced up, what Bowa discovered offered him ample reason why his pitching staff resembled a series of human golf tees on a driving range. A superball-type hard rubber sphere at the core of the 1987 ball bounces with complete abandon.

"Did you see the balls Larry cut up?" said pitcher Ed Whitson, who had allowed 10 homers and only 18 hits in his first four starts. "I don't care who it is and how hard you throw it, you're gonna give up home runs if you throw strikes. The way they've got the ball hopped up right now, it's amazing. I've been playing 14 years and I've never seen balls get out of the park the way it does. Even when I was with the 'Lumber Company' in Pittsburgh.

"You've got to see the balls Bowa cut up, to be frank with you. You've got to see it to believe it. There's an outer coating of rubber and on the inside of it, there's a superball. And the string is wound as tight as you can possibly get it."

Whitson wasn't exaggerating. Wietelmann sliced right through three of the baseballs from different eras revealing a major difference between texture and core. The last of the Spaulding balls has a three-tiered center that is two-part rubber with a solid bit of cork as its nucleus that drops dead on the floor. Not much juice in that one. Last year, Rawlings evidently changed the baseball's composition. There are six layers beneath the leather cover—three of compacted material (string and thread) and three of different colored galvanized rubber. The 1986 ball had some jump in it and the Padres were clearly affected by the change. Padres hitters set a club record by blasting 136 homers—80 at the stadium, which was once considered a pitcher's park, but recently has been dubbed, "Launching Pad West." Pitchers gave up a league-leading 150 homers—78 in the pad. That's 158 homers alone in Jack Murphy Stadium.

But that ain't nothing, really. Based on the pace of 2.5 homers per game here so far this season, as many as 203 homers could have sailed through the San Diego sky in 1987. Why? Bowa thinks he knows the reason. When Whitey Wietelmann hacked the Giamatti ball open, a little rubber ball, perhaps three-quarters of an inch in diameter, bounced to the floor and kept bouncing, bouncing and bouncing. Bowa took that core into his office and jammed it to the floor himself.

"It hit the ceiling," Bowa said. "We got suspicious when Dodgers shortstop Mariano Duncan almost hit one out to the opposite side of the field last weekend. I'm not taking anything away from Duncan. He can play. But a guy like Mariano Duncan doesn't have that kind of power to the opposite side of the field."

Bowa, of course, was picking his spots. He wasn't making any Duncan-like accusations toward the Reds, who had seven players in their regular lineup capable of hitting the ball out at any moment. "Tell Larry to cut up some baseballs in here. I don't need no hopped up baseballs. I got this," said Cincinnati slugger Dave Parker, flexing a bicep which is bigger than Bowa's thigh. "I could hit 'em out if they had putty inside 'em."

Bowa didn't doubt it. He just wondered why his club wasn't taking the same advantage of the new juiced up baseballs as the opposition. "They've got TNT inside of them and we can't do anything about it," Bowa said.

Evidently, Bowa didn't need any vote of confidence. What he needed were some power hitters.

SUNDAY, APR. 26, 1987 ◆ LOS ANGELES, CA

$\diamond\!\!\!\!I\!\!\!\!\diamond$ had just about had it with this team. What was our record going into the game, 4-15? So I closed the clubhouse door at Dodger Stadium and I went nuts. It was an all-timer.

I told them they didn't know how to win. They were going through the motions. I said if we didn't play harder, with more intensity, we'll get everybody the bleep out of here. I told them that if anybody wanted to get the bleep out of here, they should come in and see me. We'll get them out of here today. I thought I was going to have a stroke. I swear I did. My heart was pounding. I think it was the maddest I've ever got. I started out good, though. I started out by sayin' that I wanted to apologize to the seven or eight guys who are busting their butt out there for me. But the other sixteen or seventeen, this is for you. After the meeting, Tony Gwynn came up to me and said, "I hope I'm one of the seven or eight." I told him, "You're one through eight, Tony."

You know what? I can't believe you have to motivate guys every single game. That's basically what it boils down to. That's hard to do. I mean, I saw a big difference just in the intensity we played with today. Why can't we do that every game? That just upsets the hell out of me. I think it's relatively early to be throwing in the towel. Even as a player. I mean, as disappointed and disgusted as I get, each day I wake up and say, hey, we're gonna start something new today. I really believe that. And then all of a sudden, bleep, as soon as one thing happens, these guys say, ah, bleep it. Tomorrow we'll start it again. Garv had a suggestion after that bleepin' Saturday night 4-2 loss, the game that got me so upset.

He came in the office and he said, "I've got a good idea. Why don't you hit me third tomorrow afternoon?" I said, "What about Tony Gwynn?" He just looked at me and went, "Sleep on it. I'm ready to make things happen." I said, "OK, I'll think about it." I slept on it and batted him fifth.

I was talking to the coaches and Deacon Jones said he sat down with Steve during a game in which he wasn't playing and asked him, "What does a Steve Garvey day consist of?" And Steve said, "Well, I get up at eight-thirty, nine o'clock, go into the office and have a roll." I mean, he broke it down. "I have some coffee. Answer some mail. Twelve, one o'clock, it's lunch time. I go out and have lunch with somebody. A businessman or something. Go back to the office at about two, answer some more of my mail and then go to the ballpark." I said, "He does that every day?" To me, that would be draining. It's like two jobs, really. I think, especially as you get older, you've got to dedicate yourself to getting your rest and just playing. I know he doesn't go out to drink. I know he takes care of his body. But I'm just talking about mentally. When you're worried about a business you're running, it's hard to play this game. If anybody can do it, I'm sure Garvey can.

The thing with Steve is, he's been a great athlete and I think he still believes he's 24 or 25 years old. Of course, I didn't see him play last year. So I asked some coaches and other people in the organization if he has really slowed down from last year to this year. And they all said, yeah. You see, I can't compare it to anything. I know that since the last time I played against him, he has slowed down. So does everybody eventually.

Evidently, Steve is really pursuing other interests outside of playing. That's why you pick up the papers and you read that his group wants to buy the Seattle Mariners. His initial plan was that he wanted to play two or three more years. But I guess he's changing his mind and wants to consider other business interests. I think he's come to the realization that this could be the last year.

As a player, you know when it's close. If you don't, something's wrong. The thing is, he catches everything. He does. But the thing that's really hurting him right now is his bat speed.

When a guy is in a slump, usually the bat speed is there. He might not be hitting it, but you can see him fouling off pitches. The bat speed is there when a guy is in a slump. He's just not getting his hits.

But I guess when I was in the last phases of my career, I fought it for awhile too. Yeah, everybody fights it. But it only took that year—1985—to realize that it was over. And when I made up my mind that that was it, I didn't need a brick wall to fall on my head. What made me decide is that I listened to some people I respect. I watched my performance at shortstop. I watched films. I was a step late on ground balls that I knew I used to suck up. And I just said, hey, I've done what I can do. I mean, Father Time takes over. Especially at the position I played. I think when you play in the infield, it's worse because your mistakes and your lack of range really show up. I didn't want to embarrass myself. Being a manager, I can't worry about only one guy, I have to worry about the entire team. I think I've been pretty consistent with Garvey. I bet what it's going to boil down to if he doesn't start hitting the way he has proven he can, my next option is to platoon him and John Kruk. You know, we had a meeting, Jack McKeon and I, and we decided if we're going to struggle, we might as well see if guys like Kruk and Carmelo Martinez can play. Then for next year we'll have a decision. Can they play or not? I don't know if Martinez can play every day. We're going to have to find out.

Carmelo, if he hits .250 and hits 15 to 20 homers, that's all you want. Then, he's an asset to our organization. Now if he hits .250 and only hits 10 homers, we have to do something with him. It's obvious we're going to have trouble winning the division this year. So we might as well just answer some questions. Like Jimmy Jones. As bad as he's going in Las Vegas, he's gonna be called up here real soon. I know he is. Let's just throw him out there. See what happens. Dave Dravecky. He's still gonna be in the bullpen, but I think pretty soon we've got to start him and let him go five innings. Bleep it. He ain't helping us now. We're basically in the situation where our veteran players have all had it. I'm not really worried about Garry Templeton's batting average. I think he's doing a pretty good job at short. I'm not worried about Tempy, but when guys are not hitting in the middle of our lineup, it's tough. I'm looking in the papers, there are plenty of guys in both leagues with more home runs than our top guy in RBIs.

Garvey, he's been up a lot of times with men on, boy. I would think it's gotta be pretty frustrating for him. As great a career as he's had. But he hasn't come in to me once and asked me why I kept him out of the lineup. I think he knows. The funny thing is, I think he gets more respect from the opposition than he does from his teammates. I know one thing about him. He can take a negative and turn it into a positive. He's unbelievable. I mean, like the fans were booing him in San Diego. He says that means they care. They care about him being in a slump. If they didn't do anything, they wouldn't care.

We're all lucky in San Diego. What do you think would have been happening to us in Philly and Chicago during that first homestand? We'd have to put bags over our heads to get out of the stadium after the game. I'm tellin' you, they would bury you back East. When I played on Phillies teams, they let you know about it every second of the game. I'll never forget this time in Philly back in 1980. Yeah, the year we won the championship. We were playing the Chicago Cubs and we were comin' down the stretch. After eight innings, we led by something like five runs. The Cubs came back to score seven runs to take the lead into the bottom of the ninth. Now, we come off the field at the Vet after they score all those runs and the fans are booin' the hell out of us. I mean, it was merciless. Then we came back to score three and won the game.

I was pumped anyway because they gave us a standing ovation. I came into the clubhouse and exploded. I said, "These fans here tonight are the worst bleepin' fans I've ever seen in my life. The worst." The next day, the headlines blasted it all over the city: "Bowa Says Phillies Fans the Worst!" The next night, I come out to take BP and there's a big crowd there. It must have been a giveaway night. There are 40,000 people and I get the hell booed out of me. I mean, unbelievable. And that started a thing from that day on. I was hitting about .260 at the time and I went crazy.

I caught fire. Every time they'd announce me, I'd get the hell booed out of me and I'd get another hit. I'm tippin' my cap and playin' to them, too. Lovin' every minute of it.

So now we go to Montreal for the final weekend of the season and it's a gigantic series. If we win this series, we get to the playoffs. I'm oh-for-two or three. We have about 4,000 people up from Philly and they boo the hell out of me. I get a base hit. It started carrying over. Just boo him. He gets motivated by it. I was getting booed the whole month of September. I mean, it was unreal. Greg Luzinski said, "Only you could do that." But Pete Rose told him, "Let him go. Let him go. He's getting psyched up."

It's a different breed of people back there. I mean, they live, die, eat and sleep baseball. In the West, this is entertainment. You guys are horsebleep, but that's all right. Hopefully you'll get better. Basically that's what I said in the clubhouse meeting. I'm embarrassed. I'm embarrassed walking down the street. I said, "Aren't you tired of losing? Jesus!" I was burnt up. I was kicking garbage cans and garbage around the room. There were the usual boxes of autographed baseballs sitting on the table. I sent them flying. They went bouncing all over the place. I read where Tony Gwynn said, "When he's in here yellin', you keep your eyes on him. You don't drop your head. You don't look at the ceiling. You don't look at the floor. You look right at him." Mark Parent, a catcher who was with me last year in Vegas, said it was piddly stuff. Yeah, he's seen worse. Over there I once swept the food on the postgame buffet table to the floor and then two-handed the table across the room. But I got pretty worked up today. Tony said that before it was over, I had white stuff forming at the corners of my mouth.

What got it started was Saturday night's game. I think we should have won it. The intensity level was really bad. Then we've got guys always making excuses. Kruk said he can't see now because he's oh-for-seven. That's a joke. And there was a ball hit to left field that I thought he should have caught. But the last thing a player should do is let his hitting affect his defense.

These guys are just not thinking about what they're supposed to be doing. It's like, when you go up to hit, every pitch is going to be a fastball. Benito Santiago was up there looking fast-ball every pitch against the Dodgers and I don't think he's gotten a first pitch fastball yet.

Kevin Mitchell the same way. It's not because we have so many young guys. It's that we don't think. Some guys just go out and play the game. That's all they're doing. You know, it's like Mitchell. When you're with the Mets and you have Gary Carter, Darryl Strawberry, Keith Hernandez, Wally Backman and Len Dykstra, no one expects much from a Kevin Mitchell. So he just relaxes and has fun. Now he gets traded to San Diego and gets put right in the middle of the lineup. And you expect big things from him. But you don't know what the hell he's going to do. It's one thing going through the Mets lineup and facing Mitchell bat-ting seventh. The pitcher might relax a little bit. Mitch has a good year. Now he's put in the middle of our lineup. The pitchers react differently. He has never had to be the man to drive in runs, the man to hit home runs. It's always been, "Hey, I'm on a great team. Whatever I do is icing on the cake." It's different here. I'm not saying he'll never be able to do that, but right now, he's hav-ing a tough time accepting that role as the big hitter in our lineup. I don't think he's mature enough to do it yet.

Physically, I think he comes prepared to play most days. Mentally, he doesn't. But I don't think he's ever been taught that. I really don't. He has a great arm. His hands are pretty good for a big guy. But his mental preparation... I don't think he has any idea what he's doing at the plate until he steps into the batter's box. Kevin just counts on his natural ability and that's tough. If he learned the mental part, he could be a great player. Even last year, he had a lousy second half. Davey Johnson just flat out gave up on him. Never played him against right-handed pitchers. Why was that?

Joey Cora is another one. Here's a kid who doesn't know what his game plan is. He reacts to situations pretty good in the field. But he doesn't know when to go up there looking for a walk and when to be aggressive. You know, there's a time and place to look for a walk. In the eighth inning, if the score is tied nothing-nothing, and you're the leadoff hitter, battle the guy for a walk. But when you're up there down 2-1 with a runner on third, you've got to be trying for a base hit. See, he hasn't separated the two yet. He's all confused. First you're telling me to get a walk and now you're telling me to get a base hit. That's baseball sense. I could sit here and hold a baseball seminar for him all day and wonder if he'd ever understand a thing. A lot of these pitchers are throwing the first pitch down the middle because they know he gets a lot of walks. Joey is like a lot of players. They love looking at the stat sheet. To me, whoever brings those bleepin' stats down there should be fired. Stats shouldn't even be in the clubhouse. I'm serious. You should look at stats in October or Sunday when you pick up the paper. Stats to me are the most misleading things in baseball I've ever seen in my life. Sure it's great to hit 30 homers and knock in a hundred runs. Everyone needs one of those guys on your team. But guys like Cora have got to do the little things to win. They don't realize that. If they hit .300 and we come in 30 games out, they figure they're going to get a bleepin' raise. They probably would get a raise, but it ain't gonna help 'em win. Like today, the atmosphere afterward was great because we won a game. It makes for a long summer, boy, when you're going through losses. I should know. The first bleepin' Phillies team I played on back in 1970 lost 88 games. My first four years in the majors, we lost 88, 97, 95 and 91 respectively. It was brutal like that, losing all the time. Everyone is irritable. No one wants to let little things slide. It's tough. And to stress to these kids that losing sucks, they don't understand it yet. They really don't understand it.

I think if you sat down with each and every one of our young guys and just went one on one with them, they'd say, "I don't like losing either. Who is he kidding?" But do they do anything about it? Do they make adjustments? No, they don't make adjustments. They go up there and do the same thing every night. We can do the same thing every night and keep losing. But they're not doing anything about it. I'm trying to change lineups. Talk to guys. But to me, if you don't make adjustments in this game, you're going to get buried. The guys who play a long time make adjustments.

That's what the meeting was all about, really. My goal wasn't to get ticked off so they would play harder. My goal was to let them know that we were playing horsebleep. We're not thinking. We're not executing. When you go up there with runners on second and third we're not thinking about what we're supposed to do. Instead of hitting a ground ball when the second baseman and shortstop are back, we're trying to hit the wall. Then we pop the ball up to the infield. To me, the physical part of this game is tough. It's hard to hit a baseball. But if you think about what you're supposed to do, you should be able to execute. I'm not saying you've got to hit .300. I'm just saying, execute. We've been layin' down some bunts lately. We never did that. They didn't do it all last year, I've heard. But I've been harping on it and harping on it. That's a plus. That's something I can see. All the work we did in spring training is not going down the tubes.

The hardest thing for me is to be patient when I keep getting my butt kicked every night. I hate it. When we don't hit and our starting pitching gets rocked, we look like crap. There are even rumors now that they're not going to give the franchise to George Argyros. Somebody told me there's already four owners who don't want Argyros in the National League. I don't think they want him to go from league to league. So it looks like Joan Kroc is going to keep the team unless Garvey's group gets in. But really, I don't think that's going to happen. He's making her angry—very angry—with his quotes about the club not opening the books up for him. She's not too happy right now. As far as I'm concerned, I can't worry about that. I've just got to hope that the baseball people feel I know what I'm doin'. I know this will all directly reflect on me. Even though you're human, you can't think about it. It's like beating my head up against a wall. I can talk all day to these guys, but the bottom line is we just have to go out there and do it.

WEDNESDAY, APR. 29, 1987 ✦
ST. LOUIS, MO

eneral manager Jack McKeon called it all a crazy coincidence, but pitcher Tom Gorman wasn't so sure. It was just
another in a series of off-field problems that had plagued the Padres in recent days. On Tuesday, the National League president
had taken it upon himself to contact Steve Garvey about his reported involvement with a group interested in purchasing the Seattle Mariners franchise, which became available when Mariners
owner George Argyros decided to buy the Padres. Are you following all this?

Gorman claimed to have a bad left elbow. McKeon said he
didn't know about the injury when Gorman cleared waivers and
was outrighted to Las Vegas. Both Larry Bowa and McKeon
thought Gorman was trying to pull a fast one.

"It would be a whole different story if I came up with this after I found out I was going down," Gorman said. "This isn't something that was premeditated by me. And that's the way they're
making it sound."

About the Garvey situation, Bart Giamatti called the intrepid
first baseman prior to a game in which Garvey broke out of a
deep slump. Garvey had a double, single and three RBIs to double his season RBI output as the Padres beat the St. Louis Cardinals 5-2. The gist of Giamatti's comments was simple:

"My intent is clarity of the situation," Giamatti said. "Mr.
Argyros still owns the Seattle club in the American League. Mrs.
Kroc still owns the San Diego club in the National League. I want
it clear that there should be no comment, substance or commerce between the two situations. Steve now knows that. I trust
that George knows that too."

Garvey, who for the first time mentioned that his hitting slump might be related to a nagging sore left shoulder, evidently understood Giamatti's intentions. "He had read something and I told him what I told the press," Garvey said about a story written by *Tacoma News Tribune* reporter Steve Buckley. "I had been contacted by a Tacoma paper. They had found out that there had been some preliminary contact with the Mariners by some associates of mine. They wanted to know if I was involved in it. I told them that these are the same gentlemen that were involved with me and the Padres. But I, of course, couldn't have anything to do with it now. I told Mr. Giamatti that I thought the Northwest was still a good location. That these people were interested in the Mariners and keeping the team in Seattle.

"He just said that probably the best thing I could do was try to avoid the situation. He just wanted me to know his feelings on the entire subject. It was just one of those things. All I was doing was commenting on my knowledge that there are people interested who I know. I was just trying to communicate."

The Gorman situation cast a further pall over an evening in which the Padres bullpen blew two leads as San Diego lost 10-6 to a Cardinals team that, like the Padres, was depleted by injury. "I've got Willie McGee day to day, Tony Pena month to month and Jeff Lahti year to year," quipped Cardinals manager Whitey Herzog. After having won two games in a row for the second time, the loss put the Padres anemic record at 6-16.

The Gorman fiasco had begun innocently enough several weeks ago during the home opener against San Francisco. Gorman came on, allowed a Robby Thompson grand slam, pitched another inning, and asked out because of a sore elbow. Team doctors indicated that he had slight tendinitis in the elbow and told him to rest for a few days. The incident infuriated Bowa. The manager felt that Gorman had begged out of a runaway ballgame, forcing him to use another pitcher. Bowa, who played with Gorman briefly in New York, had added him to the team as a ninth or tenth pitcher to replace Greg Booker, another pitcher suffering from elbow problems. Trying to head off any more flap, McKeon elected to send Gorman back to San Diego for another visit with team doctors. According to baseball rules, a player may not be moved off a major-league roster during the course of an injury. That was the question. Was Gorman injured? If he was, McKeon would have to put him on the disabled list before he could ship Gorman to Vegas. The situation did nothing to mollify Bowa, who was in no mood for any more controversy.

"The thing that put the icing on the cake was him knowing what his role was as far as being a long man," Bowa said. "You've got to suck it up. And then he comes out of the Giants game. That really ticked me off. Whether he was hurt or not, he knew what his role on the team was. I told him right from the start: 'As a ninth or tenth pitcher on this team you've got to suck it up. And you can't worry about your ERA because we don't care.' So the first opportunity he has to go out there, he gives up a grand slam and comes in and says his arm hurts. That's bull. I'd rather have a guy here who would suck it up.

"From that point on, I just told Jack that I think this guy is worrying about his stats. And that's not going to be his role here. You know, you're the 10th pitcher, if you come on and pitch every time in a blow out game or something, chances are at the end of the year we're gonna say that this guy did a good job. He sucked it up. He didn't give a damn how many home runs he gave up, how many earned runs. That role takes a special makeup. It's hard to go out there and get your butt kicked."

Bowa's assessment was that Gorman didn't have the necessary temperament—an assessment Gorman challenged along with all the other allegations. "This has left a terrible taste in my mouth. I know one thing, I have 24 guys behind me right now," Gorman said. "Because tomorrow it could be one of them. I can handle being demoted. My main concern is being sound. I know I can't pitch. I can't pitch right now if I wanted to. Under these circumstances, they're not supposed to send me down. But they're doing a lot of things they're not supposed to do. It hurts. I don't like people thinking I'm being dishonest. One thing I'm not and that's a liar."

Said Bowa: "He just doesn't seem to understand that hurt or not the decision to send him down has been made."

Added McKeon: "Why would we care? If he was hurt we would just put him on the disabled list. I just didn't know he was really hurt."

What complicated the matter even more was that the Padres had a packed disabled list. Major-league teams are allowed two players on the 15-day list and three more on the 21-day list at any given time. Goose Gossage and Bruce Bochy were on the 15-day list and Stanley Jefferson was on the 21-day list. Pending diagnosis, Gorman could still be placed on the 21-day list.

"Although as of now, he's gone," McKeon said. "He's been outrighted."

Said Gorman: "I'll probably go down, but it's just a bad situation. It makes me sick. I'm so upset about it I can hardly eat. The last thing I want to do is sit out. If I was healthy, I'd go to the minor leagues and pitch. I don't care. I've been demoted before."

This final Gorman remark seemed to support Bowa's contention that the pitcher was too interested in his own stats: "I'm 29. I need to put some numbers on the board. I've got to show somebody something. I think I can pitch in the major leagues even if it isn't in San Diego."

The diagnosis on Gorman's arm was positive and he was eventually placed on the 21-day disabled list. He never pitched for the Padres again. He was outrighted to Vegas on May 15. On June 4, Gorman's contract was traded to the Minnesota Twins triple-A Portland club for another minor-league player who was released by the Padres at the end of the season.

Perhaps even more significant than the Gorman situation was Garvey's revelation that he was suffering from some sort of shoulder problem. How, Bowa was asked, did Garvey sustain that? Bowa said, "I don't know how he did it."

A homecoming in Chicago, where Bowa played nearly the final four years of his career, was next on the Padres itinerary.

SUNDAY, OCT. 7, 1984 ◆
SAN DIEGO, CA

I t is the seventh inning of Game 5 of the National League Championship Series and The Murph is absolute pandemonium. The Chicago Cubs, once leading 3-0 in the game, once leading two games to none in the series, are about to watch the pennant slip away. It is 3-2 as Chicago's big right-hander Rick Sutcliffe faces Carmelo Martinez to open the inning. Ball one. Sutcliffe drops behind the mound in a crouch to catch his breath as the noise accelerates. Ball two. He bends over and ties his shoes. He adjusts his cap and looks in to catcher Jody Davis for the sign. Ball three. Relievers are heating up feverishly in the bullpen. Larry Bowa sprints over from his position at shortstop to calm Sutcliffe down.

"I couldn't believe it," Bowa recalled later about the decision by manager Jim Frey to leave Sutcliffe in the game. "Sutcliffe was all but tellin' him he was through. He's doing a hell of a job, but he's tiring. He's tying his bleepin' shoes. He's doin' everything. I go to the mound and I say, 'How ya doin' Rick?' He's such a competitor, but I can see he's dead. And all the bleepin' relievers are up. We've got them all going and ready. Damn if he doesn't leave him in there. He was tired. He was trying to give somebody a bleepin' sign.

"No pitcher who is as competitive as he is is going to say he's tired. You can go out there and ask him how he feels. He'll tell you, 'I feel great.' No way he's going to say he's tired. You've got to know as a manager that he's had it. He did everything but send up a flag. When I went to the mound, I could tell he was done. There's a look in a guy's eyes. You can look right through him and say, 'You've had it.'

"Did anybody ever ask Frey about it? Oh, he had a bleepin' answer I'm sure."

Frey's answer: "When people say I bleeped it up by leaving Sutcliffe in too long, I think they're assholes. Anybody who would suggest that, I think is an asshole. You're telling me that Sutcliffe was tired. How the bleep do you know Sutcliffe was tired? You mean when people walk hitters, they're tired? Is that what you're sayin'? I didn't think he was.

"Every time I let him fight his way out of a jam in June and July and August and September it was great. But in this particular instance... And who knows? If the ball was caught at first, maybe we would have still won."

Sutcliffe didn't pitch out of this particular jam and Tim Flannery's grounder did indeed shoot through first baseman Leon Durham's legs for the error that tied the score. What appeared to be a routine doubleplay grounder hit by Tony Gwynn took a bad hop and skipped over second baseman Ryne Sandberg's shoulder for the double that gave the Padres enough runs to win the series. What happened in one short weekend to the 1984 Cubs is still a matter of debate years later. It has evidently left some scars.

Frey: "What I remember most about '84 is coming to Chicago and managing a team that hadn't won in awhile and winning a division. I remember the excitement that was created and the fans and the attendance. That was an exciting and very interesting experience. And nobody is going to make me feel bad about it because a couple of balls went into the outfield. No one. There isn't anybody in the world who is going to make me think we didn't do a good job with that team."

Bowa: "I knew we were in trouble after we won two straight in Chicago. I mean, we're flying from Chicago to San Diego and there are wives on the flight. And the majority of the wives are along with the players who have never been in the playoffs. They're there. And they're bleepin' drinking champagne and wine. I'm sitting next to Gary Matthews and I'm sayin', "You've got to be kidding me. What the bleep have we done? We've still got to win the last game in San Diego.' Sure as hell, man. Just a little thing like that can change everything. Momentum plays such a big part in it. Mentally, you're mind relaxes a little bit. When Steve Garvey hit that home run to win Game 4, I said, 'Bleep, we're in trouble.' I knew we were in trouble."

Frey: "I said at the moment that the fourth game was more important than the fifth. We had three leads, but Steve Garvey, three times with two out, gets base hits to get em' back in the game. And then he hits that home run. Those hits he got in the middle of the game, getting them back into it when it appeared we were putting them away, that was the difference. We had a lot of scoring opportunities. Some of my ballplayers came up in situations where another base hit would have put them away. All of those things to me, when I go over that series, are more important than the fifth game. We really should have won the fourth game. But Garvey was the big man."

Bowa: "We screwed up not pitching Sutcliffe in Game 4. When we scored those five runs? We win that with Sutcliffe on the mound. Frey's setting up his rotation so Sutcliffe can face Detroit in the first game of the World Series if we win it in four. You see what happens? You don't do that. You let the guy pitch when he's supposed to pitch. If he pitches that night, we win. They don't get six runs off Sutcliffe in a night game. I'm telling you, we would have won that game. But we're gonna set it up. We're gonna have Sutcliffe ready to open the World Series in Detroit. We don't even get to bleepin' Detroit."

Of course it all depends on your perspective. For Padres fans, that weekend of baseball was undoubtedly the most electrifying anyone in San Diego had ever witnessed. For Chicago fans, it simply fulfilled a legacy. The Cubs hadn't won a pennant since 1945. They still haven't.

"Obviously things could have worked out better for the Chicago ballclub and the Chicago fans and Jim Frey," Frey said. "Most importantly to me at that time, we had players who had played very well for six months and within a few minutes we let it all get away. Everything we had done was forgotten because of a couple of ground balls. It doesn't seem right, to me, if you put things in proper perspective, that for six or seven months everybody's jumpin' up and down and screaming about how great the Cubs are and what a wonderful year we're having and 15 minutes later someone tells you that you bleepin' blew it.

"The '84 playoffs is something I don't dwell on. I don't have any big, strong second guesses about what I did. A lot more disappointing things have happened to me since that day. Getting fired is a lot worse than losing the playoffs, believe me. Some of those moments are more dramatic and have a more lasting effect on you than a game or a series."

The 1984 playoffs began with a blast for the Cubs, who tortured the Padres and starter Eric Show with a 13-0 blitz in Game 1. Show looked up at the flags on the roof behind homeplate at Wrigley Field prior to the game. They were blowing straight out. It was a death knell. Bob Dernier and Gary Matthews hit homers off Show in the first inning. And when Sutcliffe planted one out on Sheffield Avenue, the carnage was complete. The Cubs hit five homers in Game 1 and played a good solid second game to win 4-2 and take a 2-0 lead in the final best of five playoff series.

Padres obits were being written. Cubs World Series tickets were being scalped. But that ending was far too pat, too contrived, too conservative. Three games were left to be played in California and the San Diego fans wouldn't let the Padres die. Stirred up by a Mike Royko column which alleged that San Diego didn't deserve a pennant winner because it was chocked with surfers and white wine drinkers, fans came out in the thousands to welcome the weary Padres home.

The next night, the stadium was bonkers. During pregame introductions, shortstop Garry Templeton stepped out of character and waved a towel over his head to further incite a mob which didn't need inciting. The comeback was on. "I think Garry Templeton had more of an effect on the fans than they did on him," said Frey. "He did something that was so unnatural for Garry Templeton to do at that particular time. It kind of aroused the fans, I thought. The waving of the towel when the players were introduced. Otherwise, I have no idea what got anything started. I don't know anything more about it. I don't give a bleep about psychology or anything like that. And I don't think any of this means a shit anyway. This absolutely doesn't mean anything to me. It's not an important issue to me."

Perhaps not now. In Game 3 Templeton did more than towel wave. He snared a Leon Durham line drive to blunt a first-inning Cubs rally. And his fifth-inning double knocked in two runs and gave the Padres their first lead of the series. Ed Whitson finally offered the Padres some decent frontline pitching. It all added up to a 7-1 win.

Then came that miraculous Game 4. Garvey's two-out double in the third inning gave the Padres a 2-0 lead off starter Scott Sanderson. Jody Davis and Durham hit back-to-back homers off Tim Lollar in the fourth to hoist the Cubs ahead 3-2. Garvey's two-out single in the fifth made it 3-3. In the seventh, another two-out Garvey single made it San Diego 5, Chicago, 3. The Cubs tied it with two runs off Goose Gossage in the eighth. That set up Garvey's incredible heroics in the home half of the ninth. Lee Smith opened the inning by striking out Alan Wiggins. Tony Gwynn singled to center. That brought up Garvey. To cap an almost superhuman performance, Garvey lined a two-run homer over the right-center field fence to tie the series at two games apiece. He had hit only eight homers all season. That single swing, met with explosive delirium, may long be remembered as the greatest moment in San Diego sports history. Garvey: four clutch hits worth five RBIs. Immediately afterward, while being congratulated on nationwide TV by Tim McCarver, Garvey told the country: "It was my pleasure."

It certainly was. That brought the series down to a one-game playoff on Sunday afternoon with Sutcliffe going against Show in a Game 1 rematch. There was no wind, but for Show, the results were the same. Durham homered in the first. Davis homered in the second. Before manager Dick Williams could go out and get Show, the Cubs were leading 3-0. Show, in almost a gesture of defiance, tossed Williams the ball before he could reach the mound. The Cubs never scored another run. They didn't pick up another hit until the eighth inning when all the damage had already been done. There was the ball that inexplicably bounced through Durham's legs. There was the ball that skipped by Sandberg. Was it a century worth of Cubs pathos coming to roost? Or was it simply fate?

"I couldn't believe it," said Bowa, who was really a non-factor with just three hits in the series. "I had never seen a ball go through Durham's legs. I'd seen some ground balls bounce off him, but he's a pretty good first baseman. And the one that went over Sandberg, he didn't miss a ball like that either. Gwynn's ball. It came up, but I've seen him catch it. He got a double out of it, but it should have been a double play. It was one of those where you're looking for the ball low and it comes right up. It was a bad hop, but the kind of athlete he is, I never expect him to miss any ball."

That game set in motion some life-altering changes for a number of key Chicago Cubs characters. Bowa, who would openly feud with Frey, would not make it through the 1985 season in Chicago. Frey would be fired as manager in June of 1986. Frey's buddy and coach Don Zimmer, would be shown the gate along with the manager. Dallas Green, the club's president, would fall out with management of the Tribune Company (which owns the Cubs) and resign after the 1987 season despite two years remaining on his contract.

The ironies? Frey, who was signed by WGN to do color commentary on Cubs broadcasts in 1987, would replace Green, the man who fired him, at the end of that season. Zimmer would be brought back to manage the team in 1988. Bowa would be hired to manage the Padres a little more than two years after those chilling playoffs.

Last summer, Frey left no doubt that his 1984 experience with the Cubs was well behind him. "If people think I'm going to my grave blaming myself for that, they've got another thing coming," Frey said. "I thought we did a great job with a team that wasn't supposed to win." And this time around in the organization, Frey won't have to contend with Bowa either.

Bowa's feud with Frey began in the spring of '85 when he arrived at camp in Mesa, Arizona to find a rookie named Shawon Dunston about to take over his job. Bowa, at 39, felt that Frey was treating him with disrespect by offering his position to an untested rookie without at least a competition. "My feeling was, we won in '84," Bowa said. "Now in '85, unless Dunston had an outstanding spring training, which he did not, my feeling was that I should have that job. We won. Now if I lose it, great. But that wasn't the case. He called me in, but all spring he kept saying to the press, 'I'm not telling you who my shortstop is.' Finally, near the end, I went in and said, 'Look, you don't have to tell the writers, but how about bleepin' telling me? Who's the bleepin' shortstop?' When I went in there, that's when he said that Dunston was the shortstop. I said, 'Good. I'll just be the utility player, then.' That's the only season in 16 years I didn't start on opening day. I thought that was weak."

Frey's version?

"What happened between us?" he said. "Ask him. He's the guy who's been doin' all the talking. I never said one word about Larry Bowa. I spent six weeks of spring training, once a week, reading what Bowa said about Jim Frey. You've never read anything about Jim Frey saying anything about Bowa. When I took Larry Bowa out of the lineup, he bitched. That's all there is to it. There's no more to it. I didn't bitch. He did. I never bitched about it. He did. When he went to the press and said, 'How the bleep can he take me out of the lineup?' they'd come to me, I'd say, 'Because I'm going to play somebody else today.' I never said anything else.

"Let me tell you this: I'm going to tell you this one time and you're only going to choose what you want to write anyway. And if you don't do this one right, don't ask me no more bleepin' questions. The first thing I did in the spring of '85. The very first thing I did was to call Larry Bowa in my office and explain to him that there was a good chance that he wasn't going to play every day on the ballclub. He might play part time. I am going to see if Dunston has a chance to be a major-league baseball player. That was the very first thing I did on the very first morning. The rest of the spring he said, 'The man has never told me what the situation is.' This is the first time I'm telling anyone this. I never answered the question before because I didn't think I had to."

Bowa's blitz in the Chicago papers so rankled Frey that he finally sent out Don Zimmer with a written statement attacking the veteran player. Only days before the Cubs were scheduled to break camp, Zimmer summoned *Chicago Tribune* beat writer Fred Mitchell into the Cubs dugout for a solo press conference. Mitchell recorded the entire diatribe on tape.

This Bowa comment is what started it all: "I have no dialogue with the man. None. I just come in every day and read the board to see if I'm playing. I wish I knew how he was thinking. How he planned to use me. I want him to be honest with me, not try to pull the wool over my eyes. The bottom line is that Dunston really didn't do that well in triple-A. If he tore up triple-A, I'd say there's no doubt he should be up here."

Zimmer put on his reading specs and let fly:

"Larry Bowa is the most selfish player I have ever known. He is not a team player and he cares for no one but himself. If I were Jody Davis, I might have choked him. On throws to second that should have been stopped, Bowa made no attempt. Do you know that Captain Bowa did not speak to Ryne Sandberg for a week to 10 days during the season last year? Well, I know it and other guys on the team know it. Sandberg must have been going too good. If you can't get along with Sandberg, you can't get along with your wife.

"He has now taken off on the manager for about the fourth time in the press. One time last year, his name wasn't on the lineup card. He didn't come on the field. He didn't come in the dugout. He hid. Captain Bowa. I thought the captain was supposed to help the manager keep things together. His locker was behind mine. When he was going good, he couldn't wait for you guys to come in the locker room for some more of his bull. When things went bad for him, like the day he made two or three errors and we lost the game, he hid from you guys. You find him. Larry Bowa style."

And on and on and on. Bowa countered Zimmer recently by saying, "I've never shied away from any questions whether I've done bad or good. And I've never made three errors in a game. I don't know what he was talking about."

As far as the Sandberg falling out goes, the National League's

Most Valuable Player in 1984 tells a somewhat different story.

"When I was traded over here with him from the Phillies in 1982, I was just out of triple-A," Sandberg said. "I remember that first spring training. He just showed a lot of support for me. Not only on the field, but off the field. That year, I played third base next to him all year. We just had pretty good communications between each other. I learned a lot of the basic fundamentals of playing infield from him. The next year, they had said I was moving to second base, so he suggested we both show up to spring training about two weeks early. He showed up. It was no big deal for me because I lived down there.

"I thought it was neat that a veteran guy, who knows his position so well, would show up early with somebody else. He had incredible work habits as a player. They rubbed off on me. Definitely. He's a firm believer of getting into a routine during the season. He worked extra hard in spring training. He'd stay after workouts to take ground balls. He showed up early before workouts and took grounders. I just kind of followed him. He was one of the biggest early influences on my career. It was a big disappointment the day they finally released him here.

"They didn't want Shawon to feel like he was being pressured to play outstanding because if Larry was on the bench, he'd go in and replace him. That was the main reason. It wasn't that he was a bad influence on the team or anything. Larry even worked with Shawon during spring training. I don't think it was a big bitter thing between the two of them."

About Sandberg, Bowa said: "I worked his butt off. I told him, 'You've got to work hard if you want to get up in this game. You can do it. You've got great tools.' We worked, we worked, we worked. They didn't know where he was gonna play. The harder he worked, the more you could see that, hey, this guy was going to be a stud. He was still skinny. He didn't lift weights or anything.

"I remember one year in Philly, he got called up in September. This guy is standing behind me while I'm takin' my ground balls. Sandberg is not sayin' shit. I'm waiting for him to say, 'Can I take some with you?' So I keep takin' them. Finally, I say, 'Do you want some ground balls? Well, bleep, just jump in here. Let's go.' He was so shy. But he's come out of his shell now. He's a gamer and now he's teachin' all the other guys. Now he's got great work habits. But the rap on him in Philly was that he was lazy. They didn't think he'd be anything but a utility player."

Dunston did open the season at short, but when he bombed out and was sent back to the minors, Frey reluctantly had to go back to Bowa. It was a safe bet that Frey had no further use for Bowa. His days with the Cubs were numbered. Frey was so incensed at Bowa that he even ridiculed certain people in the organization who he felt were siding with Bowa. Frey was livid at the public relations department for trying to find a positive in a season going down the drain. Bowa was batting about .150, but each day the press notes would indicate that the Cubs were far better than a .500 team with Bowa in the lineup. Frey eventually exploded at the public relations director, who is now the club's director of publications. The Cubs were on a mid-summer road trip to Philadelphia when the 1985 season began to unravel. After a game at the Vet, broadcaster Harry Caray set up a dinner at a local establishment named Morton's for the upper brass. Frey was not in a sociable mood when the p.r. director joined the party. Out of nowhere, Frey pointedly growled at him, "Everywhere we go on this road trip, everyone wants to know why we keep winning with Larry Bowa in the lineup. That's the question I most often have to answer. And you know why? Because they read about it every day in your bleepin' press notes." The hosing down caused such a stir that the p.r. director had to leave the restaurant.

When Bowa surpassed Rabbit Maranville for the most games played by a shortstop in National League history, the Cubs promotion department considered holding a ceremony for Bowa at home plate in Wrigley Field. But it never happened, allegedly, because Frey stopped it. That's how badly the relationship between player and manager had deteriorated. Along the way, Bowa kept reiterating that there were no open lines of communication between him and the manager.

"You'd go into his office and ask him something and he'd hit you with his favorite line," Bowa said. " 'I have the only pencil in town.' He makes out the bleepin' lineup. Big bleepin' deal. He says that instead of saying, 'You have some merit. I have some merit. Let me toss it around.' Instead he says, 'I have the only pencil in town.' What are you supposed to say to that?" Bowa felt that his hole card against Frey in the organization was Dallas Green, his former Phillies manager and the guy who brought him to Chicago from Philadelphia. But eventually, even that card was played out. When Dunston was recalled from the minors, Frey pushed Green into releasing Bowa six weeks before the end of the season. At a tearful press conference, Bowa said goodbye to the Windy City for good. The parting of the ways came little more than 10 months from the day the Cubs lost the pennant in San Diego.

SUNDAY, MAY 3, 1987 ◆ CHICAGO, IL

I had put off my most painful decision as long as I could. But it couldn't wait any longer. I finally called Steve Garvey into my office and told him what I'm sure he knew already: "I'm gonna have to go with the kids."

He took it super. I've got to tell you, the man has a lot of class.

It was one of those cold and gray Midwestern days that just chills you. And what I told Garv didn't make it any more pleasant. John Kruk and Carmelo Martinez would platoon at first base when the club returns home to San Diego. Garvey would be my right-handed pinch-hitter and a spot starter against certain left-handed pitchers. That was it. We talked a little about it, but he said he understood what I had to do. You know, we were going with young guys. Garvey took the news with his usual grace. You've got to remember, this is a man who was not only used to playing every day, but he was used to playing just about every inning of every game. He was the iron man. In his heyday with the Dodgers, Garvey built up that National League record 1,207 consecutive game-playing streak. He passed Billy Williams' old mark in 1983—his first year in San Diego. I wasn't here at that time, but it had to be ironic that he broke the record on an April night when the Padres were playing the Dodgers in Los Angeles.

So this was no small benching. This was the end of an era. Every manager he had played for in the last six years—Tommy Lasorda, Dick Williams and Steve Boros—had talked about reducing Garvey's playing time, if not his role. But I was the man who ultimately had to make the decision.

Garvey was amazing. After it was done, he told writers: "It

was something that was a realistic possibility. Like I told Larry, anything I can do on or off the field to get us back on track, I'll be glad to do it. I had two goals when I came here: To help the team win and build a winning tradition. The team did win and the winning tradition has been a little sidetracked, but I think I've fulfilled my obligation. And so, Chapter Two unfolds in this year's book."

It was a horrible weekend for us at Wrigley Field. Now we're 6-20 and with three losses here, we're going home on a five-game losing streak. I've been looking around for answers. I reached the decision on Garvey Saturday afternoon during that 7-3 loss in which we blew another lead—this one 3-2 when the Cubs scored four runs in the seventh. A misplay by Garvey was a big factor in the inning. Dave Martinez hit a sharp two-out grounder down the first-base line. I know it took a wicked hop and exploded by Garvey for a double, but the play could have ended the inning. And Garvey had trouble getting in front of the ball.

And look at his numbers: He was 1-for-11 with one RBI since coming out of it to knock in those three runs last Tuesday night in St. Louis. That's when he told someone that he was playing with a sore left shoulder all season.

"It's something you just have to stay on top of every day," Garvey said. "I've had it since last season, but for some reason it really started getting bad at the end of spring training. Really, I'd appreciate it if you don't make a big deal about it. I don't want it, in any shape or form, to be used as an excuse." I wasn't looking for excuses, I was looking at Garvey's production. So I told him, "I think it's time."

I wish it was my only problem of the weekend. On Friday, I brought in reliever Lance McCullers and he blew another eighth-inning lead—the second time he's done that in the last three games.

Afterwards, I was pretty upset. I told writers: "I'm watching him. I'm observing. We were in a perfect situation. We've got McCullers on the mound, our best right-hander. They've got Ryne Sandberg and Andre Dawson coming up, both right-handed hitters. To me, if we can't get those guys out with our best bleepin' pitcher, then we're in trouble. It could be a long bleepin' year... The bottom line is, the man is not doing his damned job. You can sit here and go over the whole game. But if you don't do the job, you don't win the game. It's as simple as that."

So Sandberg flies out, but Dawson homers to start another Cubs rally. A 5-3 lead turns into a 7-5 loss. I told the writers to go ask McCullers what the problem was. But he wouldn't talk to any of them. After the game, I felt like I was turning into a basket case myself. I told them:

"I really believe I've done everything I could. I really think I've made all the right moves. But I look at the record and we're 6-18. That reflects directly on me. Maybe I'm just losing confidence in my ability to do the job. I don't know."

It was no better today. How can you have any kind words for anybody with the mistakes Joey Cora made at second base and my starting right-hander made on the mound after a 4-2 loss? Andy Hawkins did a great job, pitching to Dawson during the first inning. I mean, he struck him out with a runner on second and one out. But then Leon Durham beats Hawkins with a two-out RBI-double on a 3-and-0 pitch.

You know, what's disheartening is that our pitchers making these mistakes are not rookie pitchers. They're veteran pitchers. You would think that a manager wouldn't have to tell a guy like Hawkins to put Durham on in the first inning. Durham, a left-handed hitter, is hot. And he's got Keith Moreland, a right-handed hitter, who's struggling, right behind him. If Moreland beats you with a home run, well, you've played the percentages. I'm not saying this is the answer, but maybe we'll have to start calling pitches.

Cora had to make the most ridiculous play of the game, if not the season. Here, Tony Gwynn doubles in the eighth inning with Cora on first and Joey gets called out on an appeal play at second base. I mean, this was a beauty. Cora was already running toward second when Gwynn knocked Rick Sutcliffe for a pea into left field. Cora had already crossed the bag with his head down and he gets suckered by shortstop Manny Trillo. Trillo looks up in the air. It's the oldest trick in the world. I don't know what Cora was thinking. I do know that at that instant, he figures Gwynn had hit a fly ball. Now Cora crosses over second base on his way back to first. But when he sees that the ball had fallen in, he turns around and cuts back in front of the bag on his way to third. And what does he say to that?

"You learn from those things. If I ever do it again, I should be shot." What are you supposed to think?

I mean this was a great way to come back to Wrigley Field as a manager. After the game, I figured the best thing I could do was to try and get these guys to keep their heads up. So I went into the clubhouse and told them how I felt. "This is the lowest we can go right now," I said. "I'm seeing things that I've never seen in this game. It just seems like everything we're doing is coming up wrong." I told them, "You've busted your butts. As a whole, the effort has never disappeared. I can't ask for any more than that." I'm burning up inside here right now. But I'm trying to stay calm. It's like a sinking ship. I've just got to back off and say, hey, losing my composure now is not going to help.

The Padres had certainly not reached their low-water mark. Neither, in fact, had Steve Garvey. When the club returned home, Garvey decided to undergo a battery of tests with the team physicians to find a cause for his shoulder problems. He would learn that a biceps tendon had severed in his left shoulder and needed to be surgically repaired if he wanted to continue his baseball career. On Saturday, May 23, in San Diego, Garvey took what may very well have been his last major-league at bat—a ninth-inning pinch-hit appearance against Montreal's Neal Heaton. He flew out lazily to center. A day later, Garvey began to prepare for surgery. He was through for the year. Perhaps he was through for good. His 17th major-league season would offer these sad numbers: a .211 average, 16 hits in 76 at bats, nine RBIs, five runs scored and just one home run.

THURSDAY, MAY 7, 1987 ♦
SAN DIEGO, CA

This whole thing started Sunday because Andy Hawkins popped off. We've got two outs, runners on first and third. It's the fourth inning. Garry Templeton hitting. Two strikes on Tempy, Marvell Wynne is on first, so I send him. And I knew they were going to walk Tempy. So that loads the bases with Hawkins coming up. He pops out to end the inning. The next day, I pick up the paper and I read Hawkins questioning my decision. "I mean, letting Marvell steal with two out," Hawkins says. "Who's going to pitch to Tempy with me on deck?"

What I wanted to do was try to get him some runs and a win. But he didn't understand that. He's thinking I'm trying to run us out of an inning. I'm trying to keep him in the rotation. I'm trying to keep him in the game so he can pitch another few innings and get a win. I could have pinch-hit for him. But he's more concerned about why I would send the guy. Some guys worry too much about me instead of worrying about getting people out. Today against St. Louis, it was unbelievable. It was pathetic. It's a nothing-nothing game in the fourth inning. Hawkins walks Ozzie Smith to open the inning. Gets an out. Then before I can even turn around, we're down 8-0. We lose 17-10. Tell me about it. Did he give up out there on the mound? I don't believe that, maybe he was hurt. I don't know what he did, but as far as I'm concerned, he's got to make some adjustments. We all have to make some adjustments. What are we, 7-23?

These guys are getting paid a lot of money to get people out. And they're not doing it. Hawkins, Storm Davis, Eric Show. Davis is out of the rotation. He's in the bullpen. We've got Jimmy Jones up here now. Let's see how he does. He was off in relief today, but that's OK. He can't do any worse than Storm. Give him a shot at it. Also, I've got to get Dave Dravecky into the rotation to see what he can do. So what am I supposed to do with Hawkins? I'll just keep running him out there.

Right now, I don't think the bullpen is doing so bad. I had two guys today who had to suck it up because our starter couldn't get us into the seventh inning. I've got two guys—Goose Gossage and Craig Lefferts—who aren't feeling too good down there. Gossage is coming off the disabled list. Lefferts needs an extra day. Why should I jeopardize them? I take my hat off to Jimmy Jones and Greg Booker. I don't give a damn how many hits they gave up. How many runs they gave up. They showed a lot of class staying out there and taking a whipping. They don't complain. And I'm sorry I had to do it. But basically my hands were tied.

Like I said, it's a shame a starting pitcher can't get you into the sixth or seventh inning. That's a shame. We don't even have to go to a five-man rotation. The way some guys are pitching, they could pitch every other day. Two innings, one inning, four innings. . . .

You get 10 runs in a ballgame and you're not even close?

If we get decent pitching this year, I'm not saying we'd be a contender, but we wouldn't be 16 games under .500. Not if the starting pitching does what it's supposed to do. If these guys were only one- or two-year players, you could understand it, I think. You've got people that are so-called established pitchers doing what they're doing. It's very embarrassing. That's what I told them at a meeting of the pitchers we had yesterday. You don't make any adjustments. If you go to the store every day and you drive the same piece of road, but you keep hitting the same pot-hole and that screws up your tires, you'd think after five or six days in a row you're gonna go around that hole. I would think. I would think.

Maybe some resentment is being built up against me, I don't know. Maybe they're doing it out of spite. Maybe they don't like the way they're being handled. What am I supposed to do? They're going out there every fourth day. I'm leavin' them in. I'm not taking them out with the score 1-0. Show me where I've mishandled them. When I took this job I heard one of our pitchers had problems with Dick Williams. Didn't Dick Williams call him a timid Texan or something? If a pitcher has a problem with one manager, you'd think the manager would make the adjustment for the player. But when he has a problem with more than one manager, wouldn't the player say, "Hey, maybe it's me"? Don't you think it's time the guy took a look in the mirror and said, "Maybe I should make some adjustments"? Maybe I'm wrong. I don't know. He didn't like Dick Williams and we're having problems right now.

I don't think any of those starters have been taken out of the game when he shouldn't have been taken out. In fact, if anything, I give them the benefit of the doubt to try to work out their problems because our bullpen is dead tired and we've only played 30 games. I'm probably going the other way. I'm leavin' them in there and saying, "You're gonna get it together. You're gonna get it together." One game I leave the guy in there to try and get him the win and Hawkins rips the way I manage. I mean, I'm trying to let the guy get up to bat so we can turn the whole lineup over again. So maybe we might be able to score three runs or four runs. And the next day, I read in the paper, "How can you run there?" That's bush. What is he, oh-and-four? I think I've bent over backwards trying to get him on the board. There comes a time in everyone's career when he's got to say, "Hey, I ain't doin' the job." And I think that time has come. They need to grow up a little bit. There's a couple of other guys who aren't tearing up the world either. Show has had a couple of good outings. And to me, Ed Whitson, with the exception of the home runs he's given up, has done fine. He's kept us in a lot of games. If you want to talk about quality starts, he's had some quality starts. That basically leaves you Hawkins and Davis.

All I'm saying is I think it's about time to quit talkin' and do something about it. I can sit here all day and procrastinate and everything, but the bottom line is they're not doing the job. They can't blame the pitching coach. They can't blame the manager. They can't blame the coaches. They can't blame the people behind them. They're not doing the job. Period. When I screw up, I'll be the first to tell you. I screwed up the other day, on Saturday, leaving Whitson in for the seventh inning in Chicago. But basically, my hands were tied because of the bullpen. Ryne Sandberg hit a home run off him, but he shouldn't have been left in that long. I take the blame for that. Now I think it's time some of these guys take the blame.

What are you going to do? You've got to be realistic. You can't bring up raw kids from triple-A to replace them if they aren't ready. You just destroy 'em. That wouldn't be fair. So you keep throwing the so-called established pitcher up there and you would think that out of pride or if they wanted to get traded, they'd at least try to impress other scouts. That's got to come into play sometime. You know, the biggest cop-out a player has is saying that I can't play for the manager. Because that shows what the man is made of. Because basically, when you go out between those lines, you're not playing for anybody but yourself. When the ball is hit to you as the shortstop, you catch it. You don't have the second baseman come over and help you. When there's a fly ball to left field, you don't have all eight other guys come over to help you to catch it. You catch it. Same as the pitcher. When he's on the mound, he has the ball in his hand. Not the manager.

You don't play for the manager. You play for yourself, you play for your ballclub, your peers.

At that meeting yesterday I gave all the pitchers one message: Get your act together. It's about time, don't you think?

WEDNESDAY, MAY 13, 1987 ◆
PITTSBURGH, PA

T he great snap was coming. Nobody really knew where or when it would occur or who it would be directed at. Not even Larry Bowa himself. But as sure as another Padres loss, it was coming. It finally happened just after another dismal performance, this one at Three Rivers Stadium against the Pittsburgh Pirates. And not surprisingly, it was directed at Stanley Jefferson. Jefferson had just recently been reactivated from the disabled list, but was playing with his bad ankle and a budding sore shoulder that would become another serious problem. The May 14 edition of the *San Diego Tribune* told the story:

PITTSBURGH—Despite claims to the contrary last night, neither the walls nor the clubhouse door could hide manager Larry Bowa's most serious confrontation of the season.

Angered by another in a series of putrid performances by the Padres, Bowa tried to hold the media at bay for 20 minutes in the corridor outside the locker room at Three Rivers Stadium. What went on inside sounded like a page out of "One Flew Over the Cuckoo's Nest" with Bowa playing the cuckoo and Stanley Jefferson all but bouncing off padded walls.

"Let's put it this way: It sounded worse than it was," said a calm and collected Bowa not long after the doors to this asylum were swung open.

Oh really? Jefferson literally was carried out of the locker room by five players—Marvell Wynne, Tony Gwynn, Carmelo Martinez, Joey Cora and Kevin Mitchell. Jefferson was ranting and raving as he was ushered down a dark hallway to the dugout. The group was followed closely by coach Deacon Jones, Garry Templeton and Rich Gossage.

"He's a temperamental kid," Bowa said about Jefferson, who spent about 10 minutes cooling down in the dugout. "It really wasn't fair because he's one of the guys who is busting his butt out there."

All this happened because the Padres had blown a 5-2 lead in the sixth inning on their way to a 9-5 loss to the Pirates—the Padres 27th loss in the first 35 games. This one was complete with missed pop-ups, a blown suicide squeeze by Cora and a balk by loser Craig Lefferts that brought home the go-ahead run. Jefferson seemed to have no direct effect on the outcome. His sin, apparently, was that he didn't show up for an early workout before the game. Bowa thought Jefferson had been told by Jones. Jefferson said he had not. Jones, though, claimed he had notified the rookie outfielder. "In my mind, I told him," said Jones.

Countered Jefferson: "It was a miscommunication between me and a coach. That's all it was."

Asked what had happened between himself and Jefferson, Bowa said simply: "I told him he was fined a hundred bucks."

Bowa said later he would rescind the fine. "He was supposed to be out here early today, and Deacon didn't tell him. So it wasn't his fault," Bowa said.

Bowa, whose club has been battered here by the Bucs for 21 runs and 28 hits in two games, also said he told the club, "It seems like every team we play must have the best hitters in baseball, because we can't seem to get anybody out!"

Other mouths were zipped shut in the Padres locker room. Templeton, Gwynn and Steve Garvey refused to answer questions, as did coaches Greg Riddoch and Sandy Alomar.

"Don't ask me," Alomar said. "I don't speak a word of English."

Said Jones: "We're just trying to keep it in the family."

The decibel level of the discussion made that impossible. Bowa was working up into a good froth when reporters were stopped outside the clubhouse door only minutes after the game. He went over the litany of errors before turning his attention on Jefferson. "Is that a smile I see on your face?" Bowa shouted, apparently addressing Jefferson.

Jefferson said he was not smiling.

"You're smiling," Bowa continued. "What do you think this is, a joke? I told you and Cora to be out here early."

"Nobody told me to be out here early," Jefferson said, his voice now rising.

"You were told to be out here," Bowa countered.

"I wasn't."

"You were."

"Nobody told me to be out here," Jefferson screamed in a

loud shrill. "I'll pay the damned fine. I bust my butt out here for you."

With that, there was a momentary pause and what sounded like a crush of bodies. From within the depths of the locker room, somebody yelled, "Break it up." A split-second later, Jefferson was being pushed from the clubhouse by his teammates. Bowa, quickly cooling down after another major blowup, shut himself behind the door of his office.

"I tried to hold Jefferson on the other side of the door," Jones said. "I didn't want him running out past you guys. That's the truth." Asked for more details about the miscommunication, Jones said: "I'm pretty sure I told him; he just didn't hear it. But he's supposed to be out there early every day just like the rest of the rookies."

When had he told Jefferson?

"Last night," he said. "At least I think I did or maybe it was just that I wrote it down and then thought I told him. I don't know."

Why did Jefferson have to be restrained?

"He didn't have to be restrained," Bowa said. "He was screaming that no one told him. I'll take the blame for that. . . He and Joey are supposed to be out there every day to work on the little things, and I just asked why he wasn't there. He said he wasn't told."

Bowa's other major clubhouse blowup occurred before an April 26 game against the Dodgers in Los Angeles when he tossed a box of autographed baseballs around the locker room and kicked a few trash cans. Most of the players seemed to take that meeting with a sense of humor. There was no such humor last night around a club that has won just twice in 14 games.

"I told them, 'I don't think we can play any worse than that,'" Bowa said. "I asked them if anybody had any suggestions. I said, 'Hey, does anybody have any ideas? Maybe I'm overreacting. I don't know what to do. We can't hold leads. We have trouble catching balls.'"

Asked if he thought he was losing the respect of some of his players, Bowa said: "No, because what can I do? You can only do so much. I mean, I'll take some of the responsibility, but I'm not the one throwing the pitches."

The next day, Bowa called another team meeting, this one prior to the game. He apologized to Jefferson individually and to the team in general. In order to head off what he sensed was an impending coup, Bowa suspended his hundred dollar fine structure and his sequence of signs. The message was simple: Just go out there and have some fun. The Padres lost again anyway—their 15th loss in 17 games. Their record stood at 8-28.

THURSDAY, MAY 14, 1987 ◆
PITTSBURGH, PA

◇B◇ rutal. That's the only way I can explain how I feel. It's like my hands are tied. I mean, despite the good drills we had in spring training, with a start like this it's better to tell them to just take batting practice and forget about it. I don't think you can play any worse. We look like they didn't even work on fundamentals. That's what's discouraging. It's lack of concentration. Or maybe it's just a bad year. I really have never seen as many pitches thrown above the waist as I've seen here. It almost looks like we're saying, here, hit it. That's what it looks like from where I'm sitting. What happens is, the not so good hitters get on and then there's no room to pitch around the good hitters. What drills can you do to make a pitcher pitch down? You say, "Come on out tomorrow at two o'clock and practice throwing the ball in the dirt?" That's got to come from within, I would think. You can't teach concentration. Sometimes I don't even say anything to them. I go through periods where I just sit on the bench and watch. Ten games. And it's the same.

I've been callin' in guys and talking to them. After Hawkins and I had our differences in San Diego, he came in to talk to me the next day—when he saw the papers. As far as I'm concerned, that's over. He just said he needed to get into a groove. I think he was worried about getting taken out of the rotation. But he's starting. I told him, "You'll get 40 starts or whatever, just find it." Basically he said, "I guarantee you I will. I'm the best pitcher on the staff." You've got to like that kind of attitude. You want all of them to feel they're the best. At least I do.

As far as the pitchers in general go, maybe it's time some of them started paying a little bit more attention to Benito Santiago behind the plate. Some of them keep shaking off his signs. Let him call the game. I think that's a built in excuse. Some of them say, "He doesn't know the hitters that well, so we're going to do it our way." Maybe they've got to give him a little credit. But he's not really catching good right now. He's missing a lot of balls in critical situations. He didn't do that all last year in Vegas. He went through a week when he was shaky and then he was good. But he's been a mystery for like two weeks now.

About the thing with Jefferson. He's gonna play. I talked to him last night. I said, hey, that was my fault. You shouldn't have been fined. We said, every day we have the field early, we want Jefferson and Joey Cora out there to work on little things—bunts, Stanley stretching his arm out, practicing leads. They don't even have to hit. I just said, "Come on out. Work 10 to 15 minutes on every aspect. And then we'll go in." They've been doing that. And so the other day, I told Joey, "Same time tomorrow." And I said, "Make sure Jefferson knows." But he didn't know. Because he's temperamental, Jefferson took it wrong. That's the difference between guys who played 20 years ago and now. Now, if you even think about criticizing anybody, they go into a shell for a week. It's like, you're not supposed to do that. And then, if you let it go without saying anything, it's as if you don't care. So it's a Catch 22. You don't say anything to anybody. Don't bring up their mistakes. Just let them play. Then he thinks, "If he doesn't say anything to me, he doesn't care." But if you bring up something, he'll think, "Oh, he's too critical. I can't play like that."

Last night, me and Stanley were screamin', but we weren't even close to blows. The meeting in L.A. was 50 times worse. He yelled, "I bust my butt for you." Well, nobody has ever said he was doggin' it. This may sound funny, but to this day, I don't think there's a guy out there who's doggin' it. I really don't. And that's the part that hurts. Because they're giving me everything they've got. I keep saying, "Well, we'll get better, we'll get better, we'll get better." Now we're into 35 games and no matter how long you analyze it, how long you break it down, no matter how many nights' sleep you lose, it all comes down to one thing: If our pitchers don't get people out, we're not gonna win. That's as simple as it's gonna get. You can't make a pitcher get somebody out.

That's not in your hands. All you can do is help get the pitchers in the right situations. Maybe I'm bleepin' up there.

It's discouraging because you feel like you're the failure. And you have to take some of the responsibility. Regardless of what happens, you're in charge of the ship. And it's not playing good.

I'm frustrated. Just as frustrated as everybody else. But I've never quit at anything and I'm not about to quit at this. I do come to the point when I'm so frustrated, I begin to wonder why I do lose sleep over it, why I do get so upset about it. It basically doesn't matter how bad your pitching is, how bad your hitting is, how bad your fielding is. If you don't do the job, after awhile, you're gone. It's that simple.

The thing with Jefferson, I really don't think it's going to set him back. It's hard to tell with him, though, because he's really different. He was upset because he thought he was being blamed for our loss last night. That's how he took it. But basically, the meeting was just to get some response out of them. After the game, I said, "Does anybody have any idea why we're playing so bad?" That's how I started out. And I was ready for somebody to say something. But nobody said a thing. So I said, "Well, I think we're making a lot of mental mistakes. I don't think we're con-centrating. I think the other team's hitters are intimidating our pitchers. When we play other teams, either they have the best hitting in the league or we've got the worst pitching. I don't know what it is. Maybe they do have the best hitters. I don't know."

And then I went into, "And it's amazing that we get the field for people to get extra work in and a guy who has played only two months doesn't even bother to show up." And you know, I looked at him. And I said, "But I guess with two months in the big leagues we know how to play. We don't need the extra work."

Then he got up with his, "No one told me, no one told me." And I said, "It doesn't matter if someone told you or not. You would think that being a rookie, you'd just want to come out and do some extra work." That's when he went, "I bust my butt for you. I try. I give you my best." I said, "No one is telling you you don't bust your butt. But it's still going to cost you a hundred." He took that like we lost the game because he didn't show up for practice. He kept screamin' and I said, "Take it outside." And he said, "You don't want to make me mad."

See, I think him and Cora . . . I don't think they can be good players, I know they can be good players. I really do. But it's not gonna come easy. To me, they're really going to have to work at it. Like I told them, "You can make a million dollars in this game easy. A million dollars a year. But you're gonna have to work a little harder. You're gonna have to push yourselves. You're gonna have to drive yourselves." The player today probably has more talent. Better speed. Better tools. But you question his work habits. His work ethics.

When I was a kid in this game, I'd never say anything when a manager talked. No matter if he was right or wrong. What I'd do afterwards—like after Dallas Green used to rip the hell out of me—I'd go in and say, "Were you talking about me? What instance are we talking about?" And then we'd get into it like that. But during a meeting, I would never say a thing. First of all, you usually have meetings when you're playing horsebleep. You don't need meetings when you play good.

And we're playing horsebleep. That's an understatement. I hate it right now. You really try to be optimistic. You go to the park and say this is going to be the day. Every day you say that no matter how bad things are going. And you might be winning and you still remain high and then all of a sudden something like last night happens. They get three runs. Then you go back to thinking, now what's gonna happen. You get a balk. You just keep wondering what's going to make them make a pitch in the right situation. Get a hit in a situation. It's very difficult right now because something happens every night. Like I said, what do you do to get a pitcher's concentration? There's nothing you can do. What do you do on passed balls with Benny? I've taken him out every day and had him block balls. But what do you do when he does it in a game anyway? What can you do? I'm trying to think of drills you can do to improve. I've got a new philosophy that I'm starting today. We're not getting the field early anymore. If anyone wants extra work, come and ask the coaches and if we think there's enough guys who want it, we'll get a field. It's stupid to get a field every day when you know the guy doesn't want to come out. To me, it doesn't make sense. If a lot of these guys want to come out, we'll come out. That's got to come from within. I can tell a guy to come out every day and if I know that deep down inside he doesn't want to do it, he's not going to get anything out of it. So if we get six or seven guys who want to work, I'll call and see if we can get the field. Because it's stupid for me and the coaches to go out every day and beat our heads against the wall when I know that maybe one or two guys are listening.

Like Tony Gwynn, he loves going out there. And you watch him hit. But before he hits, he plays right field and catches the ball off the bat. You know that he's getting something out of that drill. That's what I was thinking about last night in bed. I'm trying to help them, but if they don't want to be helped then you've just got to bite the bullet and say, "OK, you tell us when you want to take some extra work."

It's a problem. The same guys who blamed it on Dick Williams and Steve Boros are blaming their problems on me. I'm to the point now where I'll listen to anybody. We've tried every avenue, I think. We've given most guys a chance to play. God knows, every pitcher has had an opportunity. We've used all of them. Even though some of those guys have been hurt, the guys around them have been hurting us more. The middle of the lineup is basically kids. It's an inexperienced lineup. That's basically what it is. Like I said, you try to be optimistic, but before you even take the field, you look at the lineup card of the team you're playing against, you go position by position and just talent wise—raw talent—we're outmatched. Then we make these mistakes and we get buried. The thing is, you expect some guy to step up there and say to the rest of his teammates, "Hey, come on guys. We're better than this." I can say that until I'm blue in the face. So can the coaches. To me, it means more if a player says, "God, we're not this bad, are we?" It just seems like every time we get past the fifth inning, we find some way to self-destruct. It seems like when one thing happens, it snowballs. The entire team deflates. Nobody wants to listen. It's like Goose Gossage. I think he can physically do it if he just tries to stay within himself. Ten years ago, he could throw fastballs. Last night, he made Jim Morrison look sick on those breaking balls. I think he's still able to dominate hitters if he throws his breaking ball to set up his fastball. I really do. To me, that's one of the reasons we are struggling—because of the inability to adjust. We're not making adjustments on the spot. The pitchers, especially. I would think that our pitchers have been around long enough to realize what we are doing wrong. I can see a Jimmy Jones, maybe, being completely lost. Or a Greg Booker being completely lost. But Storm Davis has had a lot of success. Hawkins has won a lot of games. Eric Show. To me, they should know right away what they're doing wrong by just looking at what the ball is doing.

That's like when I played, went into a batting slump and hit a lot of fly balls. The first thing I was doing was pulling my shoulder out. So you've got to make a conscious effort when you go out there to drive that shoulder down. To me, the pitchers are making no adjustment. When you hang a breaking ball, you're either doing one of two things: You're dropping your elbow or you're letting the ball go way behind your shoulder. Those are the only two things you can be doing. So you would think after 35 games, after seven starts apiece, that somewhere along the line it's going to kick in. I don't like to say that they don't give a bleep, because I know they do care. But it's that mental part, it's that mental toughness that's not there. And you can't teach mental toughness. When you continue to struggle, and what worked for you when you were successful isn't working now, you've got to be a little hard-headed not to make a change. I mean, if a guy has the biggest batting flaw in the world, but he's hitting .300, I don't think anybody should say jack to him. But if he's hitting .200 or .180, I think it's time to make an adjustment. That's the point I'm trying to make. If you check Storm Davis' record in the American League, his won and lost record was very good. OK, obviously he's come over here and something isn't right. But he continues to do the same thing. He continues to throw the first two pitches for balls. He continues to throw fastballs right down the shitter, when they're layin' on the fastball. That's what's confusing me. The thing that really baffles me about the Storm Davis for Terry Kennedy trade—I can't believe an organization that needs pitching as bad as Baltimore does would get rid of a young kid like that. That's what stymies me. I mean, even though they needed a catcher, you still don't give up an arm if it's decent. I don't think we've seen the real Storm Davis. If in fact we have. . . .

You look to your pitching coach and batting coach to try to do something about all this, but in all fairness to them, how much can they really do? I think a pitching coach can help more than a batting instructor. But when the game starts, he can't stand behind the mound and say, "OK, here's what you've got to do. Now do it!" I definitely think Galen Cisco knows a lot about pitching, I really do. But when you're in a situation for so long, maybe you're not as objective as you should be. He's been the Padres pitching coach for almost three years. He knows these guys. He constantly sticks up for his pitchers. I think every pitching coach should. In fact, I admire a guy who continuously sticks up for his pitchers whether or not they get the crap kicked out of them. I've never heard him say anything bad about them. He might when he has his meetings with them, but I've never heard it. I would want all my instructors to stick up for their players. But I also think you've got to be realistic. I mean, if the job is not getting done. . . Again, I keep using the word adjustments. Somebody has got to do something. I said during spring training that I didn't think our pitching was deep enough. Nobody wanted to listen to me. We were told, "Don't worry about your pitching. That's going to be the least of your worries." Right.

And another thing that baffles me: If you notice, no matter who's starting, we get through the opposing lineup relatively easy one time. Then the second time around is when we're getting bleepin' killed. Maybe it's just my imagination, but that's the way it seems to me.

I know it's rough when you take the whole thing personal. Jimmy Leyland, the Pirates manager, came over to the clubhouse after last night's game. "For what it's worth," he said, "and I know you probably don't want to hear it, but this looks like a carbon copy of what I went through last year. The only thing I knew I had going for me is that I had Rick Rhoden on my pitching staff. Every fourth day, I knew he'd keep you in the game. I knew we had a chance to win." Jimmy was basically trying to sympathize with me. It was nice of him. I think he's a pretty good baseball man. You know, like he said, you can only do so bleepin' much. I've made mistakes. I know that. Like bringing in a couple of pitchers when I shouldn't have. But really, I don't think I've made a lot of mistakes. Yet the record indicates something else. I can't look past that. I can agree that it is not a great team. I can agree that we're short in certain areas. But I figure that even if you didn't have anybody running the team—no manager—if you just threw the bats out there and said, "Hit and run when you want, squeeze when you want, you change pitchers," I would say you should win more than eight games. I'm serious. That's how I feel. And that's what's discouraging. That's what's really discouraging. One night, maybe I should do that. Take the guy who I think is the smartest and let him run the team. My luck, we'd probably rattle off about eight wins in a row.

See, I don't have the power right now to go into Jack McKeon and tell him that I don't want a certain guy playing for me anymore. I don't think a first-year manager should have that kind of power. But I also think that just to show people in the clubhouse that we're not screwing around, there should be some changes made. Regardless of whether they're going to help you or hurt you. Just to change. I don't even know what I'm supposed to say anymore in the situation. Are you just supposed to keep telling the writers that it will come around? That gets old. If there was another manager around now, he might have buried these bleepin' guys. Like Stanley and I had our differences, but I talked to him today. I asked him, "How's your ankle?" See, I forget about it. I don't hold a grudge. If something happens one day, you let it out and then it's over. That's the way I am.

But what am I supposed to say about how they're playing? Numbers don't lie, do they? A guy will probably be ticked off at you for saying it, but if he is really playing horsebleep, if it really is his fault, in his heart he should be saying, "The man is right."

SATURDAY, MAY 16, 1987 ◆
PHILADELPHIA, PA

Mike Schmidt took his seat in the Philadelphia Phillies dugout hours before that evening's game. The topic was former teammate Larry Bowa, who only the day before, had returned to Philadelphia as Padres manager for the first time. Philadelphia. Bowa's Philadelphia, where he had played the most productive years of his career—12, to be exact—where he had only recently returned to establish his year-round residence. He had moved his wife, Sheena, and his daughter, Tori, lock, stock and pussy cat from Clearwater, Florida, to Philadelphia's Bryn Mawr section. Talk about sacrificing warmth for style. . . .

Bowa's homecoming had been a strange one. Home with his wife and daughter for the first time in three months, Bowa was awakened early Friday morning for an appearance on NBC's Today Show. Whisked toward downtown, Bowa fell asleep in the back seat of a stretch limousine. When he awoke, he was near the airport, some 25 minutes from NBC affiliate KYW. He missed the spot.

That was only the beginning. By midday, a rumor had spread east from San Diego that Bowa had resigned as manager. Found in the dugout at the Vet before the game, Bowa reacted with lusty fervor: "What? Resign? They're going to have to rip this uniform off me."

When the game began, second baseman Randy Ready strode to the plate. On the giant video board looming high above the cavernous stadium, a color slide of Bowa was offered for popular consumption. But Ready's name was mistakenly inscribed below the picture.

Quite a homecoming.

For the nine years Schmidt and Bowa teamed up to solidify the left-side of the Phillies infield, Bowa was by far the aggressor. Bowa was clubhouse agitator, mouthpiece and self-proclaimed team leader. The more reserved Schmidt seemed to be, the more outspoken Bowa seemed to be.

"Larry was a great clubhouse needler, but Larry didn't have great timing," Schmidt said from his perch in the dugout. "There were times when he didn't needle people and I think he should have. There were times when he did needle me that I thought it would be best to lay off. One time, I got so angry in a clubhouse in Houston that I almost wanted to kill him. I probably would have if there weren't four other players there. I'd probably be in prison right now." But Mike Schmidt at 39 is far more outgoing than Mike Schmidt had been a decade earlier. With 530 lifetime homers, he has clearly established his path to the Hall of Fame. With his 15 years in a local uniform, in Philly, he has clearly established himself as the man. Schmidt is now unequivocally the team leader. Two days earlier, at a press conference hyping a video tape honoring his 500th home run, Schmidt hammered Phillies upper management.

"My overriding goal is to do whatever it takes to get this Phillies organization back on top," Schmidt told *Philadelphia Daily News* columnist Stan Hochman. "We're not polished anymore. The minor-league system is depleted. The front office has a little to be desired in terms of positions that are held. And the jobs they're doing. . . The fields are the worst in the league. The dugouts are filthy. The clubhouse is dirty. The pride factor is not what it used to be. We used to have the best field, now it's the worst. We used to have the cleanest dugouts, now they're the dirtiest. We used to have the best minor-league system. . ."

When Schmidt arrived at the Vet that night, he found lush, green ferns hanging from his locker and candles surrounding his folding chair. Workmen were scrubbing down the runway from the clubhouse to the dugout where only minutes earlier Schmidt had whiffed the telltale signs of "cat piss." The next night, as

Schmidt sat in the dugout, the cleanup on the field continued. Someone seemed to have listened.

"Eye wash," Schmidt said. "You know what I mean? Now they're trying to make me look bad. To stick it to me because I opened my big mouth."

Schmidt didn't have to say it, but like Bowa, he suspects that the decline of the Phillies began on that fateful day in 1981 when the Carpenter family sold the team to a group headed by former marketing director Bill Giles, who is now the president.

"Yeah, the guy was in charge of fun and games back then," said Bill Conlin, who covered the Phillies for the *Daily News* for more than a decade and is now a columnist.

In one of Giles' first moves, he engaged in a public battle with Bowa about the length of the contract Ruly Carpenter had promised Bowa before Carpenter sold the club. Carpenter promised Bowa a three-year deal or a trade. Giles would not honor the promise. Bowa eventually forced his trade to the Chicago Cubs with a verbal onslaught in print. The situation created bitter feelings then that have all but dissipated now. Bowa has since been a guest at the Giles home. "That's all history," Giles said recently when asked to recount his end of the story. "I don't want to get into it again with Larry Bowa."

Since the Giles era began, the Phillies have won one National League pennant—with a decaying team nicknamed the "Wheez Kids" back in 1983. They've gone through four managers and in the last four years, haven't come close to leading the National League's Eastern Division.

Schmidt has been the club's lone fixture. Respected by one and all. Finally. "In his early career, I think he let the fans really get to him in Philly," Bowa said about Schmidt. "Now he deals with it about as good as anybody. I think he put so much pressure on himself when he came up. He was the No. 1 pick. Anything he does, he does great. He could play golf with you and he'd shoot par. You could play basketball with him and he'd shoot the eyes out of it. You could bowl with him and he'd bowl 200. He's a great athlete. I think one of the reasons why he wasn't successful early in his career was that everything came easy to him.

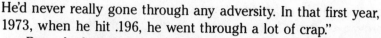

He'd never really gone through any adversity. In that first year, 1973, when he hit .196, he went through a lot of crap."

Bowa had established himself as the club's young shortstop by the time Schmidt emerged on the scene. Bowa, a natural right-handed hitter, had learned how to switch-hit in his last year at the triple-A level. Bowa had been groomed by Frank Lucchesi, who managed Bowa for three seasons, both in the minors and major leagues. It was Lucchesi who had stuck with Bowa at shortstop when Bowa wasn't hitting his weight during that trying rookie 1970 season.

"Because I knew what he was made of," Lucchesi said, recalling all the criticism that mounted at the time in the Philly papers. And so, when the Phillies drafted Schmidt as a shortstop, a heated rivalry between the two young players was born.

"When they signed Schmitty, this is what the scout told him," Bowa recalled. " 'The shortstop there isn't going to be there very long and you're going to be the shortstop.'"

One can only imagine how that went over in the Bowa household.

"Right away, I've got a chip on my shoulder," Bowa said. "So they flew him into Philly. I said, 'Bleep this guy Mike Schmidt. Big deal.' So he comes in and he's stylin'. He's a college kid. Everything's cool. He takes ground balls with me and everything. So after he worked out for three days, they sent him to Reading—double-A. And he tore it up. He hit a lot of home runs. I was having my good years then.

"I remember a comment he made: 'I plan on playing shortstop in Philadelphia.' And my reply was, 'Not as long as I'm here.' So I kept going and the more I read about Mike Schmidt, the harder I worked. And you know the rest of it. He ended up playing third."

Schmidt said it took years for his relationship with Bowa to thaw. "It took me probably five or six years to get into good graces with Larry Bowa as an individual," Schmidt said. "I think there was a great deal of jealousy evident in our relationship. I don't know what it was, but I think Larry harbored some inner jealousy toward me. That's just what I sensed. I think after, say, 1976, he got a little older and I got a little more mature and I had proven worthy of his respect, I think he sort of changed. He looked at me more in terms of a potentially great player.

"I think when Pete Rose came to the Phillies in 1979, Larry's relationship with me changed greatly because he sensed the way Pete and I got along. He sensed the respect with which Pete and I treated each other."

Schmidt and Bowa were always at opposite ends of the spectrum. When Schmidt slumped, he would turn his rage inward and become sullen.

"That was the one thing I didn't like about him," Bowa said. "I knew it was killing him inside. I'd say, 'Why don't you show some emotion? Hit something. Go mad. Go beserk.'

"Oh yeah, I did a good job. I'd get on players. But I'd know who to get on. I got on Greg Luzinski a lot more than I ever got on Schmidt. He was probably my biggest sounding board. He'd locker next to me and I would get all over him. If he wasn't hitting good, I'd say, 'Well, why don't you do something you big bleepin' hog?' And everyone would look at him like, 'Why don't you just knock the hell out of this guy?' But Greg knew me . . .

"He took a lot of crap from the fans and in my opinion, not deservedly. I thought he was a much better clutch hitter than Schmidt. Schmidt is a good clutch hitter now, but in those days when we were behind, Bull would come up and hit one. Schmitty would always hit his when the score was 7-1, 7-2. But now Schmitty has gone into that mold where he'll break a game open for you."

Bowa wanted Schmidt to be more expressive, but it just wasn't going to happen. Bowa had already become infamous for his snaps. One day in Houston after a particularly bad plate appearance, Bowa climbed the stairs through the winding walkway that connects the visitor's clubhouse and dugout in the Astrodome and shattered all the light bulbs with his bat. His teammates weren't too happy groping back to the locker room in the dark. One night in the midst of a slump, Bowa, who is not much of a drinker, was drowning his sorrows at the hotel bar when he joined a group of players for a stroll. They encountered a thick glass fire door that Bowa decided to open with the butt end of a fire extinguisher. That's the way Bowa has always discharged his anger.

It's safe to say that the two men were on different planets, viewing an alien species from light years away. In Schmidt's opinion, Bowa's basic tenet as a manager—team over the individual—was not the way Bowa acted as a player. "Except for when we won the championship in 1980, I don't think Larry Bowa as a regular player ever came to grips with the value of team success over individual success," Schmidt said. "Now that's not a rip. What I'm saying is that some people need to have that kind of focus to succeed. Some people really have to care extra how they're doing individually. To be honest with you, I guess there are times when I'm no different than that."

Schmidt wasn't the only observer of the Phillies scene to share that opinion of Larry Bowa, the player. In 1978, when Bowa batted .294 and came in second to Dave Parker in the National League MVP balloting, Bowa was blasted for his clubhouse and playing style by a beat writer, Ray "Buzzy" Kelly, Jr., who covered the team for the *Camden Courier Post.* The next day, Bowa set up Kelly by having him paged for a phone call in a nearly empty Veterans Stadium locker room. Bowa and Kelly railed against each other until the argument became so heated, the two men had to be separated by pitcher Ron Reed. In the brief scuffle, Kelly came away with a small mark on his cheek that was treated by physicians.

The incident blew over quickly with Kelly and Bowa resolving their differences. As usual, Bowa did not allow the harsh words to carry over. Today, Bowa insists that he never hit Kelly. "The entire incident was blown out of proportion," Bowa says.

Still, Schmidt's characterization of Bowa as a hardnosed individualist may not be so displaced. Bowa worked so hard and so long to develop, he was always leary of other players who could just skate in and operate on natural ability. Like Schmidt.

"Larry was always quick to criticize other people's work habits," Schmidt said. "There's an average type of worker, a guy with poor habits, and there's the hard worker. And hard working people, the people who are consumed by their profession, always seem to feel they should get more out of it because they put more into it. Sometimes, a guy comes along who gets a lot more out of it than he puts into it. To be honest with you, I probably put a hell of a lot more into it now than I did in my first four or five years. All of a sudden, I started setting standards as a player that I eventually understood couldn't be kept up without hard work.

"I don't think I've ever had the kind of work habits that Bowa had. Bowa hit endlessly, endlessly, extra hitting, trying to make himself into a good switch-hitter. And he became a .300 hitter. He got the most of his talent. I don't have to tell you that. Those are all things you've heard players say before. He got the maximum out of the talent he had. He came to an organization that was really hurting as a young player. He was forced into the big leagues and had to learn to play and to win at the big-league level. I think the same thing is true about Pete Rose. Whatever he lacked in ability he made up for in desire and hard work.

"Bowa made himself a great shortstop. We jelled. We were as good a left side of the infield as there was at the time. He never did anything really, really fluidly, he just caught everything. He caught everything and everything got to first base. It never looked real fluid and pretty and graceful, but it always got done."

WEDNESDAY, MAY 20, 1987 ♦
NEW YORK, NY

J oey Cora was walking around the Padres locker room at Shea Stadium saying goodbye to all his friends and acquaintances. Joey figured the word was out. He was being shipped to the minor leagues. Perhaps Joey was wishing and hoping. The move certainly wasn't reality, but since the Padres were playing an exhibition game in Las Vegas the next day, Joey had already decided Nevada might be a nice place to stay.

"Maybe that's the problem," said manager Larry Bowa.

The Padres were without old reliable Tim Flannery, who had sustained another in a series of injuries that had plagued the club all season. Flannery, the once and forever Padres second baseman, was working on his bunting during batting practice in San Diego several weeks earlier when he jumped out of the cage and wrenched his foot on a baseball that had somehow slithered under the dark green batting practice tarp. Flannery was carried into the locker room screaming in pain, the ligaments having detached themselves from both sides of his right ankle. For better or worse, Cora was now the second baseman. It had proven to be worse.

"The disappointing thing is that if you ask all the coaches, they'd tell you we thought he was one of our most intelligent players," Bowa said. "Maybe it's the pressure of trying to make it in the big leagues. I don't know. All I know is that every double-play ball has been an adventure. Every steal, every hit and run. Benito Santiago has a half dozen throwing errors just because he has been late getting to the bag on his throws from behind the plate.

"If we did send him down, it wouldn't be to shock him. It

would be to let him work on some things so that when he makes a mistake, 20,000 or 30,000 people don't see him make it. The game last Sunday in Philadelphia was the most incredible thing I've ever seen. He must have run into everybody. He looked like a linebacker."

The game in question—a 6-5 Padres win in Philadelphia that broke a 10-game road losing streak—would have been a horror story for anyone. Cora collided with left-fielder James Steels and shortstop Garry Templeton on one pop fly, bowled over first baseman John Kruk on another one, and sped by right-fielder Tony Gwynn when he lost the ball in the sun for an error. Toss in a throwing error and a missed tag on a potential double play. What a day.

Said Cora: "But I did have three hits."

"Joey is going through some weird stuff right now," Bowa said. "It's either going to make or break him, but he's going right back out there. He's on that roller coaster ride right now. Well, he's taking me along with him."

Talk about excruciating endings to a particular game, with two outs in the ninth and nobody on, Lance McCullers walked the next two Phillies batters just so he'd have the pleasure of facing Mike Schmidt with the winning run on first base. Schmidt didn't disappoint. He hit a towering drive toward the left-field seats that looked like it was ticketed for Wilmington. Stanley Jefferson, coming over from center field, looked toward the bleachers. Marvell Wynne in left back-peddled toward the fence. "When that ball went up, a hundred negative things went through my mind," said Kruk.

But Wynne caught the ball with his back planted firmly against the fence, breaking the Padres five-game losing streak and saving the post-game buffet from Bowa's possible wrath.

"Those ribs wouldn't have looked too good all over the floor," said one bystander.

The next night, the Padres won in New York when Jefferson, returning to the stadium where he once peddled soft drinks at New York Jets football games, had three hits and three stolen bases against the Mets, his former team. But it was back to the norm for the final two games of the road trip—both losses. Bowa was thrown out of this night's game when he jawed it out with the late Dick Stello, the umpire who met an untimely death last winter when he was crushed between two cars near his Florida home.

Bowa, who had already been peeved by one Stello call during the series, contested the back end of a double play. In his belief, pitcher Terry Leach's foot was off the base.

"I told him, well, that's two blown calls in two nights," Bowa said. "I didn't curse at him or nothing. Not until afterward."

It was Bowa's third ejection of the season. The first two had cost him $400 in fines, a figure that was sure to escalate. The Padres were heading home, by way of Las Vegas, with a 10-32 record. It was no wonder that neither Bowa nor general manager Jack McKeon was interested in listening to Cora's moaning. "It might not be a bad idea," McKeon said about sending Cora out. "Joey can go down and work on some things without the pressure of learning in the big leagues. . . . But there's no chance I'll leave him in Vegas tomorrow. I'll make a bet on that."

Cora's 22-year-old mind never seemed to be all there. During training camp, Cora claimed he wouldn't have been disappointed if he had been sent to triple-A for a little more seasoning.

"And it wouldn't bother me now," Cora said.

Cora noted that he had only played in 124 pro games during the two seasons after San Diego selected him No. 1 in the 1985 June draft out of Vanderbilt University. Cora, who grew up in Caguas, Puerto Rico, had played in just 81 games the year before at Class AA Beaumont during a season that had been cut short by a bizarre knifing incident. Cora and several of his teammates had strolled out to the team bus after a game in San Antonio. Because his father recently had undergone cancer surgery, Cora was in a nasty mood anyway when he became involved in a bout of verbal fisticuffs with a local tough.

Walking quickly away from the bus, Cora's adversary returned with a gang of about a dozen roughnecks. Cora was grabbed from behind and stabbed in the abdomen. He was rushed to the hospital where he underwent two hours' worth of surgery. To his good fortune, the only thing Cora lost was a piece of an intestine and the season. "The doctors told me 10 days later that an inch in either direction and it would have been over," Cora said. "That's how lucky I was."

The new manager took a liking to Cora, who, at five-feet-eight inches and just 150 pounds, was the image of a young Bowa—that kid so many experts said would never make it as a big-league player. As it turned out, Bowa showed more confidence in Cora than Cora showed in himself. Thrown into a losing situation, Cora took much of the blame for the club's incredibly dismal start. Nearly seven weeks into the season, Cora had lost most of his confidence and desire. "It's pretty disappointing, but I know I'm not doing the job they expected of me," Cora said. "That's the way it is. When you're losing, everything gets this big. When I go down, I've got to improve some things and do my job. You never know. I may never make it back. But I'm going to try."

The club was on the precipice of granting Cora his wish. But not just yet.

FRIDAY, MAY 29, 1987 ♦
SAN DIEGO, CA

○C⟩ hristmas had come early to those members of the Padres
front office who felt as if their heads were about to be dis-
connected from their jobs. At a stunning 10 a.m. press conference in the Stadium Club, Ballard Smith stood before the public
for what would be the last time. Joan Kroc, the Padres owner,
was back in. George Argyros, the Seattle Mariners owner, was
out. After so many months of speculation and dickering, the Padres would remain in the hands of the Kroc family. Why?

"When Joan got into this thing, she didn't know George
Argyros from Adam," a highly placed source in the club hierarchy said recently. "As things progressed, despite assurances to
the contrary, she realized what was going to happen. There
would be a lot of firings. The Padres would have a skeletal staff
just like they have right now in Seattle. City officials were getting
nervous about the lease. It was not the kind of legacy Joan Kroc
wanted to leave San Diego. George is fond of telling everyone
that he pulled out of the deal. He didn't pull out of the deal. Joan
did. There was no way in hell he would have had enough votes
to get into the National League."

When Joan called the office staff together to tell them about
her decision, there was an outpouring of positive emotion that
surprised even her. She received a similar response from the usually stoic ballplayers, whom she visited in the clubhouse prior to
that night's game against the New York Mets. During the press
conference, she made mention of a recent disclosure that right-
fielder Tony Gwynn, a .380 hitter and the rock of the team, had
filed for bankruptcy because of various problems involving his

former agent. The agent apparently co-signed sizeable loans in Gwynn's name, took the money, and left Gwynn to handle the bills.

When asked what had made her change her mind about keeping the team, Kroc said: "The agony of defeat. I don't like what's happening. Ray Kroc wouldn't like what's happening. . . . I haven't had much fun the last year. I can tell you that. But I want to tell you that when we have young men like Tony Gwynn who have had adversity that none of us realized and has been out there pounding his butt day in and day out—I love him. And I think we've got the nucleus of a good team. I think we're heading in the right direction.

"You know, it takes more than one tuba player to make a symphony. It takes more than one ballplayer to win a pennant or have a winning attitude. I'm asking these young men to get together in spirit. Adversity can tear a community apart or it can bring it together. I love this community. There is no way in the world this team will ever be moved."

In the locker room, Joan gave the players a similarly motivational speech. "She told us that all our hard work was appreciated," Gwynn said. "She turned to Goose and said, 'Come on Goose, let me see a smile.' Goose kind of looked around at us and then broke into a smile. We all smiled. Then she came over to me and asked for a hug. It really meant a lot to me. I mean, how many times does the owner come to the clubhouse and ask for a hug?"

At that same morning press conference, Smith announced that he would step down as club president as soon as a successor was found. That successor was already waiting in the wings. It was former National League president Charles "Chub" Feeney, who had resigned his post at the end of the 1986 season after 20 years of service. Feeney, a long-time baseball executive, at 67, had enjoyed close personal ties to Joan and Ray Kroc during Feeney's years as league president. His front office experience included 20 years as general manager of the Giants under his uncle, club owner Horace Stoneham. Feeney, who went to work at

New York's old Polo Grounds in 1947, presided over the Giants move to San Francisco 10 years later. Smith, who had been battered enough by the media in recent years, would remain an active member of the Padres Board of Directors and would ultimately give thanks that he had made such a wise decision.

But it was Joan who gave so many people the words they really wanted to hear:

"Our first priority is to negotiate a new lease with the city," Joan said about a lease that was indeed extended until the turn of the century prior to the 1988 season. "I want this community to be assured that whatever happens in the future that this team will not leave San Diego. I promised you that. I'm reiterating that promise now and it's going to be signed, sealed and delivered so there will be no more speculation. The team will not be sold this season. We're going to concentrate on the lease. We're going to concentrate on the field. We're going to do everything possible to turn this thing around. Selling the team is the last thing I'm looking for now."

About the negotiations with Argyros, she said:

"I think when we signed the deal, we both figured it would be relatively simple, uncomplicated, and ready to be completed by June 10, when the National League meeting is. George and I had a meeting last Tuesday and it became quite clear that neither of our goals would be accomplished by that time. I feel that it is not fair to the community in either Seattle or here to keep things in limbo. So we made a joint decision, very cordial, that we would just discontinue negotiations. We ran out of time. The clock ran out. I can say we've had a good relationship. He's a tough business man. He'd probably say the same thing about me."

What Argyros did say months later about the collapse of the deal was quite simple and not very reflective about the plight of the common man: "Don't ever leave your wife $500 million dollars."

What he didn't say is that at least six of the twelve National League owners had already ganged up to block his purchase in a move that may have been as much anti-Argyros as it was anti-Ueberroth—the man who was the alleged architect of this ill-fated deal.

On a baseball level, the sudden decision promised a fresh start for a team that had already been counter-punched into oblivion by all their incessant on and off field miseries. Perhaps the resolution of the ownership would mark a turning point for the team.

"Maybe I'm wrong, but I don't see how who's buying the team should affect the way we're playing," Larry Bowa said. "I mean, when you put on the baseball uniform, you don't worry about how much money you're making, you don't worry about who your boss is, you don't worry about what you're doing after the game. Basically, you go out there and try to do whatever you can to beat the other team. If you've got that other stuff on your mind, you're not really concentrating."

Bowa may have been right at least for the one night. The Padres dropped a 5-4 decision to the Mets. With the new Kroc era having just begun, the club's record was 11-38, and in all the joy, no one had bothered to mention extending Bowa's contract.

THURSDAY, JUNE 4, 1987 ♦
MONTREAL, QUEBEC–
OLYMPIC STADIUM

This was gonna be no bleepin' scream job. I wasn't in the mood to do any ranting and raving about anything. This time, when I called the bleepin' team together for a meeting, I wasn't going to do it off the top of my head. I wanted to be prepared. And so I jotted down some bleepin' notes. I felt like a high school coach going in there or something. But we had reached the end of the line. The night before we lost another bleepin' one-run ballgame. What was our record—12-41? What a disgrace. I was beginning to feel like nobody was listening to me anymore. That nobody even cared. Benny, you know, Benito Santiago, has just been inconsistent. I mean, that passed ball the other night and his excuse for missing it: "I lost it in the scoreboard." That was weak.

I'm going to bench Benny. Sit him down because he's gotten so complacent.

That's how you handle Benny. The only thing that disappoints me about Benny is that he went to Carmelo instead of me. But they're from the same country, they both speak the same language. I guess that's natural. He's older than Benny. I had a long talk with Benny at the hotel today. I just called him up to my room.

Basically, I said, "When things go bad and you're not playing well, you don't stay out past curfew. Sure there's gonna be nights when you're just gonna want to go out and have a few beers on the road. But what's wrong with coming in at one o'clock in the morning? That's a decent time. I caught him and a couple of other players coming in much later than that. I don't care about that night's starter going out. But Benny should know better. I happened to be sitting there in the lobby bar with Frank Pulli, Bobby Wine and Hank King long after last call. Pulli is an umpire. King is the advance scout for the Phillies. Wino, who played with me in Philadelphia, is now the advance scout for the Braves. We just started talking baseball and I literally did not know what time it was when I saw those guys coming in. There were other guys comin' down the elevators. They'd give me a quick look and they'd get back in. Who do they think they're fooling? There's nothing wrong with going out after a game and having a few beers. There ain't nothing wrong at all. Go out, have a good meal. Whatever. But when it's after hours, when you're supposed to be in bed and the manager is sitting there—it's like you're caught red-handed. I'd much rather have a guy come down the elevator and say, "I'm going to get something to drink," rather than duck back in like a little kid.

I fined Benny a hundred bucks. And that's what I told the team before the game tonight: "I've tried it your way for three weeks. No fines. What have we won, four games? It hasn't worked. So I might as well do it my way." If I'm gonna go down with this thing, I might as well do it by my own rules. Not theirs. You try to treat them like bleepin' men, well I guess you can't. We've got to find another way.

As far as Benny goes, he said I was right. But I got his butt out of there this time. Bleep it. He's not playing for the next three days. Let him think about it. I really believe that the only thing wrong with Benny is a lack of concentration. He can't maintain for nine innings. He'll go for five or six, lose it, then maybe pick it up again in the eighth or ninth. There's a period of time in games when he just. . .I don't know what he does. And until he learns how to keep that mental edge for nine innings, he's gonna be inconsistent. The pitchers must notice it because certain guys keep shaking him off. That's not right. They've got to cut that stuff out. That's got to hurt his confidence. He's blaming their mistakes on himself. That's wrong. Maybe now that he's aired it out in the papers, it'll get better.

He told Tom Friend of the *Los Angeles Times* that our pitching staff stinks. It's hard not to disagree with him. He said that our only decent pitchers are Goose Gossage, Ed Whitson and Andy Hawkins. "Other than those three, they stink," Benny said. "Pitching is why we're terrible. When have you seen one of our pitchers knock somebody down? Not this year. If you don't pitch inside, my brother, who never plays ball, could come in here and get a hit."

And then I saw in the article where Goose backed him up. "I think we've got guys who are afraid," Goose said. "They're afraid to screw up. We've got guys who can pitch on teams that are going good, but this is when true colors come out. It's twice as hard to go out there when you're losing. Our guys are afraid. They know who they are. And the Padres ought to release them because they're worthless. Trade 'em. Do whatever they want to 'em."

It's hard to argue with any of that. Except pitching isn't our only problem. It may be our main problem. But there's plenty of reasons why this club is not playing well. Like I called in Carmelo Martinez before last night's game. I didn't tell him anything. I just thought he had something on his mind or had a problem at home or something. The way he's playing. I dropped him down to seventh in the lineup and did you see his act around the batting cage? He took some half-hearted swings like he didn't give a damn.

We've got Stanley Jefferson out again, he's on the disabled list for the second time with that bad right shoulder. We just told him, get your ankle and your shoulder together and when you're ready, come back. But maybe until Jefferson comes back, I'll just bench Carmelo and put John Kruk at first for awhile. We've got Shane Mack now doing a pretty good job in center. We brought him up when Garvey had to have the shoulder surgery. The injuries have just been unbelievable. I've never seen anything like it. Dick Dent, the trainer, tells me that they had seven guys on the disabled list here in the last three years. We must have had at least seven guys this year already. That's been part of the problem. That's been a big part of the problem. We've never had the whole team out there ready to play.

As far as doing anything with this team, making it win, I

don't know if I can do anything. I just think we're too inexperienced. What you've really got to do now is just let the kids play. I was thinking of giving Mack a rest tonight, but then I figured, what the hell for? When you go day in and day out and the majority of your lineup is young and inexperienced and has not shown what it can do in the big leagues, you've got to be realistic. Those are hard facts. You know, what they've got to do here to me—whoever they have as manager, whether it's me or someone else—they have to let the players know that the guy is going to be here for awhile so you better do it his way or it's going to be a tough road to hoe. I mean, a rough road. What you have here is so many managers coming in and out that they're saying, "Oh bleep, we'll just get another one." And players react that way. You set some standards and if they don't like it, it's always, "We'll get someone else to run the team." What they need to say is that the manager is going to be here so you better just listen to the man and do what he expects or it's going to be a long two or three years here for you guys.

They did that with Dick Williams for awhile and he got some response, too, even though you hear all the guys say they hated his guts. They learned to deal with him and instead of fightin' him they went out and said, "It's too hard to fight for two or three years. We might as well just go out there and do our thing." I think half the time right now they're trying to fight the new manager. You know, "I'm gonna show him. He's not gonna do that to us." You can do that for a year. You can scrap and scrape with a guy for a year—little nitpicking and all that crap. But when a guy is going to be here two or three years, you're gonna say, "It ain't worth it. I better concentrate on what I'm doin' or I'm gonna get bleepin' buried here."

I think guys are testing me and that's more important now than what they're doing on the field. I'm not saying it's more important to them, but it's in their minds. And if you don't have total concentration on the field, you get buried. Yeah, I think they're still testing me. You see, when me and Stanley had that little incident, I apologized. I said I was wrong—which I was. And I cut back on a few things. Tempy came in and said, "I think that guys are really scared. They're concentrating on signs. Screwing up. But they're not playing." So I said, "You've got a valid point." And from that day on I said, "No more fines. You guys just relax and play." Now it's been, what, three weeks? And I've seen no change. So like I said, if I'm gonna get boxed here, I'm gonna go back to my way. It's not working. Let's go back to my way and maybe we'll concentrate a little more. Maybe we won't win many more games, but we won't make as many mental mistakes either.

Basically, I think I made an adjustment. I said, OK. Tempy came in and talked to me. I went home and thought about it. The next day, I said, "You know, you made some good valid points. And I'm willing to adjust." Now I'm not stupid. If we had played good baseball, I would have kept it that way. But we haven't. I think it's been ample time. When Templeton made that point, I thought maybe I am losing them. Maybe they are scared to play for me. Which I didn't want. Like Joey last night. He starts the game off against the Expos with a triple. I mean, no outs man on third. We can't score. They get two out, nobody on, they score. There's a good case in point right there. With no out, Joey gets thrown out in a rundown on a grounder back to the mound. Normally, I would have gone right up to him and said, "Jesus, what are you thinking about?" But I waited until the third inning when he was going to hit for the second time.

I said, "Joey, what happened on that play?" Then I let him think about it until he said, "It was my fault." But he walked away like it was no big deal. That's why I think the manager needs more than a one-year contract in this type of situation. Now if you have a veteran team, you're supposed to win with a veteran team. You better win. If you have guys who know how to play the game, you better win or get the bleep out. But when you have kids with a few veterans sprinkled in . . . Like right now, you're getting the guys who are unhappy trying to go with the young guys who don't know.

Being an experienced manager definitely has its advantages. I'm just like any other first-year manager. I have to pay my dues. If I was a Dick Williams or a Chuck Tanner or a Tommy Lasorda, then I could say, get him the hell out of here. I don't care how you do it. Out of here. I can't do that. But if I could, I would suggest we make a couple of changes right now. Jack McKeon, who has been very patient with me, told me to keep my cool. But it would be that easy if I had 10 or 15 years in managing. Because what I would say is, "If you don't get him the bleep out of here, then I'm out of here." But there's no way I could ever say that now. When you're experienced, you can go in and say, "Does that mean I have control over what goes on? Does that mean if I want a guy out of here you're going to get him the bleep out of here? Regardless of how much money he makes. If I think he's hurting the ballclub, get him the bleep out of here."

At least I'm fortunate here that I'm working with Jack whose years of experience outnumber my years of impatience. When I got here, there was no discipline. I think there's more discipline here now, but the fact remains, discipline doesn't win any more games. *We* win games. . . .

Like *USA Today* graded the managers. I think I got a D. It said, if Larry Bowa prevails, he'll be a very good manager. But right now he has to take part of the blame for this record. I agree. I'm the manager. It graded the pitchers F, infield F, outfield got a D—with the exception of Tony Gwynn who got an A. Bench strength got an F—because they said if they were good enough, they'd be playing. Then they gave Jack McKeon a C. They said he's doing a great job. He's sending the team in the right direction. I just hope I'm around to see it instead of sitting home watching on the Game of the Week.

Here's a team that's had the manager talk to them, I don't know how many times, it's had the general manager talk to them and the owner talk to them. And not a thing has worked. It just shows you that we don't have the right ingredients. Something is missing, either physically or from the psyche of the team. Let's be honest. This is the only team in the league that doesn't have a lot of power. Every one of the other 11 teams has two or three guys in the middle of the lineup who on any given night can come to bat and make you say, "Oh, no. There it goes." You look at our lineup, our top guy has 20 RBIs. That's a joke. I mean Eric Davis almost has as many home runs as our entire team.

When teams make changes, it's usually one or two player changes. What's happened here is a complete facelift. We might be going overboard. We have so many kids out there, it's scary—Mack, Santiago, Cora, Jefferson, when he plays. I know the Mets knew about Stanley not playing. They didn't want to give up on Stanley, but they knew he wasn't going to go out there regularly because of various injuries. I think Stanley wants to play, basically, I really do. But I think he has a very low pain tolerance and you can't get on a guy for something like that. Everyone is going to be different. If somebody steps on your toe, it's gonna hurt you more than it's gonna hurt me. You can't change that. That's instilled in somebody. You can't say that's not supposed to hurt as bad as it does. But I can honestly say, when Stanley puts on the uniform, he busts his butt. He's a very exciting player. You know how trades are. Whenever they're made the other team brings up the negative. It's like they said Shawn Abner couldn't hit the curveball. Well, who the bleep hits the curveball when they're 18 years old? You learn how to hit a curveball. Mike Schmidt couldn't touch a curveball when he started. Now he kills them.

And Joey, what are we going to do about Joey? The thing is, he's making mistakes in the mental part of the game. I think by playing him, he's going to correct that. I don't know. All I'd have to do is say, "Jack, let's send him out." That's how close he is to going down. Just recently, when Stanley went on the disabled list again, we didn't know if we were going to send him out. I said, "I'd just as soon keep Joey here. I got a feeling he's going to come into his own."

Joey will be a good player. I really believe that. If I'm wrong, then I just can't judge talent. I like some of the things he does. He's a contact hitter. He hits the ball sharp. He's not an easy out. He's not a great hitter yet, but he's gonna be a good hitter. He's never gonna be a home run hitter, but he's gonna be one of those pesky guys who always gets on base. He shows signs of brilliance in the field.

The thing is, because of our inexperience and youthfulness, I don't think we put any fear into the opposing manager. There's not one guy who watches our team and goes, "Oh, hell," when almost anybody in our lineup comes up. They might with Tony Gwynn and John Kruk. What Tony Gwynn has done this year is more amazing than anything else. Tony Gwynn is a great player. I respect the hell out of him. And he gives you the same effort whether you're 42-10 or 10-42. That's what's amazing about him.

I still think that the day Ballard Smith announced that Tim Raines was not coming to the team, it took a big piece out of people. It deflated everybody. From Jack down to the last player on the bench. And in my mind, nobody has ever got it back. The only thing I can hope for as a manager is that the kids are going to start maturing a little bit and not make as many mistakes. It's hard for me to put it all into perspective. It just seems to me that we're making as many mistakes now as we did in April. It really does.

This Week's Cover

"Hey, don't fence me in!" says Duluth's No. 1 junior baseball fan, 16-months-old Larry Bowa, clinging to the grandstand netting at the Municipal stadium. News-Tribune Staff Photographer Glenn Fitzgerald snapped this picture of him at a practice session of the ball club the other day. Larry is the son of Paul Bowa, manager of the Duluth Dukes, and Mrs. Bowa, and is a regular at all the Dukes' home games.

Duluth News-Tribune, May 11, 1947

Although I was a little squirt in high school, I still managed to lead the team in scoring.

Even starting out on my little league team in Sacramento, (kneeling, second from left) I was the smallest of the small.

At Sacramento City College in 1965
I received the trophy for MVP. Later
that year I signed as a free agent
with the Phillies organization.

I didn't have a great year at the plate in Reading in
1968, but I was on my way. (First row, second left)
By 1970, I was starting as shortstop in Philadelphia.

I had most of my 318 stolen bases with the Phillies. Here I make
it safely into second base . . .

. . . and home.

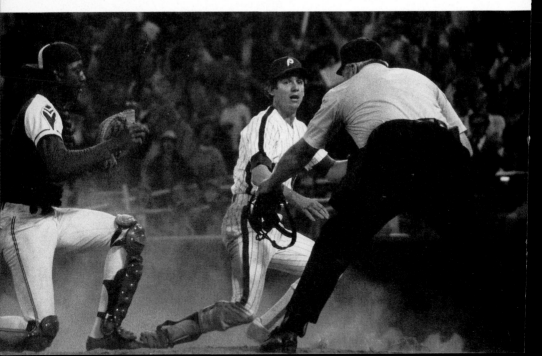

The Phillies finished last in 1972. Steve Carlton (left) won 27 games to earn the Cy Young Award, and I won the Golden Glove award.

Presenting me with my second Golden Glove award, in 1978, was Frank Torre. Guess who still holds the Major League record for the highest life time fielding percentage for a shortstop—a .980 mark?

I tried to provide some payback to the cities where I played by working with groups like the Philadelphia Child Guidance Clinic.

My wife, Sheena, looks much better
than I do in the field . . .

. . . and in the dugout at an exhibition game between the
players and their wives.

In Philadelphia I tried it both ways:
with a mustache and without.

In the field, I tried to be consistent. I didn't always look pretty but I made the plays.

At the plate I choked up a little more from the left side and did my share of bunting.

To Larry,
a guy who has made
himself a good player
(my kind of guy)
Joe Morgan

Joe Morgan of Cincinnati called
me his kind of ball player at the
1978 All Star game. I didn't
mind that a bit.

Practice and more practice from the left side
made me a switch hitter and extended my stay in
the big leagues. My career high was .305 in
1975.

To celebrate the Phillies division championship my teammates made an album. Here's the front and back of it . . . and us.

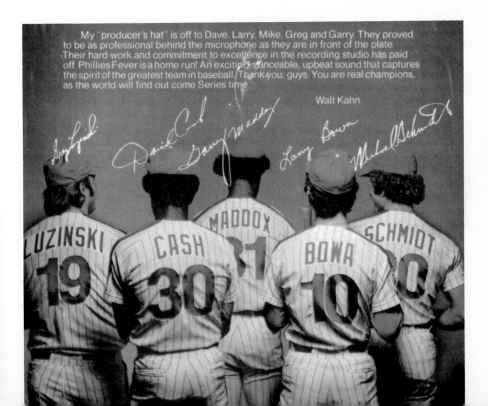

To Larry Bowa
With best wishes,

Gerald R. Ford

When President Ford visited the locker room before the 1976 All Star game I got his autograph. I was lucky enough to play in five All Star games.

A little of the bubbly helped us celebrate the Phillies division championship in 1977. Greg Luzinski is in the center and Jay Johnstone is on the right.

I was never known for being an offensive player. I got labeled as a good glove, no hit. I got over 2,000 hits and had a lifetime average of .260. I'm not gonna say I was a great hitter, but I wasn't a ''no-hit'' either.

A jubilant moment in Chicago in 1984. Hit number 2,000 off of Fernando Valenzuela.

I always tried to be where I should have been. Here I tag out the fleet Willie McGee of the Cardinals.

My year as manager of the Las Vegas Stars in 1986 was turbulent but successful. We won it all. That's my daughter Tori with Sheena and me.

One of the most pleasant aspects of my first year was the maturing of our catcher, Benito Santiago. He came on like gangbusters, hit in 34 straight games, and was rookie of the year.

Here's what I hope is the first of many group shots with 10 of the other National League managers in June of 1987. From left, front row: Tommy Lasorda (Dodgers), Buck Rodgers (Expos), Whitey Herzog (Cardinals), Chuck Tanner (Braves), Me, Jim Leyland (Pirates); second row: John Felske (Phillies), Roger Craig (Giants), Gene Michael (Cubs), Hal Lanier (Astros), Davey Johnson (Mets). Pete Rose (Cincinnati) was missing.

Right now, if you talked to ten people in San Diego, nine of them would say the Padres are going to be contenders in the National League West next year. Maybe we are. But with the team we have, everything is going to have to fall in place. Everyone has to have good years. The pitchers have to do well for us to be contenders.

THURSDAY, JUNE 4, 1987 ◆
MONTREAL, QUEBEC—
DORVAL AIRPORT

As if this particular day hadn't been long enough already, Larry Bowa had one more incident to deal with. This incident didn't involve mental errors on a baseball field. It involved Kevin Mitchell and the United States Customs Service.

After Bowa's most solemn team meeting of the season, the Padres dropped an 8-5 decision to the Montreal Expos. Facing the specter of a game the next night in Atlanta, the team bus made its quick escape to Dorval Airport where the usual charter flight would whisk the club overnight back to the States. Unlike most American cities, Dorval has a strict midnight curfew on all departures, making it a tight fit to get out that night anyway. The prospect of pushing 24 ballplayers through customs in their re-entry from Canada to the United States was no thriller either. Normally, these return voyages are no problem. But on this late night, Mitchell took care of that. With 20 minutes remaining before curfew, Mitchell was stopped at the gate by customs agents checking a plastic carrying bag containing $2,000 worth of newly purchased suits. In an attempt to skirt the duty tax, Mitchell told the agents he had purchased those suits on a trip to Canada a year earlier and had brought them back simply for alterations. Customs agents asked Mitchell to produce the receipt and that's when the fun began. Mitchell started shouting at the agents, claiming that he was being harassed. One agent told Mitchell:

"You better watch it or you'll stay here."

Mitchell: "Fine. All I need is a pillow."

Customs agent: "Where you're going, you won't need a pillow."

Bowa and Doc Mattei, the Padres scruffy traveling secretary, were then summoned off the plane. Curfew was now just fifteen minutes away. One option being considered was flying the plane to Mirabel Airport, some 30 miles away, where there was no such curfew. Bowa and Mitchell would cab it there if the dispute could be mediated.

It was just what Bowa needed. "I was sitting on the airplane," Bowa recalled. "A guy comes on the plane and yells, 'Mr. Bowa, Mr. Bowa, where's Mr. Bowa?' The guy says, 'You've got to come with me.' We've got about 15 minutes to a midnight curfew. If we don't get out of there, we don't leave. So we go out there and there's Mitchell standing there with all his bags open and all his clothes. He's holding a receipt. And the receipt is dated something like, June 3, 1987. He told the customs agent that he got the suits altered and they gave him that receipt.

"The customs agent said, 'Well, we're not stupid.'

"So I asked, what are our alternatives? One alternative was, he goes to jail for resisting this. The other alternative is that he pays the duty on it. Something like 150 bucks. So I say, 'I don't think there's any alternative.'

"Mitch says, 'I'm not payin' any money.' I thought he was kidding. We're down to about eight minutes, seven minutes." At that point, Mattei took out a billfold and offered to pay the duty. "I'm not blowing a $20,000 charter because of $150," was Mattei's rationale.

Bowa: "Now the guy asks Mitch for his social security number. Mitch says, 'I don't have it.' That makes the agent even angrier. I mean, Mitch has already given him a lot of crap. He says, 'Then you're still going to jail.' That's when I said to myself that we're not getting out of here."

It should be noted that Mitchell is one tough character. He has various scars on his face and caps on his teeth from childhood altercations. Mitchell grew up in rough southeast San Diego where he was a gang member. Mitch knew the streets and had plenty of crazy stories to back up his exploits—some of which had long since proven to be unfounded.

Case in point: When Mitchell joined the New York Mets, he

told publicity people that he had played football for and had graduated from Clairemont High School in San Diego. They dutifully noted such in the club's 1986 media guide. A bit of investigation proved that not only had Mitchell not played football for Clairemont, but he had never graduated. In fact, he was listed on the rolls of several San Diego high schools, but had never graduated. Also during his one-year tenure in New York, Mitchell was fond of telling people that he had not played baseball until he was 18 years old. Mitchell, who was estranged from his mother and still lived with his grandmother in one of San Diego's toughest neighborhoods, could not pass that bit of malarkey by his maternal grandmother, who claimed to have driven Mitch to little-league games. In his short Padres stay, Mitchell had already been fined and chastised by Bowa for a number of missed curfews and practices. He reported to camp—late—with painful back problems, sustained, he said, when he was knocked off his bicycle by an automobile in a hit and run accident. Since the season began, he had hurt his leg running down a fly ball. He currently was nursing a toe that was broken when he was hit by a pitch during the club's recent exhibition game in Las Vegas. Mitchell had clearly been Bowa's most quizzical problem during a first two months rife with problems. Mitchell had immense talent, but Bowa viewed him as overweight and not mentally prepared to play the game. Bowa seemed to have no reading on the man who was supposed to have solved long-term Padres problems at third base.

"The only read I've got on Mitch is that it doesn't seem like his priorities are in order," Bowa said. "I think he's had a rough childhood. You know, I sit down and talk to him, I think he's a pretty good kid. I think the big mistake we made was, you make a trade and then right away you say the guy is your third baseman. It shouldn't be that way. You should say he's going to have the opportunity to win a job. Not unless you get an established player. You can't give away jobs to players who aren't established."

The Padres did make it out of Dorval with both Bowa and Mitchell on board their chartered flight.

Bowa: "I told him, 'Why don't you start cooperating with them a little bit and get it out of the way?' So he started cooperating a little bit. He asked the guy, 'Why are you always picking on guys like me?' I don't think he used any swear words. At least, when I was there he didn't. If he did I think the guy would have thrown him in. They were upset. But the guy finally took the money, let him go and we sprinted toward the airplane. When we got on the plane, Mitch gave Doc the $150 back. Before we left, the customs agent told Mitch, 'You'll be hearing from us.' So I can't imagine what's going to happen the next time we go up."

As it turned out, Mitchell's next trip to Canada would be his last with the Padres. And this bit of trouble was over. Nobody knew it yet, but so were many of the problems that had plagued the Padres this season. As they winged south from Canada, though, there was one thing that nobody could change: This team was horse(bleep)—12-42 horse(bleep).

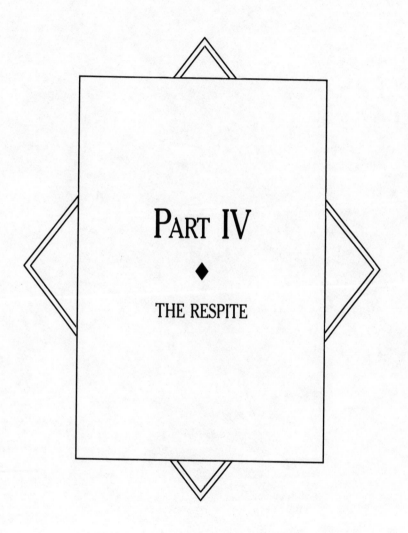

PART IV

◆

THE RESPITE

Oct. 17, 1970 ♦
Clearwater, FL

$\langle T \rangle$ he first two months of the season were the worst of my life. Those were the worst two months I've ever spent in a baseball uniform because no matter what we did, no matter what I did, no matter what the players did, it was wrong. We would invent ways to lose games. Missing bags. Not tagging up. Leaving early. A double play ball, the second baseman not touching the bag. I'm glad my family was back in the East because I would have been horrible to live with. I didn't like myself much. I was bouncing off walls.

But who knows? Sheena has always been good for me. I don't know where I'd be without her. She's led me down the straight road as far as my temper. You know, I flip out so easy on a baseball field. She'll see it on TV or something and when I go home she'll say, "What did you do that for? Let's sit down and talk about it." She keeps everything in the right perspective all the time. She'll say, "Well, let's look at the other side of the story." When I flip, I don't have time to go into both sides of the story. I only look at my side.

We got married at the end of my rookie year in Philadelphia and have been together for 17 years. Man, that seems like such a long time. I met her in Clearwater, Florida, about three years earlier when I was in the instructional league. She said she'll never forget it. It was after a game. I went down to the beach and I had on polyester slacks and a polyester shirt. Something real loud. We used to dress like we were in a band.

So I was walking on the beach and I saw her on the beach laying there. And I just went up to her and said, "I will have a date with you."

She looked at me like, "What? You've got to be crazy." You know, I thought I was a big stud then.

I said, "Do you know who I am?"

She said, "No, uh, uh."

I said, "I play baseball with the Philadelphia Phillies." The Philadelphia Phillies? She had no idea.

She said, "Big deal. What's the big deal about that?" So I backed off a little.

I sort of said, "It's not too many days you get to meet a baseball player."

She was with a friend and when Sheena went into the water, I asked her friend for her telephone number. She said, "I'm not going to give you that." I said, "Come on." So she gave me Sheena's phone number and I remember I called her every day for about two weeks. She kept saying, "Get out of here. I'm not going out with you."

Then finally, her mom said, "Why don't you just go out to dinner with him to get him off your back?" So we did and that's the way our relationship started. It didn't really get going for three years. It was on and off. I'd see her every time I went down to Florida to the instructional league. In 1969 I was playing in Eugene, Oregon, and she flew out to meet me. That's when it started getting serious and we began thinking about getting married. All that time, I really didn't want to get married on a minor-league salary. It was tough enough myself, riding buses and eating greasy food all the time. It would have been brutal having a wife do it too. Other guys were married, I don't know how they did it.

My dad told me it was no bed of roses to go through something like that. He would know. He had my mom and me bouncing all over the country when I was a little kid. I figured once I was in the big leagues that would be a good starting point. Once I got up there, I wasn't positive I would stick around for the first four or five years. But being up there was good enough.

When we got married after my rookie season, Greg Luzinski was my best man and Bob Boone was in the wedding party. They weren't in the big leagues yet. They were still in triple-A. I was lucky enough to stay one step ahead of them. But we had all gotten to be good friends when they came up to the majors that past September.

Sheena was born in Germany and raised in Scotland. I can tell you this, she was never impressed by the professional aspect of baseball. I could have been a banker or a teacher as far as she was concerned. Her mom knew what I did for a living and when she told the family over in Scotland that her daughter was marrying a ballplayer their reaction was pretty funny. They said it would be nice if I got a job before we got married. They thought it was sort of a hobby. They hadn't met me yet. If they only knew. Some hobby.

Her dad was in the service and they eventually settled in Clearwater. He was in the army. He died of Lou Gehrig's disease when she was eight or nine years old. She has a brother. A retarded brother, who is still alive and living in Florida. She went to school at the University of South Florida. She got her degree in special education. She's used it, too. One year, she worked with retarded kids. Now we've got a healthy little girl, Tori, who is four years old.

About having a family as late as we did, we planned it. When I was playing early in my career, it seemed like all the guys on our team were married. And all the wives complained: "Yeah, they leave us home. We're pregnant. We're stuck with the baby all summer. When they come home from that road trip..."

Sheena said, "I don't want to do that. I want it to be when our priorities are in the right place. We've got a solid marriage. That comes first. The family will come when we're both ready."

You know, we saw all kinds of people getting divorced. Friends of ours. She could only go to school during the winter. We wanted to get all our running out of our system. We did a lot of traveling and took a lot of cruises. We didn't want our kid brought up by a baby-sitter. And she wanted to get that degree. She's a very independent person, which is great. She learned to take care of so many things when I was on the road. She can handle herself better than any man. As you can guess, we've had our ups and downs like everybody. We've struggled. But we're still together. We've survived. She'd like to have another baby now, but we're getting close to the deadline. She's 35 or 36.

I was really lucky. I had to have somebody different. Somebody special. If I had nine different women married to me they would all have left me by now because of my personality. I go through so many ups and downs. I know there were times when Sheena wondered, "What do I need this for?" But it never got to her enough that she would want to do anything about it.

Not so much as a manager, but as a player, I would literally come home and not talk for days. If I was on an oh-for-15 it might go four or five days like that. I don't mean no talking, but really minimal talking. You know, like a quick, "Hello," in the morning and an even quicker good night before we went to bed. Sometimes I would get too wrapped up in what I was doing and I wouldn't see other problems around me. Her outlet was shopping. When I was acting like that, she wouldn't want to hang around. She'd go out and buy herself a suit.

I always respected the way she could separate the real world and the baseball world. She did it a lot better than me. That's not to say she wouldn't go through slumps with me. But she used to hate it. She'd sit behind the screen at the ballpark and she'd know something wasn't right. And she'd say, "I hate to get so involved in it because there's nothing I can do." You know, when you have a cough, you take some cough medicine. When you have a headache, you take aspirin. But when you're in a slump, all you can give someone is support, which she always gave me. I mean, I was hell to live with during those times. If I could do it over, I'd try to keep it in better perspective. I was too obsessed with how I was doing and how the team was doing. Especially when I was younger, I used to get sick. I look at the way some of our young guys handle it on the Padres—when the game is over, they turn the page. I wish I could handle it that well now. But I always had a knack for forgetting about it the next day. When I woke up to face the new day, I was usually fine. The hardest part was getting from the last out to when the new day would begin.

Sheena always said, "If you can't deal with it, quit." You shouldn't make yourself sick over something you supposedly love to do. She'd remind me about someone who was sick in the family or tell me about someone in the news who got his leg cut off. That made me realize an oh-for-20 wasn't the worst thing in the world. Hey, some people don't have food on the table. I can't thank her enough for helping me work on that.

WEDNESDAY, JUNE 10, 1987 ♦
HOUSTON, TX

(S) omething had to be done about the Joey Cora situation. I think Joey was reaching out and really wanted to go down. I really do. I went with him as far as I could. I'm not at all upset as far as his physical ability goes. But he made so many rookie mistakes, it was really starting to show up. It seemed to be getting worse and worse instead of better and better. In that 11-2 game last Sunday in Atlanta, I came that close to getting Tim Flannery out of the game because of his ankle and letting Joey play. But for some reason I didn't. That game was just a disaster. We had won two in a row and were up by nine runs going into the sixth inning. I'm feeling so good about it, I even pull Tony Gwynn out to give him a rest. He's playing with that bad hand and sore legs and all. Then the roof caves in on Jimmy Jones. Storm Davis did not have anything and I had to leave Craig Lefferts in to be shelled. He says his arm is bothering him or something. He asked Jack McKeon to put him on the disabled list a few weeks ago, but we were so short, we couldn't do it. We've tried to just bring him slowly around.

I wound up using Greg Booker in the ninth inning with the score tied 12-12. I felt bad about that because he's not used to working in those sort of situations. He walked three guys and walked in the winning run. We lost 13-12. What a complete bleepin' disaster. We were 14-43 after the game. Doesn't that tell the story of the whole season?

Afterward, Storm was complaining to some of the writers about pitching out of the bullpen. He tells them: "What I'm really hoping would happen, and it looks like it could happen, is that if

I sit around in the bullpen long enough maybe somebody in the race will pick me up. It's crossed my mind a few times."

You've got to be kidding me! What has he done to work his way out of the bullpen? And if he doesn't like it in San Diego, maybe we should talk with Jack and get him the bleep out. As for now, I've thrown him back out there as a starter. Jimmy Jones hasn't been real consistent. Who knows, maybe somebody will step forward and do something. Of course, Storm didn't do too well tonight as a starter either. He was blown out of there in the fourth inning and the Astros blew us out 10-1. But I'm sure he'll have some sort of excuse. Now we're 15-45. There's this joke going around baseball, "Who'll win 20 games first, the Padres or Bret Saberhagen?" At this point, my money might be on bleepin' Saberhagen.

Anyway, I knew after that Atlanta game that we had to make some changes. Joey was the first to go. Maybe more are coming because I heard Joan Kroc announced that Chub Feeney is the new club president at the league meetings in Philadelphia today. Ballard's out. Who knows what that will mean?

Back to Joey, on Monday when we got to Houston, I called him into my office. He sat down. And he hasn't looked at me yet. I said, "We're going to make a move and I don't want you to think this is punishment or failure. Physically, you can make all the plays. You have a nice hitting stroke. You put the ball in play. But you're pressing in the field and it's hurting us. Do you have anything to ask me?"

He says, "Nope."

I said, "Do you think I'm being fair with you?"

He says, "Yep."

I said, "You've got to feel something. Are you upset? Are you hurt?"

He just wouldn't answer me.

So then I said, "You can do one of two things: You can go down to Vegas for two or three weeks and you can play your butt off and be back up here or you can go down there and we might not ever hear from you again. It's up to you."

He got up out of the chair—and I literally had to grab his hand to shake hands with him. All his friends were in the locker room—I think there were 10 people in there—and he didn't say a word to anybody. He was really upset and left. Maybe I saw Garry Templeton say something, he was right next to his locker, and that was it. I sort of wish he was striking out and making errors instead of making mental mistakes. I really do. Because then he would still be playing.

I guess I feel for him because I see a lot of me in him. I was very moody as a player. I had a lousy temperament. Like I said, I might be dead wrong, but I think he's going to be a good player—if he plays relaxed. I'm watching us play now. We're still not playing great, but we're making all the plays. I knew you had to have veteran players up the middle, but I really thought that Joey, going to college and all, was going to be better prepared. I mean he played all those years at Vanderbilt. I could have sent him down a couple of weeks ago. I thought he'd come around. I really did.

But he was very sensitive, and there's too many guys on this team that are too sensitive. They want to be praised for everything they do. It's hard to praise all the time when a team is 30 games under .500. The other guys I'm having a hard time figuring out are Carmelo Martinez, Tempy and Eric Show. With Eric, it's not because of his ability, it's because of his personality. I just think he thinks too much, I really do. I mean, I like him as an individual, but . . . I've seen him in games—I know he doesn't give up—he just gets disgusted. Like I know our defense cost him three wins with bad plays. I know it. And after awhile I could see him getting disgusted, discouraged. I'm not saying he's taking the team down, but he's a perfectionist. He worries about things that are completely out of his hands. If a guy makes an error, you can't do anything about that. But he'll carry it over to the next hitter by either walking him or hanging something.

He's so much different than his buddy Dave Dravecky. Both of them had bad elbows. Both of them are Christians. Both of them belong to the John Birch Society. Physically, Eric started out the season way ahead of Dravecky. Now Dave's elbow is fine.

He seems to be the Dravecky of old. What is he, 1-6? I watch him between starts. He approaches every start like he's 7-0. I said that during that big meeting earlier this month in Montreal. I said, "I've got a guy here," and I didn't mention his name, "who's strugglin' his butt off, but you wouldn't know it the way he works in between starts. You'd think he was going for the Cy Young right now." That's why I like the guy. He's a winner. He might not ever win a game for me, but just watching his work ethic, just by watching his mannerisms on the field, he's a winner.

There's a difference when you're struggling. You can pick out the guys. You can pick out the guys who are struggling and believe in themselves, because they keep working. Or the guys when they're struggling and they get in the corner with another guy and start rippin' everybody. It's the guys who don't believe in themselves and are very insecure people, they go out there and they get a young kid, and say, "He's runnin' a horse-bleep game." They're watchin' every move: You can tell who the guys are.

It's like Carmelo. He and I were disagreeing on a few things about four days ago. And Tempy, Tempy wasn't a malcontent, but he was so depressed, if he was sitting here right now, he'd make you feel bad. Joey Cora was very sensitive. Here's a guy who was so down on himself he went through a bunch of roommates in two months. That's moody. Carmelo, I think right now he's feeling sorry for himself. He's like oh-for-27. He thought he got screwed when I took him out of the lineup a few weeks ago in San Diego. And to this day, I told him the reason I took him out of the lineup is because the fans were getting on his butt and I didn't want to see him get buried. I thought he could miss two or three games and then start it back up on the road. We go on the road and then he pulls that crap in the batting cage in Montreal because he's batting seventh. He gets ticked off. Attitude has a lot to do with whether you hit or not. Now the last four or five days, starting in Atlanta, he's been working hard. We'll see what happens.

When guys go bad, and I did it as a player, it's easy to make excuses. You're human. It's up to the manager, it's up to me to say, "I know you're going bad, but let's not bleepin' go crazy. Let's just put the blame where the blame should be blamed. You're not swinging worth a bleep." He can get mad at me. He can get mad at the hitting coach. He can get mad at hitting near the bottom of the lineup. But what really brings out what he's made of is watching him before the game. Is he sulking or is he working hard at it?

As far as Tempy is concerned, he gets down when he's not hitting. He's always been a good offensive player, but in the last two or three years I think he hasn't hit as well as he'd like to. He gets really down when he thinks he's not hitting. And he's not. What is he hitting? About .200? But I told him, "I don't give a damn what you hit. Play shortstop the way you're capable and it will help out." I think he could help a team in a pennant race just with his glove. It's only natural. Veterans don't want to go through rebuilding. Most of 'em, when they first come up, go through it. In all fairness to them, I can see them being a little frustrated. They want to play maybe two or three years on a team that has a chance to win.

I think Tempy is going through a tough time right now. Mentally he's not where he wants to be. I think he needs to lose some weight, not because he's fat but to take pressure off his knees. He's been playing on bad knees for years.

The thing that upsets me most about Tempy, and I told him when I named him captain during the spring, "There's going to be a time when you're not playing worth a damn. It happens to everybody. This is when you've got to say, 'OK, I'm going bad, but I'm going to help out in other areas.'" I told him, "Tempy, I named you captain because I think you can be an influence on these guys." He said, "You're right, you're right. I want you to jump on me. I want you to jump on me." In my mind, motivation should come from within. And it can't be inflicted by another person. You've got to inflict it upon yourself. If you don't have the motivation, you're in trouble.

The clubhouse meeting I had in Montreal—Tempy came in to see me a couple of days later. He said, "The meeting was for me, wasn't it?" I said, "Some of the things were, yeah." He said,

"You're right." And it so happened that Martinez came in and saw me too and said the same thing: "The meeting was for me, wasn't it?" And I told him the same thing I told Tempy: "Yeah, some of the things I said were for you." I mean, guys know. Guys know who you're talking about without having to bring up their names. They know they're capable of performing better. And for us to turn it around they have to play up to their ability. I may be wrong, but I still believe they can.

That's why it was so funny after the first big blowout meeting in Los Angeles when I apologized to the seven or eight guys who were busting their butts and had to listen to me. Tony Gwynn came up to me afterward with that, "I hope I was one of the seven or eight guys." I mean, Tony Gwynn is something. I always respected him when I was a player, but I respect him even more watching him work every day. Right now, he's hurt. He's hurt bad. But he's still stealing third, stealing second. He's got a great attitude. People think he hits because he's a good hitter, but he works at it. Every day we get a field, he's there. I've got to literally order him off the field. Yesterday he wanted to hit, but I told him I didn't want him shagging flies because his leg was bothering him. So he hit and went in. He felt bad. Talk about routines, he has his routine and it never changes. That's because this is his job and he knows it.

If some of these guys worked in a bank, the way they approach their jobs, they'd never get anything done. It would be like, "Monday, I'll go in. Tuesday, ahh, I don't think I'll go in today. Wednesday? I might go in for half a day. Thursday, yeah." That's the way they approach it. Instead of saying, "This is my job. I'm supposed to play 162 games. Mentally, I'm going to be ready to play." Some guys don't have that approach. There are a few guys who do: Tony Gwynn does. I think John Kruk is getting that approach. I don't think he's had it. He's getting it because he hangs around better people. Gwynn has had a tremendous effect on him. Every team John played on, when he hit .300, the manager wouldn't get on him. I jump him all the time—tellin' him he used to be a bleepin' clown out there. He hasn't done too much more clowning around. He said, "Hey, with Steve Garvey gone, this is an opportunity to play first base. I'm not lettin' it slip away."

Some guys have so much talent, but they don't work hard enough. When I think about my life, from the first time I played little league, I knew what I wanted to do. In little league, I knew I was better than everybody there even though I was the smallest guy. I had a real good arm. I could hit. I could just see I was better than everybody. And then, as I started getting older, I didn't grow that much so I knew I was going to have to work that much harder. They didn't have weights in baseball back then. In the old days, if you touched weights, you'd never played baseball. You get too tight. You can't swing a bat. You can't throw. It was a big taboo then. If I could have seen my career and known that by lifting weights I would have been stronger and better, I would have been pumping at eight. That's the kind of work habits that were ingrained in me. That's the kind of work habits I don't see today.

If you're a regular in baseball, it's very difficult to lift weights every day. Mike Schmidt says he is probably in his best physical shape when he leaves for spring training and he's probably in his worst shape around July. But he busts his butt during the winter. He gets up at 7:30 in the morning and he works out with this guy in Philadelphia named Gus Hefflin. He's unbelievable. A whole group of us used to work out together during the winter when I was playing there. We used to get up every day, be at the stadium early to work out. It didn't matter how cold it got. And it gets cold in Philly. We would run steps. We would run ramps. I mean, every day.

I was talking to Jack McKeon about it. He was telling me about all the Padres who live out in San Diego. What a great facility they have. What great weather. You're living in San Diego and our trainer, Dick Dent, has a workout program right there for you. And most of these guys don't want to use the facility. I can't understand it. But then, I don't really understand a lot of the things some guys do around here.

Sunday, June 21, 1987 ◆ San Diego, CA

s George Harrison so aptly wrote, "All Things Must Pass." And so too did the initial grief of the Padres season, albeit, temporarily. Visions of the 1962 New York Mets, those dandies who lost 120 baseball games, disappeared into the early San Diego summer, which was still quite nippy by anyone's standards.

Beginning with three straight wins over the Giants in San Francisco, the Padres, who at one time fell 14 games behind the *fifth-place* Los Angeles Dodgers, had won six games in a row.

How did they do it? It all began with that long-lost pitching. On a Friday night in San Francisco, Ed Whitson tossed his first complete-game National League shutout in almost six years. Dave Dravecky, his arm problems seemingly behind him, pitched his first complete game of the season just two days later against those same Giants. In the six games, Eric Show was the only one of the five current starters who failed to register a victory. The bullpen trio of Lance McCullers, Craig Lefferts and Goose Gossage kicked into gear. This was more like it. And suddenly, credence could be lent to the theory that with three starters and one reliever coming off dismal ends to their 1986 seasons, the Padres pitching staff just wasn't ready to open the season. It seemed ready now.

But a shadow seems always to cast its pall across Padres light. On Tuesday, baseball's special arbitrator George Nicolau ruled against the Padres release of pitcher LaMarr Hoyt, who had concluded his brief stay at the minimum security prison in Elgin Air Force Base for carrying over-the-counter prescription drugs across the Mexican-American border. At the same time, Nicolau reduced a commissioner-ordered one-year suspension of

Hoyt to 60 days. The Padres would have to begin paying Hoyt his $1.1 million, and according to the ruling, allow him to continue his career in a San Diego uniform.

Within days, Joan Kroc issued her decision—she would pay Hoyt his money, but she refused to play him. That brought the Major League Baseball Players Association into the fracas. Would a new grievance be filed? It was yet another mess that, for the umpteenth time since Alan Wiggins disappeared from the club on a drug binge in April 1985, detracted from the Padres play on the field. The six-game winning streak had ended in typical Padres fashion the previous Friday night. Leading the Giants 5-0 at home going into the seventh inning, Dravecky tired. McCullers came on to strike out Bob Brenly and Will Clark, but a double by Eddie Milner and a throwing error by third baseman Kevin Mitchell put the Giants back in the game. The bullpen then collapsed in the eighth inning and the Giants stole a 7-6 win.

The streak was over, but critics couldn't help to notice that a key run or a better pitched game in the last two weeks would have raised that streak to a far more impressive level. Recall the 11-2 lead that the Padres had blown in Atlanta, a pair of 1-0 losses in Houston and San Francisco, and Friday night's debacle. Add it all up and the Padres could have won 13 of 14 games since Larry Bowa called his last team meeting in Montreal on June 4th. Instead they had to settle for nine of the 14. It wasn't Camelot, but thank God for small favors.

Behind the scenes, though, much was going on to again disrupt the club that was now playing with some panache and cohesion. Houston, San Francisco and Cincinnati, the three teams that had emerged as clear threats to win the National League West, were in desperate need of pitching. With strong veteran arms in the rotation and strong young arms in the wings, the Padres were now openly accepting bids. Rumors that Dave Dravecky was about to be traded to the Astros had circulated so widely during a recent visit to Houston, that the pitcher called home to put a hold on a family excursion to San Francisco, San Diego's next stop on a lengthy trip. Dravecky was not traded and his family did indeed join him in San Francisco.

Show was also in constant demand, having told writers that perhaps a change of scenery might be in everyone's best interest. Both Storm Davis and Andy Hawkins were also keenly interested in the news. Ironically, Dravecky was one of the few Padres starters who wanted to remain in San Diego. Dravecky would eventually be traded, simply because he could bring the greatest price.

This weekend, Giants president Al Rosen had made the trip to San Diego and met with Jack McKeon during each game. The rumor mill had produced the information that the Giants wanted Show in a multi-player transaction. In fact, they wanted Dravecky, whom the Padres were reluctant to trade. In return, the Padres asked for third baseman Chris Brown, who had just returned from a 38-game absence caused by a Danny Cox fastball to the jaw during an early-May game in St. Louis. The Giants politely declined. For the moment, there would be no trade.

Show's actions during the day's game evidently were one reason the Giants scratched him from their list. It happened in a flash. The game opened with a Garry Templeton error. Jeffrey Leonard doubled in the first run. Will Clark grounded to Kruk at first base, who, instead of rushing to the bag for the sure out, slung a one hop throw across the diamond trying to nab Leonard at third. Both runners were safe. Leonard scored on a fielder's choice grounder. Chili Davis doubled. Brown and Brenly singled. The next thing Show knew, the Giants were leading 4-0 and Bowa was on his way to the mound to remove him from the game.

As he stomped off the mound, Show turned and briefly jawed at Bowa, not the most intelligent thing to do in front of 20,000 people, your teammates and a prospective club president. It was over in a split second, but in that second, Show had succeeded in upsetting Bowa and angering some of his teammates. Bowa would eventually fine him the usual hundred dollar note, but the one guy you would least expect to rip him, did: Tony Gwynn.

"When I came out to get him," said Bowa, "the first thing he said to me was, 'Why are you taking me out?' That had some merit to it. Only one ball was hit hard. But I said, 'I've seen this before, Eric, when it snowballs. I'm not going to let you sit out there so you can give up eight or nine runs. It's not worth it.'

"That's when he stalked off, turned back to me and said, 'Same old crap every bleepin' time.' I didn't think he swore, but he threw a bleep out there. He was really upset. That's the worst I've ever seen him."

Show's remark isn't what drew the fine. What perturbed Bowa is that Show dressed and left the ballpark long before the Giants 11-2 stomping had concluded. He was nowhere in the vicinity when Gwynn, sitting in the nearly empty locker room, decided to tear him apart.

"I fined him because he left the bleepin' clubhouse," Bowa said. "He pitched the one inning. He's out of there in the second. I told him, 'You got us into this bleepin' mess. The least you can do is sit here and watch the rest of the game.' I have a rule. If you get taken out of the game, you can shower and get your street clothes on. But I don't want anyone leavin' until the game is over.

"I told him, 'I understand you getting ticked off. I understand you getting upset. I understand you getting mad because the team is not playing well behind you. But there's no reason for you takin' a hike—you being home by the third inning while we're still getting our butts kicked in.' He said, 'You're right.' I said, 'Fine. Just give me the hundred dollars.' "

In Show's defense, the afternoon had been a culmination of some of the worst fortune in history. Why the cycle began, no one knows. But it evidently began that cool October afternoon in Chicago during the 1984 playoffs. Show would allow seven postseason homers to the Cubs and Detroit Tigers. For two straight years he had been a 15-game winner. But since then, he has had one serious elbow injury and 29 wins. Twenty-nine wins may not be awful, but when that number could have reached more than forty victories, it has to drive a pitcher crazy.

Since then, Show has tinkered with his mechanics and his psyche to try and unmask the problem. But how does one explain phenomena like this? In 1985, Show pitched 233 innings and allowed 212 hits. He walked 87, struck out 141 and registered a 3.09 ERA. In contrast, Hawkins pitched 229 innings and allowed 229 hits. He walked 65, struck out 69 and finished with a 3.15 ERA. Show was 12-11, Hawkins was 18-8. Simply, the Padres scored more runs in the games Hawkins started. Their offense was anemic when Show took the mound. It was enough to make a pitcher scream and on many occasions, Show, a free spirit, wailed.

His public image wasn't helped much when midway through the Padres 1984 pennant-winning season, Show, Dravecky and former Padres left-hander Mark Thurmond disclosed that they were card-carrying members of the John Birch Society. Each player, having to defend his position, found himself wide open to scathing editorials from the national press for belonging to an organization perceived to be both racist and anti-semitic. Show and the Society have long denied that either is the case. Show, a seemingly intelligent and thoughtful man, came away bitter from the experience, but still undaunted.

In 1985, Show was heaped with further national abuse when on September 11, he served up Pete Rose's "Big Knock" on a memorable night in Cincinnati. While Rose shed tears at first base and thousands exalted No. 4,192—the hit which pushed Rose past Ty Cobb to the top of the all-time list, Show took a seat on the mound. That action angered his teammates and later led to a brief tussle in the dugout between Show and left-fielder Carmelo Martinez. Show, talking heatedly with pitching coach Galen Cisco, pointed to left field, a gesture that was mistaken by Martinez.

Show didn't help his cause by disappearing from the clubhouse and blocking his hotel phone after that game.

From that point on, Show had to tread very delicate ground with his long-time Padres teammates. He and Dravecky became isolated from the group when Thurmond was traded to Detroit in July 1986. But Davis, a devoted Christian like the two veteran pitchers, made it a trio again when he joined the club in 1987. Perhaps they were who another veteran pitcher was talking about when, earlier in the month, he had noted that the Padres could release certain other pitchers. "They're worthless," said the veteran pitcher, supporting a claim by rookie catcher Benito Santiago that the Padres pitching staff "stinks."

Santiago, who was having trouble at the time calling games for a number of pitchers, claimed that he had gone out to the mound on several occasions to talk to Dravecky and Show. So it was no surprise when someone on the Padres publicly blasted Show. But nobody figured it would be Tony Gwynn.

"His job is to get outs," Gwynn told a group of reporters including the *San Diego Tribune's* Ed Zieralski. "Our job is to make it easier for him to get outs. There was an error and a bad decision that opened up the door for it. But that's part of the game. I don't particularly like people coming in here and saying they're not getting any support after they've been taken out of the game. Obviously, we made some mistakes and they cost us. But it just doesn't happen when he's on the mound. Sometimes you've just got to tough it out."

The next day, Show did call the *Tribune* to air his side of the story. His comments only helped broaden the issue.

"Tony has popped off before about me," Show said. "I realize that Tony is a very good player and a lot of things he says carries a lot of weight. So, I'm at a disadvantage, but Tony is not God. Yet people take what he says as gospel because he's hitting .360. . . .

"I won't deny I was frustrated about the way things were going. But I wasn't mad about physical errors. All I can say is, walk a mile in my shoes and then come talk to me personally. Quit basing it on second and third hand information. If it keeps happening, I'll start popping off about things that are happening behind closed doors. I'll open up a can of worms myself. I've never talked about my fellow players in the press. Yet, these same individuals seize every opportunity to stab me in the back to the media. I wish they'd talk to me like a man about it."

After that, Bowa called in Show to levy the fine and the issue seemed to be closed. Gwynn, noting the stir he had created, tried to backtrack about his original comments, telling one writer, who was not there for either the rip or the retort, that he thought his statements about Show were off the record. But the entire diatribe had been taped and at no time did Gwynn ever ask to go off the record.

As far as airing it out with each other, that evidently never happened. Show was to become involved in bigger problems a few short weeks away that would pre-empt that particular discussion. Gwynn, who was batting near .500 for the month, would find out just how open he had left himself to criticism. One night, jogging back to the dugout at The Murph, he would be stunned by some fans taunting him with pea-brained racial remarks.

And Bowa? He figured the entire incident had been blown out of proportion. Standing around the batting cage two nights later, he wondered why his club could cause so much negative publicity when it was on its way to winning for the eighth time in 10 games.

But as one long-time Padres broadcaster is fond of noting, "It's simple: We are the Pads."

WEDNESDAY, JULY 1, 1987 ♦ LOS ANGELES, CA

You ask me how things can turn around so bleepin' quickly, I wish I could give you the answer. A month ago, we were at our low and I thought we'd never come out of it. Then we come back and have a 15-12 month of June. We're not out of the hole we dug ourselves into by any means, but it's nice to know that you can see light at the end of this long tunnel. Eric Show came back and pitched a beauty tonight. For the second time this year, he shuts out the Dodgers at Dodger Stadium. A four-hitter. The first two months everything we did turned out wrong. Now . . .

Like the other night, Storm Davis has been having these back spasms and he'd already missed a start. Before Monday night's game against the Dodgers, I asked him, "Do you want to give it a try?" He says, "Yeah." He's sitting on the field a couple of minutes before the game and he's having a hard time stretching out. Maybe I shouldn't have let him go out there, but since he said he wanted to, I let him. That was my mistake. In the first inning, he pops something in his rib cage punching out Pedro Guerrero. He's got the same injury now that Goose Gossage had the first month of the season—torn cartilage or something. We put him on the disabled list today. So he's gone. Who knows when we'll have him back. Goose missed the whole first month. But the way it turned out, I bring Jimmy Jones out of the bullpen and he throws eight innings of two-hit ball. This, from a guy who has been struggling all year. So now Jones is in the rotation. Maybe he's ready to make it over the hump. Like I said, during the first two months, if this had happened, we would have been bombed. How can you figure it? You can analyze it all you want, but my guess is that there are two reasons for the turnaround. Obviously, the pitching has been better, which I think has been the biggest thing. That's an understatement. And then the meeting I had in Montreal early last month, I think that finally opened some eyes. I told them, "Two or three of you guys are on your last legs. You're trying to take other people down with you. The bottom line is, you probably can still play, but in your mind, you think you can't play so you want to take other people down with you."

We had some heads down. Suddenly, they all jerked up like, "What the bleep is he talking about?"

I said, "You're scared. You're scared to face the reality that it's getting near the end. If it's over, just go out with your head up instead of taking guys down with you and bleepin' around when you shouldn't be bleepin' around."

You see, in Montreal, my office is near the front of the clubhouse and the training room is right next door. I can shut my door and without trying to, I mean, I can be reading and still hear every word. You hear things like, "I'm bleepin' 21 years old and I need someone to tell me when to go to bed?" I'm hearing all that crap. So in the meeting, I threw all that crap back at them. "Yeah," I told them, "that is a shame when you need somebody to tell you when to go to bed. But you're bleepin' idiots. I'm sitting there in the bar with a bleepin' advance scout and I see eight bleepin' guys going through the elevators. And we're getting our butts kicked. Now you tell me that's professional. And the guys staying out late aren't tearing this league up either."

I mean, there's no way I should have a bed check. These guys are grown men. You've got to be a little discreet about when to go out and stay out a little late. When your team is getting its butt kicked, that isn't a good time to go out. Just give me everything you've got on the field.

I really think these guys tried fighting me in the beginning. I really do. In their own minds they tried to say, "Hey, bleep him. Let's test him." It's human. But they found out I wasn't going to give in. They realized, "Hey, this guy is crazy. He's relentless."

You see, I think I've made some adjustments, too. And it

seems like they've worked. I haven't been as critical as I was. Right now, if I see a guy bleeping up, I'm gonna call him in. Like Stanley Jefferson, the other day when he hit a doubleplay ball, I called him in and said, "Stanley, I know you're frustrated because you're not swinging the bat real well right now. But there's no way you should be thrown out on that double play. It got us a run, but there were no outs." And then two innings later, I watch him hit that slow roller to second and he beats it out. I told him, "You're either going to have to do one of two things: You're either going to have to tell me you're tired so I can sit you down or you're going to have to bust your butt."

Before, what I would have done is called a clubhouse meeting and said, "Damn it." But there's no sense calling a clubhouse meeting to reprimand one or two guys. I'll call 'em in individually now. If I see seven or eight of them bleepin' up, then I'll call a clubhouse meeting. But I'm finding that the best way of going about these individual things is one on one.

I'm trying to teach them that this game will drop you to your knees when things go bad. It's the hardest game to play when you're struggling. And when you're doing well, it's the most fun in the world. When you're struggling, you hate going out there. That's how it's been for me managing.

Last year in Vegas, I had fun. But the first two months of this season, I had no fun. I was miserable. My wife, Sheena, says I'm miserable all during the baseball season, anyway. But I mean, I was really miserable. Each road trip felt like it was eight years long. Now when you look back at it. . . I mean, we're not anywhere near over the hill, but at least we're playing a little better. If we could have gotten out of the gate just a little bit stronger, we might be seven or eight games out right now instead of 16 games out with a brutal 28-51 record.

We can be as good as we want to be, but the bottom line on this team is, if we don't get pitching, we're in trouble. We can't play catch up. We don't have a lot of power. We're not a great defensive team. Our middle relief is inconsistent. If we don't get pitching from our starters and closers—bleep! Why have we done so well the last month? It's because of our starting pitching, and because Goose Gossage and Lance McCullers—Goose in particular—have done outstanding jobs.

It didn't hurt either that Tony Gwynn batted .473 for the month of June. Every time he got up it seemed like he got a hit. I've never seen anything like it. He carried us offensively, even though I know he was uncomfortable batting third. He only knocked in 16 runs. But he's our best hitter. So I have to bat him there for now. Eventually, I'd like to get him back to hitting first or second. But we don't have a legitimate cleanup hitter.

I think things are really starting to come around. Honestly, I think I've done a pretty good job under some amazing circumstances. I'd like to have a contract extension, but that's up to Chub Feeney.

My very first meeting with Chub, something had come out in the paper that I was asking for an extension. He called me in and he wanted to talk about the team. But I said, "Before we talk, let me say one thing: I have not nor will I ask publicly for an extension. That is in your hands. I don't know how this came out. All I said is that it would be easier to manage if you know you're coming back."

He said, "Well, I don't believe in giving out new contracts until the end of the season."

I said, "Hey, that's fine. You're the boss. You do what you want to do."

Chub knows baseball. We've had a couple of talks now. It's one thing to watch the big leaguers play as president of the league. You go to this game and that game. You see one guy get three hits and you go, "This guy can play!" To watch him day in and day out and then evaluate him, it's a little different. Like I said, he knows baseball. I think the more he watches our games, he'll begin to realize what we need.

Yeah, I'd really like to be back here next year. I really would. I think with all the talent we've got comin' up, and with a trade or two, we'll have a decent team. We're not going to be the 1927 New York Yankees, but if we get a power hitter and our young kids improve, we'll surprise a lot of people. The way our division is now, there's no power house. Cincinnati, talent wise, probably has the best team, but their pitching is short. The Giants are pretty good. But the balance changes so much from year to year, you can't even speculate on it anymore.

Injuries are key. If we lost Tony Gwynn right now, we could lose 130 games. It's hard to project what's going to happen.

Saturday, July 4, 1987 ◆
Montreal, Quebec

I t was just after a rough game and I was sitting in my office. Goose Gossage had let up a ninth-inning homer to Hubie Brooks and Montreal had beat us 4-3. It was the second tough one-run loss here in a row. I wasn't feeling too good anyway when the phone in my office rang. It was Chub Feeney on the phone and he told me that we had just made a big trade with the Giants. It was almost eleven o'clock at night.

I wasn't even sure we were still talking with the Giants. The only person who had said anything to me about it was Jack McKeon. The only clue I had was that a week before, Jack had asked me if I liked Chris Brown. I said, "Yeah, do you think you can get him? I think he can be a good player." That was the last word I heard of it. They kept it quiet. Part of it was that when we were talking with the Giants a couple of weeks ago about an Eric Show deal, Al Rosen, their president, thought the press screwed it up. Too much information leaked, I guess. I don't know.

It stunned me 'cuz I didn't know we were that close to making any deal. There was Chub on the phone after a tough loss telling me that we just made a trade. He said: "Do you want to tell the people involved that we'd like them to be in Chicago tomorrow and wish 'em luck?" I said, "Yeah, I'll do that." At the end he asked me what I thought of it. I said, "I like Chris Brown, but I really haven't thought about the rest of it." He said, "OK," and hung up the phone.

It was a whopper. A seven-player deal that sent Dave Dravecky, Kevin Mitchell and Craig Lefferts to the Giants for Brown, and three pitchers—Mark Grant, a right-handed starter,

Mark Davis, a left-handed short reliever, and Keith Comstock, another left-hander who could possibly help our middle-inning relief situation. The key to the trade for us was Brown—a quality third baseman who had earned the reputation of not playing hurt with the Giants. I didn't care what they said in San Francisco. The kid was starting out fresh with me. He had just come off having his jaw broken by a Danny Cox pitch. I knew he was going to need time to get over that.

The Giants were playing the Cubs in Chicago the next afternoon, so all three of our guys had to leave early in the morning to get there. The Giants players were coming up here, which I thought was kind of ridiculous considering that we were playing in Chicago on Monday. I put Grant in the rotation right away and since he was starting against the Cubs on Monday, I told him to just stay there. I guess that's the way Chub wanted it. So that's the way it happened.

I called our three guys into my office to tell them about it and their reactions were surprising. Lefferts seemed glad to get out of here. I read a few days later where he said he couldn't have felt any better about the deal because he picked up 12 games in the standings in a single day. Dravecky was kind of thoughtful about it. He was sad to leave, because he loved living in San Diego, but he thought he was ready for the change. Mitchell was the guy that really surprised me. He was shocked. He didn't say anything. He even went back to his hotel room and threatened not to report. Maybe he was just shocked to get traded again so fast.

I figured of all of them, he'd be the one who couldn't wait to go because since he was traded here from the Mets last winter, nothing had gone right for him. I really think that because he was a homeboy, he had too many distractions in San Diego. There were too many people putting demands on his time. It didn't matter what he was going to do in San Francisco. He wasn't going to do it for us. I hated to lose Dravecky. He was a quality pitcher and quality individual. You don't find that many of those. But to get something, you have to give up something and Dravecky was the guy who was at the top of everybody's list.

I found out later how it all happened. A few weeks ago in San Diego the Giants asked for Dravecky, but couldn't get him because they didn't want to give up Brown. Jack told me that Rosen finally called him and put Brown's name on the table. That's when we started talking seriously about trading Dravecky. They said that if they traded Brown, they would need another third baseman to fill in for the short-term. We said we'd give them Mitchell. The nuts and bolts of the deal was worked out by Chub and Rosen in San Francisco. I've heard that when Ballard Smith was president, Jack worked out most of the deals. Now he had handed the ball over to Chub. Jack said he didn't care as long as everything was being done for the good of the team.

I read where Jack said: "Chub wants to be involved in everything. There's nothing wrong with that. I've had no problem working with him . . . As long as he keeps me in cigars and I keep him in cigars, we'll be fine."

I guess there were actually about a dozen names on the table before Chub and Rosen worked it down to seven guys. The Giants were calling the deal, "The Chicago 7." Some of the San Diego guys were calling it "The July 4th Massacre." Whatever you want to call it, it was a hell of a big deal.

It wasn't the most thrilling experience I've ever had, telling those three guys they had been traded, but really, it wasn't my weekend here anyway. On Friday night, I got into it with some reporter who I'd never seen before because he asked me some stupid bleepin' question. I found out later it was a guy named Lynn Henning from the *Detroit News* who was in town to do a feature on Tony Gwynn. He should have stuck to talking to Gwynn. We had just gotten beat 2-1. Herm Winningham, Montreal's center fielder, had made a great catch on a drive by Carmelo Martinez to rob us of two late runs and had thrown Tim Flannery out at the plate in the first inning. There was one inning when we stung the ball three times at their outfielders and came up with nothing but three outs to show for it.

So this guy asks me, "I haven't seen the team play yet this year, but is this an example of the way things have gone for you? I mean, there were a few times when it seemed like you had the game won."

I looked at him like he was ridiculous and said, "How did we have the game won?"

He says, "Well, you hit all those line drives at people in the fifth inning." I figured, he's got to be kiddin' me. I said, "What are you supposed to do about that? What am I supposed to do, make the outfielders sit down?" Then he walked out of the office. I wasn't in much of a mood anyway. When another guy asked me what I was so upset about, I told him, "The guy asked a stupid question." Then he comes back and tries to explain himself and I snapped.

"It was a stupid question," I said. "It was a stupid bleepin' question. Get the bleep out of here. They ought to ban all baseball writers up here. Get out of my bleepin' locker room. Get the bleep out of here."

Now he yells, "NO!"

That made it even worse. I told him, "You better get the bleep out. I'm tired of answering these stupid bleepin' questions. What are you going to do?"

I'm glad that Claude, the clubhouse attendant, finally walked him out of the locker room because that put an end to it. Then I told the three San Diego writers who usually travel with the team:

"It was a stupid question the guy asked me. What do you want me to do? We hit three line drives one inning. He saw the same game I saw. What am I supposed to do, make excuses for that? I'm tired of listening to stupid questions. The guy is watching the same game I am. Write it. We got beat 2-1. You guys act like we threw the ball all over the place. You're acting like I should make an excuse why we lost. We got beat. I don't like losing whether it's 10-0 or 2-1. Why should I get on the players? They busted their butts. Well, it seems like somebody is waiting for me to jump on somebody."

What really ticked me off about the entire thing is that the local writers went back and put it in their papers. I thought that was pretty weak. It's one thing if I rip an umpire or have an argument with a player, but another writer? I thought it should have been left alone. I think it was the only time all year I really got into it with a writer. I've been really mad at some guys, but by and large, I think I've been pretty fair to the media and the media has been pretty fair to me. I have no complaints. Most of the guys who cover the team regularly don't ask many stupid questions. That's the only thing I hate. The guys who aren't around regularly asking stupid questions.

I know they have a job to do, but damn. I think I've been pretty patient. There were times when I could have gone bonkers at some guys. Some guys, they know when they ask you a stupid question. You give the guy a double take, he knows it's a stupid question. You don't have to tell him. Some people think I'm cold to guys that I don't see around the team regularly. I'm not cold. I'm short. Some of the questions they ask me, I know why they don't travel with the team. Some of these guys come out of the woodwork. Like I said, I know they have a job to do, but even a sports writer from some small town hick paper has to have pride in some of the questions they ask. Some of them sound like they just don't know the game.

Yeah, I was pretty upset at the writers for going ahead and printing that argument I had with some reporter. I didn't even want to talk to them. Then Chub called about the trade and it changed everything. What a weekend. What a season. Will it ever end?

TUESDAY, JULY 7, 1987 ◆
CHICAGO, IL

W hen Eric Show's pitch exploded in the face of Andre Dawson, it began one of those free-for-alls which are so typical of major-league baseball. The pitch, a high inside fastball, dropped Dawson face first to the ground. Dawson had homered three times off Padres pitching in two days. No. 3 came in the first inning off Show. Paul Noce had opened the fateful third inning with another long ball—the 20th Chicago Cubs homer off Padres pitching in half a season. Did Show snap and launch a high-hard one at Dawson on purpose? Dawson thought so. Ditto his teammates. But the video replay seemed to back Show's contention that once again he was a sad victim of circumstance.

"I was in here watching it on TV when it happened and Eric's head just dropped," said close friend Storm Davis. "He didn't look like a man who wanted to hit somebody. If you go after somebody, you stand there and look at him because you know they're going to come out there after you."

Said Larry Bowa, several days later: "I think it was blown out of proportion, I really do. I don't blame Dawson for getting so mad. He's got a gash in his face. But first of all, these people don't know Eric. He wouldn't intentionally hurt anybody. Then, Joe Torre goes on some TV show and says Eric is a headhunter. Where does he come off saying something like that? He's basing it on some 1984 incident when he was managing the Atlanta Braves and his club and the Padres were involved in an all out beanball war. And from what I understand, Eric wasn't even in the game that day. The whole thing was ridiculous."

Bowa emerged as the star of a golden summer's day when he prevented an all out riot. Cubs pitcher Rick Sutcliffe charged the mound where he plowed into Show with his long arms extended to shoulder length. That emptied both benches and sent 26,615 Wrigley Field crazies into a frenzy. Sutcliffe's initial thrust was slowed by several players as Dawson continued to lie prone at the plate, his face dripping blood.

As Dawson climbed slowly to his knees, he decided to charge the mound himself, doing a neat impersonation of Walter Payton until he was gang tackled by a combined group of Chicago and San Diego players short of a sixty-foot, six-inch gain. Unknown to Dawson, Show was well behind the mound talking to pitching coach Galen Cisco when Dawson made his futile charge. It was Cisco who parried a second onslaught by Sutcliffe after Dawson was herded at the mound. Despite the recent friction involving Show and his teammates, several Padres came to Show's defense. Newcomer Chris Brown was standing next to Tony Gwynn when umpire Charlie Williams motioned Show toward the Padres dugout which is on the first base side of the field at Wrigley. Before Show could get there, Dawson, running with the abandon of a gored bull, made one last run at the offending pitcher. Show scampered into the dugout and Dawson, the front of his white pin-striped Cubs uniform streaked with red, was stopped from behind by Brown and Gwynn.

When the fracas was over, Dawson and Sutcliffe were ejected from the game. Dawson was taken to the hospital where he was administered a CAT scan and 24 stitches in his cheek and upper lip. Show was not ejected or even warned. But in a move which boded well for even wiser moves to come, Bowa took Show out of the game. Only an inning later, Bowa told Show to leave the ballpark. He was escorted by armed guards to the club's downtown hotel. Before Show left, he issued a statement through Padres traveling publicity man, Mike Swanson. "I apologize to the Cubs, the fans of Chicago and especially Andre Dawson," said the note scribbled in Show's own handwriting. "It was unfortunate and I'm sure I'll regret it for the rest of my life. I don't know any other words to express my feelings at this time."

Dawson didn't buy it and wouldn't accept Show's apology until he received a personal letter some days later. The fans certainly didn't buy it as they howled for the remainder of the series. Show did not emerge again in public, switching hotel rooms in his own form of covert activity. Once again, he took no phone calls. He showed his face only when the team bus left for O'Hare Airport several days later, having spent the time deep in reflection. He even received a death threat through the mail that was investigated by the FBI.

He was not around to witness the Cubs' retaliation that day during the top half of the fourth inning. He also missed Larry Bowa's finest hour in his short tenure as Padres manager. This writer, having witnessed it all from day one of spring training to this very moment, offered his observations in the Wednesday, July 8th editions of the *San Diego Tribune:*

CHICAGO—It was the kind of day that does nothing for baseball's already tarnished image. A national news story, the third-inning beaning of Andre Dawson was reported last night by Dan Rather on the CBS Evening News. It didn't receive positive coverage.

Steering a taxi along the lake front toward downtown long after the debacle, the driver offered this commentary:

"I don't like this. It doesn't make our city look good."

The cabbie could take solace. The day could have been worse—a lot worse. Chicago, San Diego and the National League office can thank one pint-sized former shortstop for putting the freeze on what could have been an all-out war. The guy is known well enough on the North Side. He played practically the final four years of his career here. He was the shortstop on the Cubs 1984 National League East titlists, the team that lost to the Padres in the playoffs. But Padres manager Larry Bowa made his best play ever for the Cubs yesterday at Wrigley Field. When the beanball battle could have ballooned completely out of control, he said no. The same guy who seems to snap at his own shadow, made all the right moves when cooler heads were needed.

"If you're the manager of a baseball team," Bowa said afterward, "whether it's your team or the other team, you don't want to see guys dropping like flies because you've made the thing into a circus."

Everyone in the ballpark knew the Cubs would retaliate in the top of the fourth inning. It was just a matter of when. Bowa didn't say anything to his team before it came to bat. He apparently had already made his decision. It didn't help tensions any that the first batter to face Greg Maddux was Chris Brown, who, in a San Fransisco Giants uniform on May 4, had his jaw splintered when St. Louis Cardinals pitcher Danny Cox lost control of a pitch. Brown walked cautiously to the plate. Maddux threw a curve. Brown bailed out with a meek swing.

"He had me," Brown said.

Brown struck out without incident. So did Tim Flannery. It lulled everyone into believing that the Cubs might not strike. Forget it. Maddux slammed Benito Santiago just above the left buttock. To his credit, the rookie catcher, bat dangling in hand, jawed briefly with Maddux, who immediately was tossed from the game. Catcher Jim Sundberg blocked Benny's path to the mound. Carmelo Martinez lumbered out of the dugout and gestured angrily toward Maddux.

"Benny was so mad," said Bowa, "he couldn't even see straight. I don't even think he knew what the score was."

Both teams took one step out of the dugout. Round 1 had been fought after Dawson was decked. Round 2 figured to be a lot worse.

It was a moment of truth for Bowa, who calmly strode up to Santiago with his hands characteristically tucked in his back pockets. He calmed the catcher down. He walked him to first base. As he returned to the dugout, he raised both hands in the air, palms out, to gesture his players back inside.

The danger was over, at least for the moment.

"Hey, I could have let Benny go. He was pretty upset," said Bowa, who also remained calm when Scott Sanderson uncorked a wild one behind Brown in the eighth inning. "Brown was worked up. I don't think you're going to solve anything like that. Let's put it this way. If you're going to play this game, you can't be intimidated. But you can't be ridiculous either."

Bowa wasn't around when all hell broke loose among the Padres and Braves on Aug. 12, 1984. Anyone who was there could tell you that yesterday's events paled in comparison.

Only 11 current Padres—nine players and two coaches—were there that day when Dick Williams did turn the game into a circus. Williams, who has been managing in the major leagues since 1967, couldn't do what the rookie manager did yesterday. Back off.

Williams let a host of Padres pitchers throw at Pascual Perez because Perez had the audacity to open the game by plunking

Alan Wiggins in the back. By the time Craig Lefferts hit Perez during the eighth inning, the day was so hot, so muggy and so damp that tempers were frayed to the boiling point. A pretty fair fight followed that encounter. And when Donnie Moore nailed Graig Nettles to open the ninth, it really became ugly.

That's when the fans entered the fray.

Can you imagine what might have happened yesterday with the maniacs in Wrigley Field already littering the field? Chaos. Utter chaos.

That day in Atlanta is still the sorriest day of baseball I've ever witnessed. I put the blame for those sordid events squarely on Williams, who was fined $10,000 and suspended for 10 days. (It should be noted, by then National League president Chub Feeney.)

For keeping the situation under control yesterday, I give Bowa all the credit . . . When Sanderson walked Gwynn on inside pitches in the fifth inning, Bowa let it slide. One pitch actually came so close, Gwynn barely skipped away. "Today is the first time in my life I've been scared to come to the plate," Gwynn said. "I'm glad I played basketball. That's the only reason I got away." Bowa also let it slide when Gwynn took another inside pitch from Sanderson during the seventh. And when Brown almost got it in the eighth, Bowa still held his ground. It's not as if Bowa didn't have his opinions. He was angry at Sanderson, but he felt Show wasn't guilty of trying to hit Dawson.

"If you're throwing at a guy's head, you don't do it like that," Bowa said. "You throw behind him because his first reaction is to snap his head back . . . Looking at the films, when you start diving over the plate like Dawson did, a pitch with movement on it has a chance of hitting you. In my mind, though, I think Sanderson was trying to hit Gwynn. But I can't read Sanderson's mind. I can't get into his head. Just like I can't get into Show's head or Maddux's head."

Perhaps the most important point of another dreadful day was that we were all given a glimpse into Bowa's head. What we discovered is that he isn't as hot-headed as he leads you to believe.

It goes without saying that Show was vilified as a demon in the Chicago papers. Particularly vicious were two pieces by *Chicago Sun-Times* columnist Ron Rapoport, who has since departed the Second City scene for the *Los Angeles Daily News*.

In the first column, Rapoport dissected Show's initial written apology.

"I sincerely regret...I have never intentionally...I was not intending...I apologize....It was unfortunate...I'm sure I'll regret...I don't know any words...You listen to this and you think, what am I stupid?"

In the second piece, Rapoport wrote: "Show, who is a mediocre pitcher and a worse liar...."

Aside from normal hometown fever, Show sensed at the time that his John Birch Society affiliation might have been a contributing factor to this bias. That affiliation had certainly come into play before. Rapoport has since denied any such bias.

Right or wrong, by Friday night's game in Pittsburgh, Show had graduated from apologetic. He was on the offensive. In several live, on-field television spots, Show made this high-brow reference to Rapoport that had never before and may never again slip from the lips of a man decked in baseball garb:

"He's an amoeba brain with cerebral ague and mental vertigo." You can look it up.

Show's next start was on the following Sunday in Pittsburgh just prior to the All-Star break. He pitched well enough, showing little effect from his week of trauma in a 4-2 loss to the Pirates. He did manage to allow another home run. A mammoth two-run blast to right by Bobby Bonilla that was the first ball to reach that region of the upper deck in Three Rivers Stadium since a Willie Stargell shot in 1970.

Admiring Bonilla's homer, Show waxed eloquent: "I hope when a guy hits a homer off me it's like that. I want to watch it, too."

After the break, with the Cubs scheduled to come into The Murph just after St. Louis, Show would do some more watching. Bowa would stack his rotation for the second half so that Show would sit against Dawson and the Cubs. Dawson was baited by San Diego fans, who for three days sat in the bleachers and hurled slanderous racial epithets at the National League's leading power hitter. But Show was not rushed into action.

"There was no reason for it," Bowa said, explaining his decision. "The only thing it would've created is a lot of problems. Time erases a lot of things. We don't face them anymore. If you can avoid it, why not? If we were in a pennant race, there's no doubt in my mind he would've pitched. But there's no sense in starting some trouble. To be honest with you, mentally, I don't think Eric can pitch against them right now. When I told him, his reaction was, 'That seems like a decent idea.' The kid has had a rough year. He has. I'm not trying to protect him. He's 4-11. He's not a 4-11 pitcher. Everyone knows that. It would be like Tony Gwynn hitting .220 right now. Compare it. That's what it would be like."

Of course, the lingering question will always remain, did Show go after him? To this day, Bowa believes he didn't. Only Show knows for sure. But much of the evidence, coupled with Show's own adamant posture, leads one to believe that there really was no overt intent. It was the last incredible incident of an incredible first half which the Padres just happened to conclude with five losses in their last six games. At the break, they were looking down the nasty gullet of a 30-58 record. And the season wasn't nearly over.

Sunday, July 19, 1987 ♦
San Diego, CA

I t wasn't bad enough that we lost the game in the 10th inning to the Cardinals today when Goose Gossage tried to fire that fastball by Jack Clark, it wasn't bad enough that it was our 60th loss of the year, but I had to answer telephone calls about it on my call-in radio show later in the day. I just can't believe some of the fans. The questions they ask. They've got to be kidding me. Clark, who is their biggest gun, parked the fastball into the seats to give the Cards a split for the four-game series. All the games were decided by one run and we could have won all four games.

The situation was this when Clark homered: There were two outs, none on and Goose was pitching great. He had a 2-and-2 count on him and had gotten there with a combination of breaking balls. Then he tried to beat him with his fastball. So this guy calls me up and asks me, "Why didn't you walk Jack Clark?"

I told him, "I'd just like to say that that's a very ignorant question. You have your opinion and I have mine. Anybody who wants to walk somebody with nobody on and two strikes on the batter has got to be crazy. Let's go to the next caller."

The next caller was even worse! He tells me: "I agree with the other caller. Why didn't you walk Jack Clark?"

So I just about lost it. I was livid. I said, "There are some people out there who think they know baseball. Let them call and ask stupid questions. Maybe I should give them stupid answers ...That just shows me how much they know about baseball. That's why they're there and we're at the professional end of it. I don't mind getting second guessed, but at least second guess in a situation that merits it. There's not even any merit behind that.

I'll take my chances anytime of the day with Jack Clark. Today, Clark won. Next time we go to St. Louis, Goose is liable to win. Next caller."

I mean, those kind of questions are hard for me to understand. I guess I'm always going to get upset by stupid questions. I just hope the rest of the season is better than the first part. I've never been through anything like this. I've been through losing streaks and stuff. But the inconsistencies are about the worst part of it. It's just the little things. Like last weekend in Pittsburgh, Randy Ready slides by the bag and gets tagged out. We lose a big inning. Jimmy Jones walks a number eight hitter. How many times have we done that? Nobody thinks anything of it. I don't think it registers in our guys' minds. I'm serious.

It was just like that game in Chicago the day after Eric Show hit Andre Dawson. Lance McCullers walks Manny Trillo and then Jim Sundberg hits a grand slam. We wind up blowing a 7-0 lead. If you walk him by just missing, it's understandable. But the pitches weren't even close. A quality relief pitcher can't do that. You know he didn't do it on purpose, but it's hard to digest. I think the difference between good baseball teams and baseball teams that struggle is inconsistency. You have no idea from day to day what you're going to see on a particular night. I've learned that real quick.

The one guy who is making great strides and I'm beginning to look at differently now is Benny, my rookie catcher Benito Santiago. He has come on a lot in the last month. Defensively, there's no comparison between April and now. And hitting, he's really starting to do more than I ever expected. The other night, he goes up there against the Pirates and the guy who is pitching makes him look sick on breaking balls. He comes back to the dugout after striking out and I say, "Benny, until you get two strikes, you've got to look for that pitch. You've got to look for it." So he goes up there the next time and he almost breaks his neck swinging at the first pitch—another breaking ball. I think to myself, "Damn, we just talked about that."

He steps back in there and he gets another one, but this time he was looking for it. He hits a home run. That's a bright moment because you know he's getting there. It's slow, but he's getting there. It's a breakthrough. You figure all is not lost. Stuff like that stands out in your mind when you lose. The only thing I've got to do with him during the second half is I've got to rest him. He's tired. I would have rested him this weekend but the Cardinals base runners would have been all over the place. You can tell he's tired. He's not that big. The heat is killing him right now. He looks like a POW. Take a look at him when he takes off his uniform. His chest is sunken.

The only thing we'd really like to do in the second half is see the younger kids start to improve. If they don't, then you have to start to wonder—maybe it's going to take awhile. If they progress like Benny's progressed, I would be happy. The big thing to watch is Mark Grant and Jimmy Jones. If they can come on and pitch good, I think we'll be in decent shape. If those two guys can pitch, we've got two guys who we can put right down on the drawing board for next year, for the next five years. That's the key to me if this team is going to be real competitive or not next year. If those two guys fall flat on their faces, you've got question marks.

That is, with the exception of Eric Show. Maybe Ed Whitson will have another good year, you never know. And Andy Hawkins is having trouble with his right shoulder. There may be some tendinitis in there. We're probably going to have to put him on the disabled list. When he'll be back, who knows? Storm Davis, hell, he might be out the rest of the year with that rib cage injury. I mean, Goose was out with the same thing for six weeks. He's getting better, but better and pitchable are two different things. To me, if you get him going along with Jones and Grant, now you have three young guys out there with pretty good live arms. Can they pitch? I don't know. That's what we have to find out. If they can pitch, you're starting spring training way ahead of the game with three real good arms comin' in. If they can't pitch, we're in trouble. I like Grant, though, in San Francisco they said he had a weird head. They kept bouncing him from the bullpen to the starting rotation. They did the same thing with Mark Davis. That plays games with a guy's mind. My philosophy is, give a guy a job and let him go out there and do it. Don't keep jacking him around. That bouncing back and forth works great when you're near first place like the Giants are because guys will listen to you then. That's why as soon as a ballclub starts to fall, the manager of that club is going to have problems. Hell, they put Mike Krukow in the bullpen over there. A kid like Grant figures, if you can yank a guy who has won 20 games, then you can do it to anybody. I like Grant's attitude. He's got that buzz haircut. He came in the first day and said, "I'm very easy going. I like to have a good time. But when it comes to baseball, when it's my day to start, I'm all business. This is my livelihood. I have to succeed and do well to benefit. It's no joke out there when I take the mound. I pick my spots as far as having a good time. There's time to be serious, there's time to have fun. But when it comes to having a good time, I don't cheat myself. There's nothing wrong with good, clean fun."

If he really can do that, he's my kind of kid. And so far, I haven't seen anything to tell me that he isn't.

I like all the guys we got in the trade from the Giants. They all look like they can play. It's too bad, because any time you make a trade of that magnitude it's going to disrupt things whether it's a bad trade or a good trade, especially when it happens during the middle of the season. It's all a matter of personalities. You've got new ones comin' in and old ones leavin'. Dave Dravecky was well-liked. Right now, these new kids are probably feeling uncomfortable. That happens anytime you go into a new environment. Among the people who are left, an uneasiness starts stirring. Guys figure, if they can trade a quality pitcher like Dravecky, why can't they trade me?

I said right from the beginning that you're not going to be able to judge this trade from our end of it based on one year alone. The guys that went to San Francisco, they've got to help them win the pennant right now. If they do, then it will be a successful deal for them. For us, you've got Chris Brown coming back from that broken jaw. And he had that off-season surgery to repair the torn tendon in his shoulder—the same operation Steve Garvey just had—and he missed just about all of spring training. I told him to forget about his hitting and just come in and play. I said, "Don't worry about your batting average. Just get yourself acclimated." The jury is going to be out on him for awhile. For me, I think the first half gave me a chance to grow a lot as a manager. I've learned a lot. I'm not saying I'm there by any means. I've still got a long way to go. But I think I've gotten much better dealing with people. Little problems, I think I've learned how to deal with them better. I still get angry, but it's in a different way. I've come to realize that it's up to the players. You can make all the moves you want, but it's up to the players. And if you alienate the players, you're not gonna get anything.

In my mind now, I know I can help turn this around. I don't see how they expect it to be turned around in 162 games, not with as many changes as we've made. That's the point I'm trying to make. I can see if we made one change with a guy here or a guy there, but we've made changes that have affected the whole baseball world. I mean, let's be honest, with the exception of a few veterans, we don't have too many household names on this team.

I would like to have an opportunity here because we started at ground level. I'd hate to go through all these frustrations and have some new guy come in next year and say, "This wasn't that bad a team."

I know I've made my mistakes. Maybe my biggest was trying to rush Joey Cora. That was my decision. You come to the park one day and you see the physical skills. Then the next day the physical skills are still there, but up pops four mental mistakes that just kill you. I mean, they crucify you. Yeah, that was probably my biggest mistake. In all fairness to him, maybe Joey should have gone straight to triple-A.

It just seems like there's something missing from our entire team make-up. The killer instinct isn't there. We're like a fighter who doesn't know how to put another team away. Maybe that's our problem. We've got a bunch of people who are pretty nice guys and when they put the uniform on, it doesn't matter whether they beat you or not. You can't change personalities. That's the point I'm trying to make. You cannot change personalities. I could scream. Jack McKeon could scream. Chub Feeney could scream. But it's got to come from within. Tim Flannery has that type of attitude. When he puts the uniform on he's going to try to beat you any way he can. Once he takes the uniform off, hey, it's over with. But when that uniform is on man, he's doin' everything he can to beat you. Goose is like that. You sure as hell know he was more upset than anyone about the homer he gave up to Jack Clark.

That's the way you're supposed to play the game. That's the way I played the game.

WEDNESDAY, JULY 29, 1987 ◆
CINCINNATI, OH

I f Larry Bowa was making an effort to calm down since the team had begun to play better ball, it still was not really evident. The Padres had just lost 15-5 to the Cincinnati Reds and Bowa was on a belated rampage. He tried to wait this one out. He really did. Reporters went into his office for a post-game chat several times. On their third visit, Bowa could not keep it to himself any longer. "Twenty guys will go through walls for me and, frankly, four others don't care..." Bowa said.

Months later, Bowa qualified the statement: "Maybe the words 'don't care' are wrong. I thought there were four guys whose attitudes were on a different level than the rest of the team. They're at the stage of their careers where their attitudes aren't going to change. When you're bringing up a lot of kids who see that, it's not helpful to your program. It has a tremendous effect on them. I don't have to mention any names. I'm sure those guys know who they are too."

It was evident that Bowa was upset with Storm Davis and Chris Brown because of nagging injuries. Bowa also ripped Eric Show, who allowed six runs and eight hits in two and a third innings. During the third inning with the Padres trailing 4-0, Show approached Bowa in the dugout to ask him whether or not he should take his time at bat. Bowa snapped. He openly wondered whether Show was displaying a "bad attitude." The action indicated to Bowa that the embattled Show wanted out of the game.

"How in the world he can draw that conclusion is amazing," Show said. "I mean, I've been taken out of the game before, having given up fewer runs than that."

The next day, Bowa explained his reaction: "I'm just saying

that's the impression you get as a manager. He might have been just doing it out of courtesy, but I'm just saying what a manager would think. I thought I might have overreacted, so I asked Pete Rose what his reaction would be. He said the same thing—he'd think the guy wants out of there."

It would not be the last time Show and Bowa would exchange caustic words in print before they settled their differences during a lengthy one-on-one meeting during the club's final trip to New York. Bowa ultimately respected the pitcher whose numbers were far below his capabilities. But for now, the flack was still flying.

"Larry says things to me different from what he says to other people," Show said. "I think that what he does sometimes is, he's frustrated like we all are and he'll think about isolated incidents that he can single out as a reason for why generally we're going bad. . . . Larry is a good baseball man and knows the game. I hold no anger toward him. I just wish he would confront me one time and tell me what's on his mind.

"I think you ought to figure out what you're deep down dissatisfied with and try to help the problem, rather than scream about something to try to give your argument some validity. And if you notice, he also has individuals he likes to single out, who usually are safe for him to do that with."

Interestingly enough, one of those supposed individuals, who just happened to have left the club in the July 4th Massacre, decided to take his own shots at Bowa on the very same night. On the other side of the country where the San Francisco Giants were playing the Dodgers in Los Angeles, Kevin Mitchell spoke out about his relationship with Bowa.

"Really, I could never understand his baseball," said Mitchell. "I think he scared a lot of people over there with all his screaming and yelling. When I grew up, I wasn't the kind of person who was too easily intimidated. Larry didn't intimidate me. But we really didn't talk. Just a few words back and forth. As far as I'm concerned, we really didn't get along."

It wasn't the first or last time Mitchell would blast Bowa to anybody who would listen. To an insider, it seemed strange that

Mitchell would pin his San Diego failure on Bowa. Bowa had protected him from public ridicule when Mitchell was frequently traveling back and forth from San Diego to Yuma during spring training and he had helped bail him out of all the potential trouble with the customs agents in Montreal. But the diatribes never really seemed to bother Bowa. "I can't worry about criticism like that," Bowa said. "You're gonna get criticized no matter what you do."

In any event, Bowa was having enough problems with players currently on his own team. He had come to a stalemate with pitcher Storm Davis about how his re-entry from the disabled list should be handled. Davis, who had been out for a month with torn cartilage in his rib cage, had suggested to Bowa that when he was ready to return, he would work himself back in shape out of the bullpen. Instead, Bowa wanted him to take a rehabilitative demotion to the minor leagues for several starts. Davis, who had to grant permission for that move to occur, was balking at the suggestion.

After pitching a pair of simulated games, Davis decided that he wasn't really ready to pitch yet. That left Bowa scratching his head. The matter was eventually resolved when Davis agreed to make two minor-league starts, the first for the Padres Class AA club in Wichita and the second for their single-A club in Reno. He was not impressive in either outing and Bowa's decision to reactivate him as a reliever anyway eventually led to Davis' split with the club.

As far as Chris Brown was concerned, he was in the process of missing 15 consecutive starts because of an injured left wrist. Brown claimed he had originally sustained the injury before leaving San Francisco when Giants batting coach Jose Morales inadvertently hit him in the wrist with a pitch during batting practice just a day before the trade. The Giants would not substantiate that claim.

Brown evidently re-injured the same wrist just after the All-Star game when, in a game against the Chicago Cubs in San Diego, he dove for a grounder off the bat of Keith Moreland. Teammates had been surprised by Brown's injuries before.

"The craziest injury I ever heard of," said pitcher Mark Grant, who was Brown's teammate both in San Francisco and San Diego, "was one spring when a guy missed a week because he said he slept on his eye. I don't think I have to tell you who that was, do I?"

The situation hadn't gone unnoticed to Bowa, who was trying all kinds of psychological means to reach the 25-year-old third baseman, who obviously has the physical talent to be a force in the National League for the next decade if he ever recognizes his ability. Bowa tried calling him in for meetings. He tried ignoring him. He tried penciling him into the lineup and he tried leaving him out of the lineup until Brown asked back in. It was a perplexing problem.

"There's no doubt he's taken a beating from his teammates," Bowa said. "I mean guys have gotten on him about calling him a jake. It's been rough. But he's dealt with it. He's a very complicated and sensitive person to get to know. When you talk to him one on one he seems like he's sincere and he wants to do well. Physically, I really think the guy can play. But if you're not mentally involved in the game, if there's something bothering you mentally, it's going to show up out there."

For his part, Brown admitted playing at about 60 percent of his physical capability because of the wrist injury and backlash from the Danny Cox pitch that shattered his jaw. Brown also admitted anticipating a quick end to the season. That turned out to be a self-fulfilling prophecy when former teammate Mike Krukow fractured his right hand with another pitch late in the season. For Chris Brown, 1987 was quite a year.

"I got traded," he said. "I got hit in the jaw. I had shoulder surgery. Then there's my wrist. It has just been one of those years. My 1987 hasn't been the greatest. I hope '88 is a better year. It can't help but be a better year, barring injuries."

That left the dubious matter of who actually were the four deviant players Bowa fingered in his tirade.

General manager Jack McKeon, who has been through enough managerial wars, had his own theory: "It's almost August. I would be surprised if there was one manager in the big leagues who wasn't down on at least four of his players right now. It's part of the territory when you have 24 guys for six months. When Dick Williams was managing here, he'd be ticked off at four different guys every single week."

To this day, Bowa says he has not divulged the list to anyone. As Bowa is so fond of saying, the players evidently know who they are.

TUESDAY, AUG. 11, 1987 ♦ SAN DIEGO, CA

Y ou just never know when this club is going to go on a roll. We just won our seventh in a row tonight. We scored a run in the bottom of the ninth on Benito Santiago's single and we beat the Braves. That's 10 wins in our last 12 games. God, May seems like a lifetime away. The strange thing is, because of the deep hole we put ourselves into we're still 21 games under .500. We're still in last place, but now at least we're just three and a half games out of fifth instead of 14 out. If you ask me, that's pretty remarkable. I still don't believe we've turned the corner, but since June 4 when we hit that 12-42 mark, we've won 34 games. That's not too bad.

If somebody had to ask me right now what the difference is, I'd have to say that we've done pretty well since the trade. We're starting to develop a cohesiveness on the club that just wasn't evident during most of the first half of the season.

I think the two guys in the bullpen—Mark Davis and Keith Comstock—have done a good job for us. They've really helped solidify the relief staff. Mark Grant has shown signs. Right now he might not be pitching the way he's capable of pitching, but I think he's pressing. I like his arm. He's just trying to win six games in one start and you can't do that. He's trying to make perfect pitches instead of just letting it happen. I've seen that kid pitch in triple-A, and though I know that's not the same as pitching up here, he's always had great stuff. I like his make up. I think he's going to be a good pitcher and I know he can help us. Chris Brown, like I've said all along, let him play and forget about what he hits. We can't worry about where his batting average ends up this year because of the injuries he's had. But I would like to see him play the rest of the year and start the season brand new in February. I think he can really help us. Right now, if you looked at the trade straight up, it's definitely in favor of the Giants. But I think when you're looking long range, I'm convinced more now than I was when we made the deal that it's gonna help us. That is, if these guys do what they're supposed to do. There's no guarantee, of course.

I think all the trades we made since I came here last winter—Kevin McReynolds to the Mets, Terry Kennedy to Baltimore, and the Giants trade—I think the other team has benefited for the moment. For today. But I think in the long run, we're going to benefit from them. I'm not saying that it's not going to help those teams. We gave up some quality people in Dave Dravecky and McReynolds. We gave up some quality names. McReynolds is having a real good season, but I think Stanley Jefferson is starting to play the way we expected him to play. We don't know about Shawn Abner, but he's doing things we expected of him in triple-A. And so at the end of that trade, we got Brown instead of Kevin Mitchell. But it cost us Dave Dravecky. So who knows?

I don't think losing Dravecky hurt us that much, really. Our starting rotation hasn't been all that stable lately, but it wasn't really stable back then. Dave threw some good games for us. But we still need a guy who can go out there every fifth day and I can say, "If we get one or two runs, we have a chance of winning." That's not to say that Grant or Jimmy Jones or Eric Nolte, that kid we brought up from double-A when we put Andy Hawkins on the disabled list, who won in Houston in his first major-league appearance, can't develop into something like that. To me, our most consistent pitcher is Ed Whitson. He's given us good quality starts all year.

With Dravecky, he had those elbow problems coming off last year and we had to put him in the bullpen at the start of the season because he really wasn't ready. His elbow didn't come around until right before the trade. In June. He started pitching well in June. Everyone started pitching well in June. When you look back on it, we had five guys going pretty well for a while. And all five were veteran pitchers. Then Storm Davis went down, Hawkins went down, and we traded Dravecky. We went from a veteran rotation to a young rotation all in a matter of weeks. The only thing that's bad about the young guys is that on any given day, you don't know what to expect when they go out there. It could be a shutout, it could be three innings, it could be eight innings, it could be five innings. That's youth. That's something I've got to learn to live with.

But I'm telling you, if I was the general manager of this team, I still would make that trade today. The only guy I wouldn't have wanted to give up was Dravecky. Chris Brown to me is a big-league third baseman. I know he hasn't had a Chris Brown type year, but to me, for us to get Chris Brown, we had to give up Dave Dravecky. You're not going to get Chris Brown for Craig Lefferts. You're not going to get Chris Brown for Mitchell.

All three of them are doing well up there. Dravecky and Lefferts are pitching good and Mitchell is hitting the hell out of the ball. Really, I've always thought Kevin Mitchell had talent, but I think his environment is the reason he didn't play well in San Diego. The fact that a lot of his friends were around him all the time. I mean, guys in the clubhouse, they're right outside my office in San Diego, you could hear them say to him, "How many hours of sleep did you get last night, two?" I think he felt he had to accommodate his family and he failed to take care of himself, basically, as far as rest goes. Even so, he was starting to hit the ball pretty well when he was traded. Three days before the deal came down, he hit two home runs for us in a game at L.A.

I think this trade, for us, is gonna work out if we can get Chris Brown five hundred at bats next year. I really do. Some people may think that it's all up to Chris Brown. It's all in his head. But it isn't all up to him. Some injuries can't be helped. Let's face it, the man has got a nasty scar on his left shoulder from surgery. I mean, it's nasty. Then he has the wrist. Those things right there, those are nasty ailments, boy. He has a lot of talent, you just wish he could play through a little more pain. But one thing I've learned, and I've talked to some people I respect, no one knows pain tolerance except the individual himself. You know what I'm saying? Something that hurts you, may not hurt me. Maybe something that hurts me might not hurt you. It's very difficult to say, "If I had his injury, I'd be playing."

I used to think that, I did. I used to be too critical, even when I played. When guys wouldn't play I'd say, "What the hell? Get the bleep out there and play. You're not hurt." Only that person knows if he's hurting. You can get a psychologist, you can get anybody, but that person is the only one who could tell you. If he can't go, he can't go. As a manager, you've got to learn to live with that. You may not like it, but you've got to learn to live with it because that's the facts. Brown's pain resistance could be higher than mine. It might be lower than mine. Everybody's pain tolerance is different.

I think if this were a fair and equal world and baseball salaries were in line with the rest of the society, nobody would complain about it. But I think when you're making $300,000 a year, people are going to wonder if they're getting their money's worth. Aside from what the player says, the only thing that trainers and managers have to go on is X-rays. Chris Brown had a bone scan on his wrist and it really didn't reveal anything. But if the man says he's hurt, he's hurt. Last year in San Francisco, it's my understanding that the team doctors couldn't find anything wrong with his shoulder. And everyone, from the club president down to the bat boy, thought Brown was pulling some crap. Finally, he goes to his own doctor and they find that tear in his shoulder tendon. That had to shut everybody up. Who's to say what is right? You can't look the man in the face and tell him he's lying if he says he's hurt. I've learned that you can moan and groan all you want about it, but the man with the injury has got to have the final word.

Take Tim Flannery, for instance. The doctor told me that the ligaments in his foot that he injured back in May are going to be bad all year until he just completely gets off it. And here's a guy, I know he's going out there hurt. Tony Gwynn told me once that Flannery played an entire week with broken ribs after he got hit with a pitch. Just got it taped up, didn't tell anybody and went out there and played. I believe it. Tony Gwynn has been hurt a couple of times. Even now, his legs aren't right. Randy Ready, there's a kid who's playing under tremendous pressure. His wife is a paraplegic. He has a bunch of little kids. That's what I call tough. Yet, he goes out there whenever I ask him and he busts his butt.

The point that I'm trying to make to most of the players is that maybe you are only 70 percent, but your 70 percent is better than the guy I'm throwing out there in your place who is 100 percent. Sure, it would be great to play this game at 100 percent, there's no doubt in my mind. I wish I could've played every game when I felt great. But it just doesn't happen. Not when you play day in and day out.

TUESDAY, AUG. 18, 1987 ◆
PHILADELPHIA, PA

T he inevitable had finally occurred. Storm Davis wanted out of San Diego. Fresh off the disabled list after nearly seven weeks of recuperation from that rib cage injury, Davis made his declaration in the visitor's dugout at Veterans Stadium while the Philadelphia Phillies took batting practice.

"If it's at all possible, I'd like to be traded," a solemn Davis said. "The way they're handling me makes me feel like I'm not in their plans, either now, or for next season. That's the way I read it. I told them in Atlanta two weeks ago that I was fine and I would work out of the bullpen until I was ready. They insisted that I go down to the minors for two rehabilitative appearances. I didn't want to go, but I went down there to prove to them that I was ready to pitch.

"I've never said anything like this before. I never wanted out of Baltimore, but I want out of here. I have nothing against my teammates or the city of San Diego. I have nothing against Jack McKeon or Larry Bowa, for the most part. I'm just not comfortable here."

After months of sparring, the lines had finally been drawn. Davis had never felt comfortable in the National League where he resisted making the adjustments to pitching in a lower strike zone. Unlike Eric Show, his closest friend on the team, Davis never seemed capable of communicating with Bowa. Bowa was unable to understand the rationale of a baseball player whose top priority didn't seem to be succeeding at his career. On several occasions, both Davis and former teammate Dave Dravecky had revealed their philosophy of life: baseball was, in fact, third in line behind their religious convictions and their families. During the National League Championship Series, after Dravecky pitched a two-hitter against the St. Louis Cardinals to win Game 2, San Francisco Giants manager Roger Craig made note in the postgame media briefing that anyone who deemed Christian athletes docile was sadly mistaken.

"They say Christians don't have any guts, well he's got a lot," Craig said about Dravecky.

Dravecky had long ago taken exception to the "gutless" typecasting of Born Again Christian athletes.

"I don't ever want to hear that the Christian athlete is a wimp," Dravecky had said. "I consider it to be the saddest thing when people say that as soon as a Christian athlete is injured, he just gives up. Nothing is further from the truth."

That was during spring training when Dravecky was struggling to return to form from elbow tendinitis. After the playoff win, Dravecky punctuated his convictions: "The only audience I have is Jesus Christ. As long as I please him, I'm pleased." Evidently along the way, Dravecky had also pleased Roger Craig. The entire religious question in baseball is a matter Bowa had pondered at length:

"Mental toughness is so important in baseball," Bowa said. "I think religion is an individual thing. Obviously, when you're on a baseball field, you believe in God, you believe in all your beliefs, but you're out there for one reason: To beat the other team. Like there's no way you can go out on the field and worry about other things. There's no way. Don't get me wrong, I'm not saying you're a jerk because you care about your family. I'm saying that during that two-and-a-half hour period, there shouldn't be another thing on your mind except baseball. Of course, there's going to be some isolated incidents. If your baby is sick, your wife is sick, sure you're going to worry.

"But I'm saying, if everyone is healthy at home, when you're out on that bleepin' field, there should be nothing else you're thinking about except how to beat the other team. Now, the last out of the game is over, you sit back and say I gave it my best shot. Now, all the rest of your priorities come back into play. My family, my religion is first, baseball might be fifth or sixth. But once you're on the field, if baseball is not your top priority, you're cheatin' yourself. That's how I played the game. And that doesn't mean that I don't love my wife. That doesn't mean that I don't love my daughter, my mom, my dad. That I don't love my God.

"When I was on the field for two and a half hours, I was trying to do one thing: beat the hell out of the other team any way I could. Once the game was over, I could say I gave it everything I had. Now, let's get back to the real world. If every guy had that approach, you wouldn't have to have clubhouse meetings to fire guys up."

This is not to say that the split between Davis and the Padres was solely based on religion. It was more a matter of Storm's inability to cope with failure and convey those pent up frustrations clearly to management. Davis, after all, had played for more volatile managers than Larry Bowa. He had been on a Baltimore team managed by Earl Weaver, an all-timer for spit, guts and sarcastic remarks. Part of the problem was that Davis never wanted to leave Baltimore. It was the Orioles who gave up on him.

"I could get along with Earl, but I couldn't get along with Larry," Davis said. "I could talk to Earl. He had a pretty open mind. It seems like every time I go in to talk to Larry, he has his mind made up. He doesn't listen to a word I say. It's a waste of time. I haven't seen eye to eye with Larry on a lot of things this year. About the way he has handled me and the way he's handled a lot of guys. I'm not going to get into who I'm talking about because I'm really only concerned about myself. Larry jumped on me publicly the second week I was here. Something about me not living up to my expectations. And that was the second week of spring training.

"We've had two team meetings and I've been vicariously mentioned at both of them as one of the guys who was jaking it or didn't want to play. He never mentioned me personally, but I felt like I was one of the guys he was talking about. I've never discussed it with him. I didn't want to. He made his point perfectly clear. He just happened to say it in front of my peers—all my teammates."

Just 11 days later, Davis received his wish. He was traded back to the American League, to the Oakland Athletics, the team of this childhood dreams. In return, the Padres received pitcher Dave Leiper, a left-hander of little distinction, and first baseman Rob Nelson, who had vanished into the Oakland system behind the explosive emergence of Mark McGwire. Putting it all together, it meant that the Padres had actually traded veteran catcher Terry Kennedy and pitcher Mark Williamson, a reliever who had shown some promise this season with the Orioles, for Leiper and Nelson. Davis was a brutal 2-7 with a 6.18 ERA in 21 appearances during his short, pathetic tenure with the Padres. He walked 86 batters in 63 innings.

The entire Storm Davis affair left a sour taste in everyone's mouth. Larry Bowa, who did not appreciate being made the scapegoat for Davis' problems, was particularly miffed.

"What happened to my relationship with Storm? I just think it was a combination of things," Bowa said. "Maybe Storm was right, I didn't use him right. I just thought it was an injustice to the guys who were pitching to throw him into the rotation when he came back from the injury. At the time, I think our starters were doing a pretty good job. Not great, but they were keeping their heads above water. He felt I didn't have confidence in him, and at one time, it was tough to let him go out there when he was gonna walk everybody. He was having trouble throwing strikes. Then, when I brought him in from the bullpen, he didn't do well. His big deal there was, 'I can't pitch out of the bullpen.'

"He said I was on his butt from day one, but I don't know why. I put him in the rotation the first day. Some guys, to me...He's very immature. He was pampered around here more so than anyone else. I think if you analyze it, if you ask the guys on the team, there weren't too many guys who were unhappy to see him leave. That's how I base it. If there are 23 guys on the team, or 20 guys, or even 15 guys, who are saying, "Oh man, that's a mistake," then maybe I did do something wrong. But when you have 20 or 21 guys doing back flips because he left...I don't consider that to be a mistake.

"The point I'm trying to make is, maybe I didn't get the right perspective on it. But watching guys' reactions when they found out he got traded, I knew I did the right thing."

In essence, the trade of Davis completed the purge of players Larry Bowa really did not want on his team. The weeding out process had begun in February, and through either injury or trade, the strong had indeed survived. Weeks after the deal, Davis, a thoughtful man, seemed to have put his San Diego experience into proper perspective.

"In retrospect, maybe it wasn't all Larry's fault," Davis said. "If I had it to do all over again, maybe I should have been the one to force open the lines of communication. Maybe I should have gone to him."

SATURDAY, AUG. 22, 1987 ◆ NEW YORK, NY

I t took almost an entire season, but tonight Larry Bowa finally won an argument with an umpire. Oddly enough, the discussion came a night after he had been thrown out of a game by the same crew for the second time in this tumultuous season. The dispute came on a zany play in the eighth inning. The Padres were on their way to an 8-3 win over the defending champion New York Mets—San Diego's second win at Shea Stadium in as many nights. Goose Gossage was on the mound, and with one out, he gave up a pair of singles to bring Darryl Strawberry to the plate. Strawberry foul tipped a ball off home plate that ricocheted to the backstop. The late Dick Stello, the home-plate umpire, immediately signaled foul, called time out, and handed catcher Benito Santiago a new ball.

Dead play, right? Wrong!

"He showed foul ball and then handed Benny the ball," Bowa recalled. "Then he actually took it back and tossed it to Goose. The runner was running from the outset. That's what got Stello confused."

Before the play was over, Gossage found himself holding two baseballs. Tim Teufel, who had been waved around by third base coach Sam Perlozzo, seemed to have scored all the way from second base. And Stello was standing there completely befuddled. Bowa stalked out of the dugout, but by the time he could yank his hands out of the back pockets of his trousers, his argument was won.

Here's what happened: When Stello saw Teufel streaking around from second base, he somehow neglected his own call and jumped out of the way to allow Santiago room to race to the backstop—which Santiago certainly did. There, Benny retrieved the original foul tipped baseball which had yet to be collected by the Mets' ball boys. Remember, if you will, that this all happened in a matter of seconds.

"Benny went back and got the ball," Bowa said. "At the same time, Goose had a ball in his glove and there was a ball at the backstop. I don't think I've ever seen anything like that before. I went out there to ask Stello what had actually happened. He conferred with the other umpires who told him that he had originally called a foul ball. That's when he sent the runners back." That's also when the Mets' Davey Johnson rushed the field and wound up protesting the game. To no avail, of course.

Said Stello, failing to share any more information about his indecision: "I called it foul right away, then I got confused for some reason."

Ironically, it was Stello who had issued Bowa his third ejection of the year right here on May 20 for arguing a call at first base. And it was Steve Rippley, a vacation substitute in the same crew, who had run Bowa just the night before—the rookie manager's first ejection in three months. On that one, Bowa admonished Rippley, the plate umpire, for not issuing Mets pitcher Ron Darling a warning after he threw a pitch over the head of John Kruk.

Bowa claims he harbors no ill-feelings toward any umpire after a confrontation. He says he admired Stello.

"I thought he was a really good umpire," Bowa said. "He was dedicated. I used to play golf with him a lot in Florida when I lived there during the winters. He's gonna be missed in the game. He had a lot of friends. He was one of those guys who could argue with you on Sunday and then on Monday, he'd approach you like nothing ever happened. There are some umpires, whether they want to admit it or not, who hold grudges. They don't want to look like they're being friendly with someone they just kicked out. Dick was never like that. Dick never took it personally. Some guys do. I have never taken an umpire's call personally. When a guy runs me out of a game, nine times out of ten, there's a good chance I've deserved to get kicked out. Either because I used foul language or I've stayed out there too long.

"Dick's death was a tragedy for the game."

Although Bowa's on-field run-ins with umpires—from childhood through professional ball—are legendary, he really was pretty subdued on that front during his first year as manager. For him.

"I think I really controlled myself," Bowa said.

Though he was run five times in all, a number which may seem excessive, he was ejected just two times during the final four months of the season. The fifth ejection came on September 24 against the Reds in Cincinnati when he contested a called third strike on Santiago. Bowa actually survived the argument, but he was tossed after the fact by first base umpire Dave Pallone when Bowa, standing in front of the bench, made a gyrating pelvic motion indicating to the umpires that his ballclub was being screwed.

For the record, Bob Engel, Dana DeMuth, Dick Stello, Steve Rippley and Dave Pallone had the honor of running Bowa during his first year as a big-league manager. But no major-league umpire could rival the trio of 1986 ejections issued by Pam Postema in Bowa's only year managing in the Pacific Coast League. None of Bowa's more recent incidents matched the comic relief of his final toss by Postema, who claimed in a report to the league office that Bowa spit at her as he walked to the mound.

"I was just rubbing up the ball," Bowa was reported to have said at the time. A year later, Bowa said with a devilish grin: "I rolled off a string of curse words, and every time I swore, spit came flying out of my mouth."

Actually, Bowa's most interesting confrontation with an umpire this past season came in an exchange off the field that didn't even involve the umpire. Rather, it involved some correspondence between Bowa and National League president Bart Giamatti about the umpire. The incident occurred during the fourth inning of a late-season 2-1 win in Houston and transpired innocently enough. With Randy Ready on second, Benito Santiago on first and one out, Shawn Abner hit what appeared to be a routine single to center. Except, on its journey into the outfield, the ball struck one umpire of extremely wide girth. (Names will be withheld to protect the innocent.) At the time of the obstruction, Ready was about to score and Santiago was on his way to third. But according to the rules, the ball was immediately signaled dead. Abner was awarded his single, but both runners were sent back a base, negating a Padres run and loading the bases for Garry Templeton, who promptly grounded into an inning-ending double play. Bowa was infuriated, but instead of wasting his wrath on the field, he took pen in hand and wrote Giamatti. According to Bowa, the correspondence went something like this:

"In last night's game, an incident came up that really disturbed me. One of your umpires failed to get out of the way of a ball that was not hit that hard. That literally cost us two runs. If my team was in a pennant race, they would have had to carry me off the field. I would appreciate it if you would continue to emphasize conditioning and weight programs for certain umpires." The letter was dutifully signed, Larry Bowa, manager of the San Diego Padres.

Giamatti's response was swift and to the point: "You worry about managing your players. I'll worry about the physical condition of my umpires."

Strangely enough, Giamatti had stated earlier in the year that he was unhappy with the extra weight being carred by certain umpires, particularly John McSherry and Eric Gregg. He then instructed the umpires to become involved in weight loss and physical training programs. After the season, at the winter meetings held this past December in Dallas, Bowa encountered Giamatti at the Lowes Anatole Hotel.

"He told me not to worry," Bowa said. "He's working on the umpires and their conditioning."

Bowa seemed to have driven his point home with the new tactic. Perhaps it wasn't as esoteric as former Padres manager Steve Boros marching to home plate and handing umpire Charlie Williams a video tape of a contested play in the previous night's game, but it worked. That play involved Boros' only ejection as a manager and the only toss of Steve Garvey's 17-year career.

In the letter writing instance, Bowa showed the type of maturity that club president Chub Feeney is hoping to see more of during the 1988 season.

"Larry's nature is Larry's nature," said Feeney, who as league president surveyed more than one umpire's report with shortstop Larry Bowa's name on it. "He's a maturing man at the moment. He just has to get himself in the mindset at times that he controls his anger, so it's a controlled anger, not an uncontrolled anger. There's no reason not to get angry. People always get angry. It's the way you get angry that's important."

Bowa wasn't there yet, but he was learning.

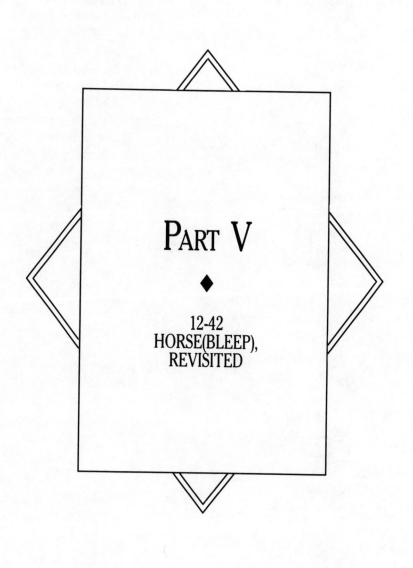

PART V

◆

12-42
HORSE(BLEEP),
REVISITED

SUNDAY, SEPT. 6, 1987 ◆
ST. LOUIS, MO

❖I❖ 've been reading all the stuff and listening to the fans about how we've turned it around. I think we're a lot better than we were, yeah, but I think people can't overreact when we beat second division teams. When we play some good teams, like when we played the New York Mets and St. Louis Cardinals recently, we still show some weaknesses. We don't make the pitch when we have to. We don't come up with the key hit. What have we just lost, five out of six to those guys? We played them pretty well in most of those games, but the bottom line is, we didn't win, did we? I think the ability is there. But we still have to get the experience and go through things. We haven't really played under pressure all year. From the beginning of the season, we've been out of it. So I don't know how these guys can say, "We're uptight." They're in a pennant race, not us. The pressure should be on them. Here we are 20 games out. I wonder how our guys would react if we were two or three out? And when that happens, that'll be a whole different set of circumstances for this team. We'll go through this whole growing process again. That's the amazing part about it.

Somebody asked me if we were going bad again. Yeah, we are. But you have to consider the teams we're playing. Those guys out here this weekend, they're basically playing for $100,000 in postseason money and the pride and the ring. We're playing to try and get out of the basement. And no matter how good athletes are, mentally, that's a big difference. You lose four in a row to the Mets and the Cards, it's a Catch 22. You're discouraged because you didn't win one of them, but we battled them tough. You've got to be pleased with that. The Cardinals are probably the toughest team to manage against. They have all those switch-hitters. It doesn't matter what pitcher you bring in. You look at their averages, they're almost the same from either side of the plate. And Whitey Herzog has got a perfect situation in his bullpen. He has three lefties and three righties. I think Whitey Herzog is as good a manager as there is in baseball. He sets up his team so he can make all the right moves. He's got guys on his bench who can run. It's a perfect team for him. That's the kind of team I would love the Padres to be. You have all those switch-hitters, who can run. You can put a hit and run on. Let 'em steal. You have one big guy—Jack Clark—in the middle of the lineup. That's definitely my kind of baseball.

We went through a period when we played real good. But when you analyze the teams we beat, they weren't pennant contending teams. You have to put everything into perspective. We swept the Houston Astros, but if you really want to analyze it, at the time they weren't playing very well. If we had come out and beat the Mets and Cardinals three out of six or four out of six, I think we'd have a right to say, "Hey, we have improved." But as far as turning the corner, I don't think we've turned it yet. I think we've made big strides, but I think we have a long way to go.

I think for me, I saw things start to click in place when we put Tim Flannery and Randy Ready at second base. They're veterans that know how to play the game. They're very consistent. They don't make mistakes—you know the rookie things that you've got to go through.

Benny—Benito Santiago—if you really want to analyze it, we might have sent him out in April or May. That's how bad he was playing. That is, if we had another frontline catcher. But we didn't have one and we elected to stay with him and Benny turned it around. To me, he may now be the best catcher in the league. Who's better? You tell me. I don't know. I don't think there is one. We had infielders. That's why we sent Joey Cora out. I realize now that the worst thing you can do is just throw a guy like him out there. That's why, when he joins the team again for the last few weeks, Cora's situation is going to be unique. I can't throw him right in there. But I can't let him just rot on the bench. I've got to see if he has improved after all those months in the minor leagues. That was one harsh lesson I really learned—how to deal with kids like Joey Cora.

Another lesson I learned was how to deal with different personalities. People who don't happen to think like me, but have developed approaches to the game that are right for them. I don't think he's been the toughest for me to deal with, but I have to say that the toughest player for me to understand has been Eric Show. I think I might have caused that problem by putting too much pressure on him early to be our stopper—the best pitcher on our team. And when he didn't live up to it every time out; when he had a so-so outing, that would upset me. That was my fault. That wasn't fair to Eric. And Eric took a lot of things I said like I was rippin' him. I had a good talk with him a couple of weeks ago in New York and ever since then everything has been all right. Sometimes it's easy for a player to think of himself, but they've got to know where I'm coming from, too. They think I'm trying to embarrass them. They have to understand that I'm trying to worry about 24 guys and not just one. The thing that gets me most frustrated, and I've got to deal with it, is you try to make the moves that best helps your baseball team. And when it doesn't work, you look like a jerk. When it works, it's the greatest feeling in the world. You're on a natural high.

The toughest thing for me has been to deal with the pitching staff. I knew that would be my biggest problem from day one. Some days you let your starters stay in longer. When your bullpen is hot, you use them quicker. That's probably been the hardest thing for me to judge because our bullpen has been so inconsistent. You start saying, "I'll give this guy one more hitter." Pow, home run. What I've got to learn to do when the bullpen is cold like that is stay longer with the starters.

I know a few of the pitchers have questioned me openly about how I've worked the staff. I've read stuff in the papers from some of the guys who we traded out of here—Dave Dravecky, Storm Davis, Craig Lefferts. I don't mind that. I never mind taking any criticism as long as it's valid. I try to listen to everybody. The only thing I don't like is being blamed for someone else's bad year. Anybody who blames a manager for a bad year is a weak individual because the player basically has his fate in his own hands. He goes up there and swings the bat. He's the one who goes out on the mound. Occasionally, I might dictate whether a starting pitcher wins or loses a game by leaving him in or taking him out. But the everyday player, anytime he complains about who the manager is, he's not a very strong person.

You see, I've had big beefs with managers I've played with—Jim Frey for one—but you don't play for the manager. You play for the baseball team and you play for yourself. You're the guy who has to drive in the runner from third, not the manager. You're the guy who has to move the runners. You're the guy who has got to come up with a man on and get a base hit. You're the guy who has to make the right pitch or catch the ground ball.

When you start pointing fingers at other people, you're a very weak individual. But I really think we've gotten rid of most those guys already. I think for the most part, right now, we have a pretty good nucleus. There are some guys I was down on earlier in the year that I've changed on.

I'll tell you what, one of those guys is Garry Templeton. I think he's played good the second half, really. He's impressed me. He's in pain. He's playin' in a lot of pain. That's what people don't understand. He hasn't had too much luck at the plate until recently, but here's a guy who goes up there and I know that because of his knees, he's in a lot of pain.

What I've got to do with Tempy if I come back, is just watch him next year. I mean, we've got to really be careful about playing him a long period of time. You can tell how bad he's hurt by the way you see him hobbling on an airplane. Sometimes he can barely move. I admire him for going out there and playing so hurt. Here's a guy who has got a legitimate out. He can say, "Hey, man, I ain't playing. I can't even walk." He goes out there and he does it.

I know he's not hitting .270, but I'll tell you what, you take a look at all the shortstops in the league, he catches the ball as well as anybody. And that's basically what you want your shortstop to do. It just so happens on our team, we don't have a lot of hitting.

We don't score a lot of runs. So his position in the lineup is always magnified. Templeton's not hitting. That's why we're not winning. That's bull. I think if your shortstop catches a ball like he does, that's a plus. I think too many people, and I might have done it earlier in the year, put too much emphasis on his offense. Plus, he showed me something. He lost 10 pounds. He wants to come in next spring even lighter. And it's not that he's overweight. We had a talk about mid-season and I said, "Your knees are so bad, you're going to have to get lighter." The fact that he's done it shows me that he cares about doin' it. I think Tempy will be a big plus for us next year.

I've even turned it around with Jefferson. That one probably was my fault. He gave me the impression that he was just going through the motions. But getting down to talk with him made me realize that I had the wrong perceptions. He came in during the last homestand and said he wanted to talk to me.

He said, "I want to apologize to you."

I said, "For what?"

And he said, "For making it a rough year for you."

I said, "You haven't made it a rough year for me. If anything, you've been a real surprise the way you've come on and played. I like the way you're playing. And you're going out there."

And he said, "Well, you know, the argument we had in Pittsburgh. Me being on the disabled list so much. That's what I'm talking about."

I told him, "You know, there's some things you have no control over. Like hurtin' your ankle just before we broke camp. That really hurt you. A big part of your game is speed. That took six, eight weeks out of you. And the argument in Pittsburgh is ancient history."

But I think we have a better understanding now. I think he's going to be a pretty good ballplayer. Especially if he can learn to cut down on the strikeouts. And I know he's giving 100 percent, which is all I've ever asked.

I've made some mistakes. Like the Andy Hawkins thing. Whether I was right or wrong, maybe my approach was wrong. One thing about Hawk is that he has a lot of pride. Because I take a guy out of a game, he thinks I have a vendetta against him. They don't understand that at that particular time, I think a fresh arm has a better chance of getting that particular batter out. And it could backfire. Like I said, when it backfires, it makes the manager look bad. In their mind they're saying, "I knew I could have gotten him out." You know, those are just the percentages you take. That's why it's easy to second guess a manager.

There's no way a manager can have 24 guys like him. It just isn't possible. You go to Cincinnati. I guarantee you you'll have eight or nine guys who'll say they don't like Pete Rose. You've got to accept that as a manager. It's hard to accept because you want to be liked. But the bottom line isn't whether you're liked. It's whether or not they perform their jobs and perform at the intensity level they should. That's it. I still have a high intensity level even though we've been getting killed again lately. I think that's my job. If I can let them know I'm still bustin' my butt maybe it'll rub off. It's hard right now. This month is probably the hardest for me. When a team is out of it, it's difficult. But you can't worry about soothing egos. That isn't my job. To me, whatever is best for the team. It might not be good for five or six guys, but if it's good for the other 18, that's what you have to go with.

When you're winning, they put up with a little more. When you're losing, you're going to see more people complain. It's been like that whether Larry Bowa is managing or Casey Stengel is managing. That's the way the game is gonna be. I asked Pete if it was the same for him over there. He said it was the same. You have to close one eye and one ear to some things or it'll drive you crazy. When you're in first place, the unhappy players are going to keep their mouths shut. When you're in last place, the unhappy players are going to pop off. That's the nature of the game. There's nothing I'm going to be able to do about it. There's nothing nobody else is going to be able to do about it. It's never going to change.

APR. 7, 1970 ◆
PHILADELPHIA, PA

(F) rank Lucchesi and Billy DeMars were the most influential baseball people during the formative stages of Larry Bowa's career. Lucchesi, a long-time manager, coach and scout, was the man who nurtured Bowa through much of the Philadelphia Phillies farm system. As the big club's new manager, Lucchesi was responsible for keeping Bowa in the lineup early in the 1970 season, Bowa's first in the major leagues. DeMars, a batting coach with a long successful career, was the man who taught Larry Bowa how to hit big-league pitching.

"I'd have to say it's pretty true. I made Larry into a hitter," DeMars said late last season. "If you asked him, he'd probably say the same thing."

DeMars, who was recently let go by the Cincinnati Reds, was like an on-field father to Bowa, picking up where his real dad, Paul, left off. Lucchesi, who was purged by the Chicago Cubs last winter in the Dallas Green fiasco, was like a mentor. If it wasn't for Lucchesi's stubbornness against growing local media pressure, Bowa would have been demoted to Class AAA Eugene not even two months into the 1970 season.

"I'll tell you, if it wasn't for Frank Lucchesi, I don't know what would have happened to Bowa," DeMars said. "He let him play every day. At the beginning, he played him every day even though the guy was only hitting .130. If it was some other manager, he might not have given him that chance."

Bowa came along in the Phillies program at absolutely the perfect time. The team that had lost 99 games in 1969 under Bob Skinner and George Myatt was in another in a series of rebuilding phases. They hadn't won a National League pennant since the "Whiz Kids" era of 20 years past and were the last of the original 16 major-league teams to still not have won a world championship during the 20th century. Talk about embarrassing...Bowa had been force fed through the minor leagues—a $2,000 bonus baby.

How bad was the neophyte Bowa as a hitter? During his first visit to Phillies camp in Florida, Bowa stepped into the batting cage before the watchful eyes of Gene Mauch, who was still the big-league manager. Recalls Bill Conlin, who covered the team at the time for the *Philadelphia Daily News:*

"It was one of the worst at bats anyone had ever seen. It looked like he was flailing at baseballs with a rolled up newspaper."

After Bowa had limped out of the box, Mauch turned to nobody in particular and said, "I couldn't HEAR him swing."

Said Conlin: "He was gone the next day."

Several years later, Bowa had already been labeled by the organization as simply a spunky utility player, who was capable of ascending to the major leagues under Skinner in 1969.

"I didn't want to make the big club that soon," Bowa recalls. "They wanted me there as a utility player. I wanted to play everyday. At the end, there were 26 guys left in camp. Skinner said, 'I want Bowa here to be a utility player.' I just went up to him, I told him, 'I don't want to play in the big leagues yet. I want to play every day. I want to be a regular.' He said, 'Well, if you feel like that, then let me suggest one thing.' It was the last day of spring training. 'I want you to go to Eugene and learn how to switch-hit. That's the only way you're going to make the big leagues as a regular. Hitting only from the right side, you can play utility right now.'

"So that's what I did. I mean, you ever do something with one hand for 20 years and now they say, do it with the other hand? It was the worst feeling I've ever had in my life. You talk about a hopeless feeling. But I kept battling. "I just wish that, as good a baseball man as my dad was, I wish he made me switch-hit as far back as the little league. But it never came up. We never even talked about it. He even says today, 'If there was one thing I could do over again, I wish I had started you out switch-hitting.' My sister, Paula, has two little boys and he already has them switch-hitting.

"In '69, Frank was the manager at Eugene. We went out everyday and we hit, hit, hit. All of a sudden, toward the middle of the year, I started getting into a groove. I ended up hitting .287 overall."

But for Bowa, the jump to the big leagues after one season as a switch-hitter turned out to be a quantum leap.

Said DeMars: "That's hard. All of a sudden you find yourself in the major leagues and you've only been a switch-hitter for one season in the minors. He was a lot weaker from the left side, but we worked so much on the left side that eventually he became a better hitter on that side than he was on the right."

Not during the early phase of that first season. Bowa was the opening day shortstop that year at Connie Mack Stadium, the last year for the Phillies in their ancient ballpark in North Philly before they moved far south to Veterans Stadium. The way Bowa played during his first few months in the majors, who could have foreseen that he would be an opening day fixture in the Phillies lineup for the next 12 years? Only the dogged Lucchesi seemed to have any foresight.

"I've been very flattered over the years," Lucchesi said late last season, when he stepped in to manage the Cubs after Gene Michael was fired. "All over the country, the press has always written nice things: 'Frank Lucchesi made Larry Bowa.' And I'll say it again. Larry Bowa made himself.

"I will say this: Of course 1970 was the big key for Bowa. He was a rookie and he started out pretty rough as far as his hitting goes and he wasn't making all the plays in the field either. I recall by mid-May, the Philly press was all over him. One Philly columnist said, 'How long can Lucchesi go with Bowa?' And then another one said, 'Is Bowa's locker already at Eugene?' Then there was another line or two that Bowa hits like a little leaguer. That's when I called him in.

"He had his head down, because he thought he was being shipped out. I was sitting down behind my desk. I stood up, walked over to him, put my hand on his shoulder and I said, 'Larry, forget what's in the paper. You're my shortstop tonight, you're my shortstop tomorrow, you're my shortstop next week. You're gonna be my shortstop all year. Someday, you're going to prove me right that you're going to be one hell of a shortstop. Just remember that. Now get out of here.'

"The reason I stuck with him is that I knew what was inside of him. I knew he had guts. I've never seen a kid with that much heart. It didn't happen right away, but in a few weeks, he started to turn it around."

What happened was that Bowa discovered the resource of Billy DeMars.

Bowa: "There we were at Connie Mack Stadium, Billy De-Mars and me. Every home game. We'd be out there at two o'clock. He'd pitch 'em. The whole bag. I'd hit 'em and go get 'em. Every single day. And in Philadelphia during the summer, you know how humid it gets. I must have weighed about 145 pounds at the end of the year. I'd like to have a dollar for every ball I hit extra. And then everything started happening on a positive note. It took me four, five years to really feel comfortable hitting left-handed."

DeMars: "We started that first year, I wasn't even the hitting coach. He was hitting .185 the latter part of May. I said, 'If you want to come out, I'll throw to you everyday. So we'd go out there on the field. What we started working on was hitting down into the ball, because he had a terrible habit of pulling away and swinging up. That's what we did everyday while we were home and at the end of the season, he wound up hitting .250.

"Once he had the success the first year, he and I would stick together. We would work almost everyday from spring training on. Once we got the batting cage, that helped a lot. And then during the winter of 1974, I was going down to Florida on vacation and he lived down there. And we went out everyday there, too. I had a batting tee. He'd hit a couple of hundred balls off the batting tee. I'd throw a couple of hundred balls to him and I'd make him bunt a hundred balls. We did that everyday until spring training started. We did that from 1974, all the way until I left in 1981. That very first year, 1974, I think he hit .275. The next year he hit .305. If you look at his stats from '74 to '81, his average is right around .285.

"It was just a case where I had the knowledge on the hitting, but he put in the time. I didn't have to go looking for Larry. We put in a lot of time. That was his approach. I was willing to work at it and he was willing to put the time in everyday. He was already a great fielder, he could run and he had a great arm. And he hustled like hell. Once he started to improve his bat, Frank's opinion of him was bared out."

Lucchesi: "I knew him pretty well. I had Bowa for a couple of years at Reading in the Eastern Pennsylvania League. I also had him at Eugene in the Pacific Coast League. And then three years in Philadelphia. He was a kid that had a lot of get up and go. He worked hard at the game. He didn't go through the motions. If there was something he had a weakness in, he would try to improve it. I remember, during infield, Bowa would take his ground balls like he was in a ballgame. I never tried to take the aggressiveness away from him. I recall, it might have been opening day his rookie year at Connie Mack Stadium. He got thrown out trying to steal. He was a little down, so I called him in the office and he thought I was going to say something negative, but it was positive. I said, 'Bowa, don't stop. Stay aggressive. I don't care if you got thrown out. Keep doing it.'

"Going way back to 1966, the Phillies brought him up from Spartanburg for the last week in San Diego, which was still triple-A at the time. I remember when he joined the ballclub we started him in a ballgame and you know, he was only about 150 pounds at the time, he wasn't too big a guy. We didn't have a uniform to fit him. They were all big. When he went out on the field it was kind of funny. The uniform was baggy. It was long. But I don't think size had anything to do with it. The kid just wanted to play."

Bowa's maturation as a player undoubtedly reached its zenith in 1980 during the Phillies run to that always elusive world championship. He batted .316 in the thrilling five-game playoff series in which the Phillies came from behind in the final two games to beat Houston for the pennant. Then he really excelled. He batted .375 against Kansas City as the Phillies finally brought the world championship trophy home to Philadelphia. In the six-game series, he set a World Series record by starting seven double plays.

"Larry had an outstanding World Series that year. He could easily have been named the MVP," recalled Mike Schmidt, who was actually voted MVP of that series. "They chose me maybe because of a little more notoriety during the regular season. I had the RBIs [seven]. Larry might have had more hits [Bowa had nine, Schmidt had seven]. He was exceptional in the field. Like I said, he could very easily have been chosen the MVP."

For Bowa, though, winning the World Series was special enough. It was the peak of his tenure in Philadelphia. And as it turned out, it was the peak of his career.

"It was more than winning a World Series," Bowa said. "It was that we'd gone through everything together. We'd gone through the downs. We'd gone through the mediocre seasons. We'd gone through the just misses. It was really something special."

And it all began, Bowa need not forget, with the confidence of Frank Lucchesi and the expertise of Billy DeMars.

MONDAY, SEPT. 7, 1987 ◆
ATLANTA, GA

What began as a rumbling, was now starting to turn into a small avalanche of rumor and innuendo. Would Larry Bowa be returning to manage the Padres in 1988? Would Chub Feeney be returning as president? General manager Jack McKeon had already made up his mind about the matter of retaining the manager.

"If I'm asked the question," McKeon said, "I'll say Larry has done a very good job."

Months ago, Bowa had decided that he would return if asked. All parties were now waiting for Feeney to give the final word. And though Feeney had obviously made up his mind to retain Bowa, he was biding his good time. Of course, Bowa was becoming a nervous wreck. Every loss seemed like another dagger to his chances. Had he said one too many times in print that Jimmy Jones can't pitch past the fifth inning? Had he ripped Stanley Jefferson one too many times? Had he participated in one too many angry confrontations with umpires? Bowa was putting himself through mental gyrations.

"I know Chub is from the old school and the old school was, you never tell your manager that he's coming back 'til the end of the year, you never give your manager a two-year contract," Bowa said. "The last thing I heard was he's making a decision by September 15. That's fine with me. I guess he just wants to establish something in the organization. I don't know.

"It's very difficult from my aspect because if you have a little talk with some player, you'd like to say, 'Hey, next year this is what I'd like you to do.' I've made some comments about what I'd do next year to the media, but to the players I've really had to bite my tongue. I'd like to call in some pitchers and tell them this is what I'd like you to work on next year, but it's tough for me to do that, knowing the situation. It would be foolish of me to tell a guy what he's got to work on if I know I'm not coming back. Another manager coming in might not think he needs that work."

But Bowa was coming back. And so was Feeney. At this point, it was a *fait accompli*. Feeney, who was in San Francisco attending the wedding of one of his sons, just hadn't worked out the fine details yet. Like a new contract for Bowa and a public announcement. But based on Feeney's observations since he officially took over the club on June 10, Bowa had done more than an acceptable job. In Feeney's estimation, Bowa had brought the Padres back from near ruin.

"Here is a highly motivated, highly intelligent man with a fine personality," Feeney said about Bowa months later. "He made himself into a good baseball player. He's highly competitive. As league president, I had only gotten to know him in an adversarial relationship, fining him a couple of times. I've really gotten to know him as a person since coming here to San Diego. I consider him to be a manager of the future. I think he obviously knows baseball. He's wrapped up in baseball. He's a fine tactician. He's not afraid to make moves. He's not afraid to do things on the field. He does what he thinks is right. He makes the game exciting by using the skills of his team. By stealing bases, using hit and runs. Things like that.

"His limitation right now, stopping him from becoming a great manager, is the fact that he has a tendency to blow his top and to not maintain his cool. That's reflected in his attitudes towards both umpires and players. I have no objections about talking to umpires when you think they're wrong. But it's the way you do it. The attitude you have. And Larry has a tendency to lose his head at that moment. I also think he has a tendency to talk about his players publicly and that's not going to help him as a manager. I think he will get over both of those things. I think he's working on it, which is the most important thing. On the few occasions I've talked to him, I think he already understood, be-

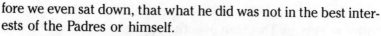

fore we even sat down, that what he did was not in the best interests of the Padres or himself.

"The best thing he did was to keep the ballplayers in a state of mind so they played as hard as they could every day. When I got here, we were obviously out of any pennant race, so everybody could have rolled over and played dead. I think they needed that motivation. I think each individual player has to motivate himself, but the manager has to have done something to put us into the position where for most of the second half of the season, we played the best baseball in the division, except for the Giants. So he had to have success in keeping these guys motivated, which is a tough thing to do."

In six months, Bowa had obviously matured as a manager. His day to day dealing with players had become less frenetic. Though he still tended to take his shots in print when he was angry, many of the comments were of a more general nature. Perhaps the difference in styles of two distinct club presidents could account for much of the change. Under Ballard Smith, a hands off president, a free-wheeling opinionated man like Bowa was able to fly free. Even in his most energetic days with the club, Smith rarely interfered with on-field personnel unless it involved a matter of front office policy. There was little accountability to the top of the organization with Smith in control.

That all changed with the coming of Feeney. Say what you will about Feeney's expertise when he was general manager of the Giants—and many critics have—but with 40 consecutive years of experience during major-league baseball's most formative stages, he is an expert on the inner workings of the game. Feeney took the job in San Diego so that for the first time in his career, he could fully saturate a club. During his final years, as Smith became more distracted with other business interests, the club began to lose focus. Like the last stages in the life of a cloud, the Padres were about to drift into clear, blue nothingness. Joan Kroc decided she should halt the process.

Under Feeney, a sense of order seemed to have been reinstituted. There was no doubt now who was to make the final decisions when it came to the baseball end of this highly complex business: Feeney. That shift of authority met with no little resistance from some of the people who were carried through the transition. But even with that, his regime had ushered in the most serene baseball era in recent Padres history.

"It's really peaceful now," said Joan last winter. "And that's the way I like it. Of course, the season hasn't started yet."

So too did Bowa feel a shift in how he had to approach his job and his attitude toward upper management. No fool and certainly a survivor, Bowa seemed to become far more conciliatory under the Feeney regime. When negative connotations toward players appeared in a Bowa newspaper quotation, Feeney picked up the telephone. Even when names appeared in print without attribution to Bowa, the manager heard about it.

"I told him, I have no control over what those guys write," Bowa said about one such conversation with Feeney.

Feeney was indeed a hands on president. And Bowa was certainly one element Feeney had his figurative hands directly on.

"When he does something wrong I'm going to tell him," Feeney said. "As far as I'm concerned, he gets a baseball team from Jack McKeon and myself—with his input—to put on the field. What he does with that team is his. We're not going to second guess him, help him strategize or tell him what players to use. But if I think he does something wrong when it involves his actions in regard to players and umpires, I'm certainly going to tell him about it."

One hundred and thirty-seven games into what seemed like an endless season, no one in the organization seemed to disagree about Bowa's expertise as a manager. It was the method that at times even he himself questioned. Without doubt, though, McKeon had grown to become Bowa's biggest fan in the front office.

"The most important thing to me about Bowa is, are we making progress even though our record is not good?" McKeon said. "And I think we're making progress. I'm not saying that just because of my feeling toward the guy. It's like the year—1981— when Frank Howard was managing the club. I recommended

Frank, but we didn't make any progress. No matter how much I liked him, I had to agree to let him go. Larry and I have become very close. That's the way it should be. He's talked me out of some things and I've talked him out of some things. I'll tell you one thing about the guy: He listens. He takes advice. Not only from me, but from a lot of people.

"In time, Larry will be a damn good big-league manager. It's like anything else, the more experience you get, the better you become. He's on track to becoming an outstanding big-league manager."

But would it be in a Padres uniform? As of now, the question still officially remained.

WEDNESDAY, SEPT. 9, 1987 ◆
ATLANTA, GA

B̲enito Santiago had just hit in his 14th consecutive game, but he seemed to be the only content player in the Padres clubhouse. Carmelo Martinez was upset. Stanley Jefferson was slumped silently in his locker. Goose Gossage was harboring a tight right shoulder and some ill feelings. And both Garry Templeton and Tim Flannery were hot about some postgame comments reporters had relayed to them from the manager.

Chalk it up to deep September last-place blues. The Padres, from the manager down, were growing awfully testy. When it was noted by one reporter that a drop in intensity seemed natural for a group of Padres playing the Braves in front of 2,501 people who somehow bumped into Atlanta-Fulton County Stadium with 23 games to go, Larry Bowa snapped:

"You've got a contract that says play 162 games. It doesn't say play 150 or until you get eliminated. Just play the schedule out. And do it with pride in your profession and all that. They're getting paid, aren't they? Tell them to quit taking paychecks. Then we won't expect them to do anything."

Templeton: "If he could come up to me and tell me that I'm having a horsebleep year, I could take that. But when he starts pointing fingers at the whole team, I don't think that's right. We talk about it every night. We hate to lose. We hate it as much as he does."

Then as an aside, Templeton added: "What do you think of this guy as a manager?"

Flannery: "That's the only thing that gets to me sometimes. He acts like he's the only one who cares. Well, it hurts us just as much as it hurts him. Even if he doesn't think so."

The mini-revolt was on, and for one of the few times all season, some of the players were sticking it right back in Bowa's face. What caught in Flannery's gut was a comment made by Bowa about a possible sixth-inning play at second base during the 3-2 loss—the Padres seventh in the last nine games. Gary Roenicke had doubled into the left-field corner where rookie Shawn Abner retrieved the ball and came up throwing. Abner's long toss short-hopped Flannery, who moved up several feet off the bag as Roenicke slid in safely. One run scored on the play and another runner stopped at third.

Said Bowa, who usually makes a point of not commenting on physical mistakes: "The throw to second, I guess Flannery didn't expect it, it was right there." The remark threw the normally affable Flannery into a tizzy. After all, Flannery had been playing all season, recovering from torn ligaments in his left ankle—an act of courage applauded often by Bowa and an injury that required arthroscopic surgery during the offseason.

Told what Bowa had said about the play, Flannery came to a slow boil. "He didn't think I was expecting it? I moved up to block the ball because if the ball gets by me, the guy on third scores. I was expecting it. This wasn't my first game in the big leagues. If I wasn't expecting it, I would have been set up in the outfield for a double cut. But I guess if the manager says I wasn't expecting it, I wasn't."

Templeton, in his role as team captain, jumped into the fray to support Flannery, who settled the matter with Bowa in a closed-door session several days later.

"I went into his office, closed the door and screamed my lungs out at him," Flannery said. "Then I felt better."

The other players rocking Bowa's boat were no less agitated. Jefferson was in one of his dour moods because he was benched in favor of Abner prior to the game. The night before, Bowa had aired out Jefferson through one of his coaches, because the rookie had swung at a 2-and-0 pitch with the bases loaded and none out against a rookie pitcher. Jefferson's sacrifice fly drove in the only run of the inning, but the manager was not pleased.

Afterward, Bowa blamed himself for not putting on the take

sign. But Bowa wanted to make it clear that the benching had nothing to do with a mental mistake in September that should have been eliminated in March.

"In no way is this punishment," Bowa said about a young player who was batting .247 with 82 strikeouts. "He's trying to get sawdust out of his bat."

Jefferson, who would barely utter a word, was not so sure. "I've given up thinking about it," he said.

As far as Carmelo was concerned, the appearance of Rob Nelson, another first baseman, sent him into a spin. Since Carmelo's arrival from the Chicago Cubs in 1984, he has been yearning to return to first base, his natural position. As a Padre, Martinez has been a serviceable left-fielder and a here-and-there first baseman. Upon his arrival, he found Steve Garvey as the incumbent at first base. No moving Garvey out. To make room for Martinez in the lineup and to fill what the Padres perceived to be another problem position, then manager Dick Williams moved Alan Wiggins, perhaps the club's best outfielder, to second base, and Martinez, a lumbering vessel, to left field. The move met with mixed reviews, but the matter remained unchanged during the year the Padres won the pennant. When Wiggins was banished from the team for renewed drug abuse in 1985, it did Martinez no good. Carmelo was waiting for the day when Garvey stepped aside. That day came in 1987, but the position was awarded to John Kruk, who promptly hit 20 homers and knocked in 91 runs. Both team highs. The arrival of Nelson from Oakland in the Storm Davis trade, was another signal to Martinez of his imminent demise. Martinez had never been comfortable in the outfield. He was jeered there mercilessly at times by San Diego fans, who rarely become rabid about anything bushier than "The Famous Chicken," their homegrown mascot of sudden international fame.

"I can see things," Martinez said earlier in the week. "I ain't blind. I think my future here is kind of in the dark right now. See, the point is, I don't want to be traded. But if I'm not going to play, I wish they'd trade me somewhere where I can play every day....I'm 27 years old and I know I can play. I've been in the big leagues now for four years. And I haven't been given a chance to play my position. I don't want to be a pinch-hitter. It's the same situation Marvell Wynne is in right now. He's 27. He wants to play. He's sitting on the bench and he's not happy about it."

Bowa's retort was a classic—a derivative of one of his best lines of the year. During the Storm Davis standoff, Bowa aptly noted: "He must think the SD on his cap stands for Storm Davis." So too with Carmelo: "I don't think it says Carmelo Martinez across his chest. It says San Diego Padres. I'm not trying to do the best for him. I'm trying to do the best for the team."

Gossage's problem was another matter entirely, as it always was with the Goose. Several weeks ago during that strange game at Shea Stadium in which Gossage held two balls in his possession while umpire Dick Stello genuflected behind the plate, the Goose reported a bit of a twinge in his pitching shoulder. The twinge turned into tendinitis and Gossage had pitched just once since. The problem was not revealed until about a week later when Bowa needed Gossage to pitch the 10th inning at home against the Mets, but found that he was unavailable. That left Bowa with Keith Comstock to pitch to Howard Johnson. No contest. Johnson won the game with a home run.

"Where was Goose?" Bowa was asked.

"Ask him," the manager said.

Gossage: "It's not that serious. I just don't want it to get serious, like Andy Hawkins. I've played too long not to know what a feeling is. It was just one of those things that needed a couple of days because it's bothering me, so I'm taking a couple of days."

The couple of days had turned into a couple of weeks. And for the second time this season, Gossage had been slow to recover from a nagging injury. The other injury being that rib cage tear which obliterated his opening six weeks of the season. Despite the physical breakdowns, Gossage had performed better than almost anyone expected. In the end, he made 40 appearances, pitched 52 innings, struck out 44 batters, posted a 3.12 ERA, and was credited with 11 saves for a team that just didn't offer that many save opportunities. Plus, he had been asked to share the stopper role with friend and teammate Lance McCullers, who had earned the nickname "Baby Goose" two years earlier when McCullers splashed onto the scene during another Gossage injury.

More interesting still, Gossage had begun to make the transition away from his once overpowering fastball to an array of stunning breaking pitches. Gossage, in his big years with the New York Yankees, had always had a tantalizing slider to set up his 98-mile per hour heat. Now, he was having success using his fastball, which had curtailed to the 92, 93 mph range, to set up his slider. But the physical problems persisted. In spotting Gossage during the course of his first season, Bowa began to realize that the vaunted right arm, at 36, was not able to bounce back as quickly as it once did after a day of work. Use Gossage for two full innings in a game, and on certain occasions he might have problems bouncing back. A few times, Bowa had called the bullpen or read the trainer's report only to find that Gossage was not available. That created a subtle problem which did nothing more than hasten Bowa's use of his other relievers.

With his starters inconsistent and middle-inning relief invisible at times, the Gossage situation made the demands on a rookie manager learning how to handle a pitching staff that much more severe.

It was ironic, then, that several weeks before the end of the season, Gossage openly questioned how Bowa had used him.

"I don't know what their plans are for me for next year, but I haven't known my role all year," Gossage calmly told Bill Plaschke of the *Los Angeles Times.* "I would like to be used more and for whatever reason, I haven't been. I don't like to be kept in the dark, but that's what it's been like. I really haven't talked to Larry all year."

When Plaschke informed Bowa about the conversation, the manager insisted that Gossage's role had not changed. "His role is our stopper," Bowa said. "But there are days, according to the reports from the trainer's room, he needs a rest. I never question those reports."

Gossage: "There are times when I say, 'If I can take a rest, I'll

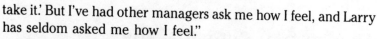
take it.' But I've had other managers ask me how I feel, and Larry has seldom asked me how I feel."

Bowa: "My door is always open."

Yes, it was quite a day and quite an end to another road trip as this raucous season wound to its conclusion. In the locker room, Greg Riddoch, Bowa's closest ally among the coaches, was watching the manager's reaction to certain pointed questions.

"You know Bow better than anybody," Riddoch said. "He wears his heart on his sleeve."

And at the moment, that heart was pounding. "They're playing like their minds are someplace else," Bowa said. "Guys don't have to wonder why they won't be starting next year. It's just making our decision easier watching them. . . . But I'm sure they'll have a reason or an excuse or will point fingers at somebody." They pointed fingers, all right. At Bowa.

Said Templeton: "When you hear things like that, it hurts. We know he doesn't like it, but he takes it personally. He's not the only one who has feelings. It has been hurting us a lot all season. A lot of us haven't been through this before. You can ask anyone around here. It hurts to lose. We want to get out of the cellar. No one is giving up."

Heading home, the Padres were 56-83 and counting.

WEDNESDAY, SEPT. 16, 1987 ✦ SAN DIEGO, CA

I never felt I was in danger of not coming back simply because Jack McKeon kept reinforcing me. He kept saying, "Don't worry about things. The club is going in the right direction and we're going to be fine." I kept saying, "Jack, are you seeing something that I'm not seeing?" I mean, if it hadn't been for Jack, I probably would have slit my throat earlier in the season. Really, he got me through April and May. There's no doubt in my mind. Every single night was like a pep talk. He kept saying, "Experience, experience, trust me."

When we were 12-42, we all could have quit right then. But you know what? We didn't. There definitely have been a lot of ups and downs, not only with the players, but with me. I'm learning as much as anyone here. I was too critical at times when I should have backed off. I've made mistakes, but I know I'm going to correct those mistakes. Now I agree with Jack. We're headed in the right direction. We've made tremendous strides in turning it around. And we're going to get a lot better.

I guess I feel a lot more humble being rehired then I did on that day late last October when I stood before the same lights and microphones and became the Padres manager. I guaranteed some things then, like the team giving 100 percent every day. I think, by and large, we did that. But seasons like this one could humble just about anybody. In my wildest imagination, I never thought my first managing job would be like this. I figured we might struggle a little getting out of the gate, but I never anticipated the kind of start we had.

We formalized my new deal yesterday before the game in San Francisco. Funny, it came on the same day we were mathematically eliminated from the division race. How's that for timing? And the night before, in his first game back at Candlestick Park since he was traded away by the Giants, Chris Brown had his right hand broken in the first inning by a Mike Krukow pitch. He's got a cast on it now and he's through for the season. Maybe that's for the best. I don't know. Now, I can really start thinking about next year. Chub Feeney was in town and we went to one of his favorite San Francisco restaurants, the Washington Square Bar and Grill. You know, it's kind of a nice little place with windows looking out on Washington Square Park. Real San Francisco.

We sat down to eat lunch and he said, "I've been thinking about next year. I am coming back. I've been thinking about you and I think you've done a good job. I want you to come back, too."

My response to him was something like this: "Sure, I'd love to come back, but I'd like to get a little security. I'd like to get a two-year deal." He said, "I agree with you about the security end of it, but I've already committed myself to signing only one-year contracts. That's all I'm giving myself. And I'm giving you one."

I could have sat there and argued with him. But what would have been the point of that? So I said, "Hey, I believe in what I'm doing. I have no problem with that." I just threw it by him and if he said no, I wasn't going to hassle with it.

He said, "We're going to give you a raise and this is what we'd like you to manage for." And I said, "Fine."

I got a $50,000 raise to $150,000. I've got some radio stuff, so that'll put me right around $200,000. I can live on that. I know that Tommy Lasorda and those guys are getting big money, but hey, they've been around. I haven't done anything yet. I've got to pay my dues. I'm not in this right now for the money. I mean, hey, the money is great. But I know exactly where I've come from. I could go back to living on the same $28,000 I made last year to manage Las Vegas. I had no problems at all living on that. I stay within my own means. I've never tried to play the role.

Incentives. I don't have any right now, but I'd like to get into that if I make it back here for another year. Right now, I want to establish myself. In fact, this year, even though we finished last, I think I have established myself as far as handling a game. I got a call from Astros general manager Dick Wagner when we left Houston the other day just to say, "You did a good job. I saw your team earlier in the year and it really improved a lot." That meant a lot to me for another general manager to say something like that. There was no reason for him to do it.

Pete Rose told me I did a good job. Billy DeMars. Those are my friends, but they also tell me when I screw up. If I make a wrong move, they'll come up and be honest with me. I don't want people stroking me just for stroking's sake. I like to see both ends of it. Pete told me one day, "You're too critical, man. You've got to back off. You're gonna kill yourself."

Chub has been honest with me, too. He tells me when I screw up, particularly when he doesn't like something I've said about a player in the papers. Ever since he's been here, my relationship with him has been good. Up until yesterday, I had only a few meetings with him, but our meetings had been of the three or four minute variety. He'll ask me about a player, I'll tell him. One meeting was about the way I argued with that umpire, Steve Rippley, in New York. But basically, the meetings had been about player personnel he hadn't seen. He'd just read the reports.

That's the way our lunch went yesterday in San Francisco. After we got the more urgent matters out of the way, we started talking about the ballclub. What areas we needed to improve in. And that's when I brought up, "Do you think I can bring in a few people?" And he said, "Yeah, we're gonna discuss that. I think you should be able to bring in some of your own coaches."

I like every single guy I've had as a coach here this year. I can honestly tell you that I didn't dislike any of them. I like them a lot. I respect them. But there's some parts of the game where their philosophy is a little different from mine. And I'm not saying mine is right. But if I'm the manager, I want guys behind me who think along my line.

Basically, that was it. We talked about our organization. Some kids he hadn't seen he wanted to talk about. We talked about Shawn Abner. I said, "I think he's going to be a good player, but I don't know if he's ready yet." The whole thing went about an hour and a half. He was tellin' me about his philosophy on contracts with players. He does not like long-term contracts. I don't know who's up for contracts in our organization, but I think for some of these guys it's going to be a rude awakening. I don't know. He's hardline, boy, when it comes to money. I think that's the old school. A dollar's wages for a dollar's day of work. You work hard for a year and you get paid for it the next year.

When you think about it, that might be the right way to go, considering the way the game has self-destructed over big player salaries. Some guys get three or four-year contracts. They're still getting paid while they're sitting at home. That doesn't make anybody look good. OK, continue to give out big money. But give it on a year-to-year basis. Earn it.

Of course, there always has to be some individuals who should be exempt from that. Like Tony Gwynn. If you gave him a one-year contract, a one-day contract, or a ten-year contract, he'd give you the same effort day in and day out. Some individuals are like that. If anybody on that ballclub is to get a long-term contract, he would be the first guy I'd give one to. I'm not saying five years, but at least three years. Nothing against Tony, but you never know what injuries are gonna do.

All in all, I think the entire situation worked out great. Now it's up to me. We made it through this first year and that was something else. I've tried to instill a winning philosophy in our players. And for this club, winning means doing the little things. For example, if we have a guy on second base with no one out, the next hitter has got to get him over to third. If a guy hits .240 and you win, it's a hell of a lot better than a guy hitting .280 and you finish last. That's what I'm trying to stress here. I think it finally got through for awhile and then we lost it again somewhere along the way.

If those guys think I was tough this year, they ain't seen nothing yet.

Saturday, Oct. 3, 1987 ◆ San Diego, CA

Benito Santiago had virtually done it all on his way to putting a lock on the Rookie of the Year award. His 34-game hitting streak was the longest ever for a Latin player, a rookie, a catcher. The 12th longest hitting streak in baseball history may also have been the most neglected item in baseball this year. It began on August 25, one day before a much more heralded 39-game streak fashioned by Milwaukee's Paul Molitor came to an end. Now, with one game to go in the season, Benny's streak was also over.

So was a nine-game Padres losing streak, the club's worst dive of the year and worst since 1974. April and May revisited. Both streaks were stopped against the Los Angeles Dodgers and right-hander Orel Hershiser, who pulled the plug on Benny in three uneventful at bats. The Padres pulled the plug on Hershiser with Stanley Jefferson's home run. The 1-0 win, No. 65, was the Padres last of the season. The next day, they lost the finale to finish 65-97. It was the club's worst finish since 1974.

"Who'd have thought Benny would get up only three times and we'd win?" Larry Bowa said. "I didn't want to be taking an 11-game losing streak into next spring. We've got enough to do next spring than to be talking and thinking about carrying over an 11-game losing streak. To me, Benny's streak was kind of a Catch 22 thing. I wish Benny could have kept going, but what if it had carried over . . . what if Benny is 0-for-3 in the season opener against Houston in the Astrodome next April and we've got the tying run on first? We've got to bunt. Do we sacrifice games early to keep the streak going or do we go for the win? And there'd be some distractions if the streak were still going.

"I'm not glad it's over. Continuing the streak would have been great for Benny. But now it's back to business."

Translation: Continuing the streak wouldn't have been great for the collective goals of the Padres—winning.

All during the season's final homestand, Bowa had brooded while both streaks continued. The homestand began with the San Francisco Giants clinching their first National League West title in 16 years. That was the final insult to a demoralizing year. But the Padres hung tough to the last out in a grueling 5-4 defeat, and for an instant right at the very end, it seemed like the Padres might force the Giants to wait another night.

Tony Gwynn was on third when reliever Don Robinson almost saw the one-run victory explode in his face. John Kruk who along with Santiago were Bowa's twin jewels for a gut-wrenching inaugural season, poked a high drive to left field that seemed to get stuck in the fog. At the first crack of the bat, Kruk thought the ball was gone.

"I think a lot of other people did too," Kruk said. "The moment I hit it, I saw Donnie's head drop."

Of course, the ball didn't go out. Jeffrey Leonard pedalled back to the fence and made a routine grab. For all intents and purposes, that catch was the final blow for the Padres, who wandered around the stadium for the next six days as if they were making a sequel to the *Night of the Living Dead*. Bowa watched his club drop its next four games. In two of those four games, Benny continued his streak with hits in his last at bat. On Tuesday, Santiago homered off Scott Garrelts in the eighth. On Thursday, he dropped a pretty bunt down the third-base line in the eighth inning against the Cincinnati Reds.

But there was no joy in Bowaville. As the Padres continued to lose, Bowa continued to talk. Here are some choice quotations, assembled with the help of John Shea of the *Escondido Times-Advocate*, from Bowa's final, desperate week:

I don't like losing six games in a row. Right now, baseball is the furthest thing from most of their minds, which is sad.

My job is to win. My job isn't to applaud streaks and forget losses.

I hope he hits in a hundred games in a row. I'd just like to win a couple of them.

I would think that when you put on a baseball uniform, your main concern would be beating the other team, not getting the game over as fast as you can.

I keep reverting to my statement about motivation. Just the fact that you have a big-league uniform in the locker should be motivation enough. If it's not, you're in trouble. I'm a manager and when I put it on, I still get goose bumps. I get excited. I get turned on by it.

I don't like losing. Obviously, they still don't realize how much I don't like losing. It's not a front, it's not a game, it's a livelihood. It's a job. An occupation.

Your approach to the game has got to be the same whether you're 20 games out, three games out or 10 games out. That's the way I learned it.

I know how I feel about the team in my heart. You have to ask them how they feel.

I'm not a quitter. I'll keep fighting until the last breath.

Watching the Giants clinch, I can't help thinking that just two years ago they lost a hundred games and that it's not impossible to turn a team around quickly with young talent. I feel a little disappointed, but I hope it rubs off on some of our young kids.

Bowa was a warrior down to the last out. For Bowa, the good seasons enjoyed by Gwynn, Kruk and Santiago had to be some sweet balm for his wounds.

Bowa simply inherited Gwynn, who had evidently made the transition from being a very good athlete to a great athlete. Playing through personal adversity, Gwynn had his best season ever in just about every department. He led the league in hitting for the second time, but better still, his .370 average was the highest mark to lead the National League since Stan Musial hit .376 in 1948. His numbers in hits (218), runs (119), doubles (36), triples (13), walks (82) and stolen bases (56) were also all career highs. His marks in overall average, hits, runs, triples and intentional walks (26) were all club records.

Bowa played little part in Gwynn's success. He watched in admiration with the same awe as everybody else. It was Gwynn himself who had made the decision to become more selective as a hitter, increasing his walk total and thus his on-base percentage to a heady .447. As Bowa was so fond of saying: "If I had eight more Tony Gwynns, then I wouldn't lose any sleep over the winter."

But it was Gwynn's work habits that enamored Bowa, among so many others, even more than his daily production.

"I very seldom take an oh-for twice in a row without extra batting practice," said Mike Schmidt. "It's just a ritual. People understand right away that if I have a bad game, I've got to hit. Tony Gwynn hits after a good game. Who works harder than Tony Gwynn?"

Perhaps Bowa worked even harder than Gwynn when he was a player, and for that reason, he has little patience for players with sloppy work habits. Many of Bowa's problems with Stanley Jefferson came simply out of his perception that Jefferson didn't spend enough time working at the game. Bowa harped so much on the reclusive Jefferson that the young man withdrew. But somewhere along the line, Bowa's message penetrated the skulls of both Santiago and Kruk.

Tabbed with the nickname "La Machine" when he arrived on the scene in Yuma during the spring of 1986, Kruk, a left-handed batter, seemed like a white version of Tony Gwynn in squat body type and swing. There was only one big difference. Kruk clowned around. He didn't work. That changed with the entrance of Bowa, who rode the usually easygoing Kruk into the turf. Kruk began hanging with Gwynn, who was of course a keen positive influence. By mid-season, they were one-two in the league in hitting and were as much a reason for the Padres resurgence as anything else.

Kruk tailed off to .313, but his homer and RBI totals far surpassed Gwynn's marks (20 to 7, 91 to 54).

At the beginning of the year, Kruk was one of the youngsters with a giant question mark next to his name. By season's end he was a "fixture," to use a word provided by club president Chub Feeney.

Bowa has to be given a large portion of the credit for that. But Santiago was his *pièce de résistance*. This was the second full season the two men spent together. The first was in Vegas, where Bowa met a talented double-A catcher with the label of being awfully lazy. In Vegas, Bowa took care of that. As soon as Bowa found Santiago's concentration level slipping, he would plant the catcher on the bench. That didn't change much in the major leagues.

After a slow start, Santiago came on to challenge Milwaukee catcher B.J. Surhoff for honors as all-star catcher in the Pacific Coast League. Surhoff was voted the all-star berth, but the Padres were convinced that Santiago was ready to join the major-league team. They were so confident in his ability, veteran catcher Terry Kennedy, who had been with the club for six years, was dispatched to Baltimore.

It's hard to say whether Santiago's wretched start was a product of the club's play or whether he might have gone through the same progression anyway. But numbers don't lie. While the Padres were sludging off to that horrible 12-42 start, Santiago was committing 14 errors and 12 passed balls.

"I tried too hard at first," Santiago explained to Bob Slocum of the *San Diego Tribune* about his poor start. "I tried to be Rookie of the Year in April or May. It messed me up, *pero*. . .it made me think. It made me concentrate on relaxing more. When I forgot about Rookie of the Year and tried to help the Padres win every day, I felt better and played better."

Bowa spent as much time in heart-to-heart talks with Santiago as a father might spend with a teenage son. Miraculously, at mid-season, Santiago began to mature. The pitchers who had questioned his game-calling ability early in the season began to allow Benny to call their games. His errors and passed balls markedly decreased. And he began to excel at the plate—a development which surprised even Bowa. Note, if you will, that Santiago batted .287 last year at Vegas and .300 during his first year in the big leagues. No easy feat.

As such, Santiago's hitting streak became a neat punctuation mark for his sudden growth as a player. Now it was over. Reduced to a blurb in a media guide, just beside the results of Larry Bowa's first chaotic season.

Epilogue ♦

No question, the development of Benito Santiago was my biggest source of pride. I really think he was one guy who I brought along. He came with me. In double-A, he had a rap of being lazy, and so, when I went to triple-A, he was like a pet project. I told him, "I see this ability, but I don't want to see this laziness." Every now and then he'll get, maybe not lazy, but complacent. And I get on him. I've been very critical of Benny. Probably more so than anybody. And he knows exactly where I'm coming from.

I've called him in on days and I've said, "Hey, Benny, you're going to be the best catcher ever. Do you understand what I'm saying? So when I get on you, take it like I just never want you to make those same mistakes again. Because I think you're that good that you shouldn't be making the mistakes you're making. Take the criticism as constructive criticism."

And he'll look at me like, "I know where you're comin' from, man." He's the guy that when he gets that Rookie of the Year Award, I'm going to feel great. I've gone through every downer with him. I told people even before we left camp that this guy was going to be a good player. And then in April and May, I'm going, "Oh, no. What happened?" And then, all of a sudden, it was just like a light went on. He just started playing his butt off.

I'll tell you the exact conversation I had with him that I think began it all. I called him in the office in May and I said, "What's going on? You're not playing the way you did in Las Vegas. What are your goals? What do you want to do here?"

He said, "I want to be Rookie of the Year."

I said, "Benny, Benny, let's not think about individual things.

Let's think about what you can do for the team. The more you think about Rookie of the Year, the more you're pressin'. " I told him, "You can't win Rookie of the Year. You can't win it. You're off to a bad start. There's no way you can win it. So let's just get that out of our minds. That's history. I don't want to hear Rookie of the Year anymore. Let's think about what you can do to help our whole team together. And you know where it starts? You've got to start catching better. You've got to start taking charge back there."

We got into that part with the pitchers shaking him off. I said, "Hey, go out there and tell them what you want them to do."

Then he came out with the rip article in Montreal. It seemed like he just woke up overnight after that. He did a turnabout, 360 degrees. Now there's no way he cannot win that award. We went from me telling him there was no way he could win it to it's a lock.

That meeting was in San Diego after a road trip. He was catching the worst I'd seen him catch in two years. Balls getting by him. Him getting crossed up by the pitchers. Him forgetting what sign he had put down. Now that he's done what he's done— won Rookie of the Year, put together that great hitting streak, it's great. But I told him, "You know, you've got to work twice as hard for next year. You've got to go out next year and prove that this wasn't a fluke." I also had Pete Rose tell him that. He may have a tough time next year, but I think he'll be all right.

He might be the best catcher in baseball right now. But when I say that, people look at me like I'm nuts. They look at his errors. I say, "They were all made in April and May, man." He's going to make errors. He's going to be a high error catcher be- cause with that great arm of his, he throws a lot. He catches some infielders off guard. He's caught John Kruk off guard at first base five or six times. He has such a good arm, if you're not on your toes, he's going to hurt you.

I really think that early in the year he put a lot of pressure on himself. I picked up every magazine during the winter and they had him as Rookie of the Year. I mean, it was a lock—Benito San- tiago in the National League and B.J. Surhoff in the American

League. They'd been rivals ever since they'd come up together. When they picked the all-star team in the Coast League, it came out that Surhoff was the catcher while we were playing Vancouver, Milwaukee's triple-A team, in a playoff game. We had a guy on third and Surhoff was catching. The guy threw a pitch and Surhoff didn't block it and it went back to the screen. We got a run. I'm sitting there watching the game and Benny comes up to me, taps me on the shoulder, and says, "All-star catcher my butt." That hurt Benny a little bit when he wasn't named the all-star catcher.

Yeah, the turn around Benny made this year, I consider that to be a significant accomplishment. But you see, Benny and I had some history. He knew what to expect from me. Last spring when I joined the Padres, training camp was just a big feeling out process. Most of the players had only heard about how I'd run the Vegas team, and I'd only heard how things were around here in 1986. I knew they had lost 88 games, so things couldn't have been too good or they wouldn't have made so many changes, including the manager. Still, when I came in, it was very difficult for me to tell guys what areas we had to work on based on what I'd heard. They're saying, "What the bleep. How do you know? You weren't even here." Well, now I do know, because I've seen it with my own eyes and I'm tellin' you this, we're going to work on some areas. We will work on it.

As far as the coaches go, I think every manager feels more comfortable with his own people. When I got the job I was only able to bring in one of my own coaches. But I was a first-year manager and I figured I'd go along with the program. Galen Cisco, Deacon Jones, Sandy Alomar and Harry Dunlop were all brought back. Only Sandy will be coming back next year and he'll be my third base coach. Last year, the guy I brought in was Greg Riddoch. Most guys usually bring their buddies in as coaches when they get a managing job. I didn't care about that. I wanted to bring in somebody who was bright, organized and knew something about the game. I really didn't know Greg. He had worked for many years in Cincinnati's minor-league system and had joined the Padres in 1986. He took over as minor-league coordinator when Steve Boros was named to manage the major-league club. As far as I could see, he did a hell of a job.

He came through Vegas a few times and he impressed me. I don't like to overreact to people, so I called Pete Rose, who knew Greg well. I found out Pete was thinking of hiring him. I said, "Pete, what kind of baseball man is he?" He said, "He's excellent." I figured, if Pete thinks that, that's good enough for me. He said he was a little too college. Not college, I guess, but really gung-ho. He was one of those guys who had been buried in baseball's system for 20 years and couldn't make it to the big leagues. Here's a guy with a masters degree. Can you beat that? Guys get labeled. It's hard to shed a label in baseball. I should know. I was never known for being an offensive player. I got labeled as a good glove, no hit. I got over 2,000 hits and had a lifetime average of .260. I'm not gonna say I was a great hitter, but I wasn't a "no hit" either. I think I made myself into a good hitter, considering what I had to do to get there. It's just like Ozzie Smith now. Ozzie is known for his fielding, not his hitting. But Ozzie has become a pretty good hitter. See what I mean? Too many baseball people look at something one time and that's their opinion. If there's one thing I hate more than anything else is that labeling system in baseball. A guy is one way and no matter how many years pass, he can never change. Greg was labeled. He was labeled as a minor leaguer. But he did a great job for me and he's coming back as my first base coach.

Those are all the kinds of guys I'm bringing in with me next year. Pat Dobson is my pitching coach. He's a former major-leaguer who spent last season as minor-league pitching coach for the Seattle Mariners. Amos Otis needs no introduction. He had a great career with the Kansas City Royals. He's our hitting coach. He was in our minor-league organization last year and spent some time with the big club on the road. He seemed to build up pretty good relationships with the kids. He's a great addition. Denny Sommers will be our bullpen coach. We didn't even have one of those last season. But I think it's a must. He's had some experience coaching in the major leagues, but he spent the last two years as a scout for the Minnesota Twins.

I don't want any of this to ever be taken as a rap against the coaches I had last year. They were all good, competent people. I liked them all. I just think the manager should be able to bring in the coaches he wants to bring in.

I don't want coaches who want to be just friends with me or the players. I want coaches who believe that what I'm doing is right. And they can still be friends with a player. They can still disagree with me. But when push comes to shove, your loyalty is to the manager, not to the player. That's I think what you get when you bring in your own people. I didn't realize as a player the importance of a manager having his own people. I thought a coach does his work, keeps his mouth shut, and helps the manager out. I never realized how important it was to have coaches thinking on your wavelength.

In retrospect, even though we played much better the second half, I really don't feel any sense of accomplishment about my first season as a big-league manager. I don't think you can ever believe you accomplished anything when you come in last. The bottom line is, we have a long way to go. If you feel any accomplishment there, you haven't set too high a goal for yourself. I think we made some big, big improvements, but we have a lot of improvements to go. I don't want people to get the wrong impression about this ballclub. Right now, if you talked to 10 people in San Diego, nine of them would say the Padres are going to be contenders in the National League West next year. Maybe we are. But with the team we have, all the parts must come together. Everyone must have good years. The pitchers have to do well for us to be contenders.

I'm being realistic. I'm taking a look at the Reds, who I think have a good team. I'm looking at the Giants, who I think have a real good team. Houston is not bad. The only other teams with us are Atlanta and the Dodgers. And the Dodgers have that outstanding pitching. You know, I don't want people to think that just because we had a decent second half, we're automatic contenders. Everything has to fall in place. The only thing I do know is that our young kids are better because they've played a year. That's all I do know. What I don't know is how they're going to react going into July or August when they're two games out of first place. Every game we played this year was a meaningless game as far as pressure was concerned. It's a lot easier to play when you're 20 games out of first. Now, what happens when you go to New York in August in front of 55,000 people, you're two games out and the Mets are two games out? How do you react? We're going to have to go through that whole scenario. And I can promise you this: It'll be different. We saw this year how the kids played in front of big-league crowds. Now, how do they play in front of big-league crowds when it means something?

And how do you know what my approach is going to be under those circumstances? I'll probably be wound up a little tighter. I let these guys run in August and September because we were 18 games out. Will I do the same thing when we're a game up or a game out? I want to think I will. I want to think I'm going to be aggressive. I think that with the talent we have, I have to be aggressive. Now, you put a thumper in the middle of the lineup, I might take a little aggressiveness away and let him swing. I don't know. That's something I've got to find out. In a crucial situation, I don't want to run us out of an inning. If I run us out of an inning with a singles hitter up, I'm not going to be upset. If I run us out of an inning with a guy who hits 35 home runs at the plate, I'm going to be ticked off. I've got to regroup there. I've got to say, wait a minute now.

Yeah, next season. It's going to be a whole new can of worms for everybody.

On Friday, Oct. 9, 1987, in San Diego, Harry Dunlop, Galen Cisco and Deacon Jones were dismissed as Padres coaches and Steve Boros was fired as the club's minor-league coordinator. Dunlop was named to replace Boros as minor-league coordinator. Cisco joined the Toronto Blue Jays as a minor-league pitching coach. Jones was hired by the Baltimore Orioles as a minor-league batting coach and liaison with minority communities. Boros was hired as an area scout by the Los Angeles Dodgers.

On Wednesday, Oct. 28, 1987, in Chicago at a press conference called to announce the hiring of John Vukovich as Chicago Cubs manager, Dallas Green suddenly resigned as club president and general manager with two years remaining on his contract. Later in the winter, rumors began to surface that Green might eventually join the Padres. He is currently out of the game.

On Thursday, Oct. 29, 1987, in San Diego, the Padres announced the rehiring of Sandy Alomar and Greg Riddoch and the additions of Pat Dobson, Amos Otis and Denny Sommers to complete the alignment for manager Larry Bowa's 1988 coaching staff.

On Thursday, Nov. 5, 1987, in New York, Benito Santiago was named National League Rookie of the Year by a unanimous vote of the Baseball Writers Association of America. He was the first member of the San Diego Padres ever to win that award.

On Wednesday, Nov. 11, 1987, in Chicago, the Cubs announced the hiring of Jim Frey as the club's director of player personnel. Frey, who had been working as a broadcaster for WGN radio commenting on Cubs games, was fired by Dallas Green as Cubs manager on June 10, 1986.

On Friday, Nov. 20, 1987, in Chicago, the Cubs announced the hiring of Don Zimmer as manager. Zimmer, who was third base coach for the National League West-winning San Francisco Giants, was fired by Green along with Frey on June 10, 1986.

On Tuesday, Dec. 22, 1987, in San Diego, Joey Cora underwent arthroscopic surgery to repair cartilage damage in his left knee. Cora sustained the injury playing winter ball in Puerto Rico.

On Wednesday, Jan. 13, 1988, in La Jolla, California, Steve Garvey, citing lack of progress in his surgically repaired left shoulder, retired from professional baseball.

On Friday, Feb. 12, 1988, in San Diego, the Padres traded pitcher Goose Gossage and minor-league pitcher Ray Hayward to the Chicago Cubs for third baseman/outfielder Keith Moreland and minor-league shortstop Mike Brumley.

On Friday, Feb. 19, 1988, in Yuma, Arizona, Padres pitchers and catchers assembled to open Bowa's second spring training. Bowa went to camp in his second year hoping to improve a team that finished 65-97 in 1987.

INDEX